ALL BUT ONE

*Dedicated
to Pete*

ALL BUT ONE

ONE WOMAN'S QUEST TO CLIMB THE
52 HIGHEST MOUNTAINS IN THE ALPS

BARBARA SWINDIN

VERTEBRATE PUBLISHING

Vertebrate Publishing, Sheffield
www.v-publishing.co.uk

ALL BUT ONE
BARBARA SWINDIN

First published in 2012 by Vertebrate Publishing.

VERTEBRATE PUBLISHING
Crescent House, 228 Psalter Lane, Sheffield S11 8UT.
www.v-publishing.co.uk

All colour photographs by Les Swindin unless otherwise indicated.
All pen and ink sketches by Barbara Swindin.

Front cover: *(Top image)* Barbara climbing in the Lake District, 1975.
(Bottom image) Mont Blanc, the Aiguille Blanche and the Aiguille Noire. *Photo: Pete Fleming.*

Back cover: Barbara and Les on the summit of the Montagne des Agneaux. *Photo: anon.*

This book is a work of non-fiction based on the life, experiences and recollections
of Barbara Swindin. In some limited cases the names of people, places, dates and sequences
or the detail of events have been changed solely to protect the privacy of others.
The author has stated to the publishers that, except in such minor respects not affecting
the substantial accuracy of the work, the contents of the book are true.

A CIP catalogue record for this book is available from the British Library.

ISBN: 978-1-906148-60-7
10 9 8 7 6 5 4 3 2 1

Designed and typeset in Arno Pro by Jane Beagley, Vertebrate Graphics Ltd.
www.v-graphics.co.uk

Printed and bound in the UK by T.J. International Ltd, Padstow, Cornwall.

CONTENTS

FOREWORD

I first met Barbara Swindin in 1976, when I was briefly a member of the Gloucestershire Mountaineering Club, and we have remained firm friends ever since. Barbara and Les, already established alpinists, were then just embarking on ski-alpinism. Since I was keen to find out how to start ski-mountaineering, Barbara advised that I enquire about the tours led by members of the Ski Club of Great Britain. I did just that and, after the Easter ski-touring season of 1977, Barbara and I had much delight in exchanging experiences of this branch of alpinism. It was to give both of us so much pleasure in the years to come; for me, those initial two spring weeks in the Vanoise and the Gran Paradiso areas had simply been the best experiences of my life. Over the next couple of years Barbara and I met on occasions to walk in the hills, or climb on British rock and, importantly, to exchange news of our respective ski-mountaineering ventures. In 1979 we both completed the High Level Route on skis in separate parties, mine culminating in an ascent of Mont Blanc, and two years later I was highly delighted when Barbara and Les invited me to join them on a ten-day ski-traverse of the Bernese Oberland. That successful venture cemented our friendship and we had several more excellent ski-tours together through the 1980s. It was also thanks to Barbara's suggestion that I joined the Pinnacle Club (for women climbers), and women's mountaineering and ski mountaineering were the main themes of my activities and mountain friendships for many years.

Roll forward several decades to Barbara's decision that the time had come to complete her book. I found I was in a position to provide her with advice on the practicalities of bringing the project to fruition. My husband, Rupert Hoare, like Barbara, was devoted to climbing in the Alps above all other mountain ranges, and was a conscientious diary writer too. On learning, in early 2011, that he had not long to live, Rupert had at once embarked on the long-planned project of putting his mountain tales and photographs together in a book for friends and family. With much credit due to his editor and publishers, Rupert's beautifully crafted book was ready just a few weeks before his death in September 2011. Over the succeeding months, as Barbara kindly kept in touch with me, we often spoke about how Rupert and I had got his book into print in time and to the very high standard of production he so much desired. Barbara soon decided to use the same team for her own book. Then, following a delightful spring walking week in the Lake District, when she and I discussed various chapters, I was taken aback to be asked to compose the Foreword.

This task, of course, led me to read the whole book. I found it most compelling and, as the chapters rolled effortlessly on, I became more and more impressed by Barbara's mountaineering achievements. The narrative presents an honest account of her development as an increasingly competent member of her alpine teams. In the early years, there were a few ascents which she admits to finding very challenging, and where she was conscious of being the weakest member of the party, particularly in difficult conditions. However, as the years passed, it was apparent that she was becoming a thoroughly proficient and self-reliant participant. I was also very impressed by the clarity of the experiences recounted and the exquisite detail of the route descriptions, which often made me feel as if I was there too. I have been aware these last two summers of very much missing a summer holiday in the Alps, but reading this book, whilst further awakening my desire to revisit the Alps, has provided an alternative to actually being there, so vivid are the descriptions and the portrayal of the intense feelings of joy engendered by alpine climbing. Barbara's evocative writing will bring happy memories flooding back to many of her readers. Others will be inspired to build up their own store of memories of unforgettable alpine ascents.

Some recent books by women mountaineers rightly focus on their roles in leading climbs and taking part in bold exploration of remote mountain regions. Barbara's story is in quite a different genre. She is telling her readers about the classic Alpine ridge and face routes which she and her husband Les climbed on their annual long summer holidays. When a couple share such a love of mountains and each other, it is natural that they should mainly spend the precious good days of an Alpine summer on the same routes in each other's company. Twenty years after the zenith of the Swindins' long climbing partnership, there are now climbing couples where the lead may be shared more equally, as some women have developed the confidence, skills and opportunity to be equal partners. Nevertheless, it is abundantly clear from Barbara's writing that she can in no sense be described as a 'passenger' on the climbs she did with Les, once her apprenticeship was complete. Her thoughtful writing demonstrates a full involvement in the continuous decision-making required by the weather, climbing conditions and route-finding in the Alps, together with the changing human factors of fitness and motivation.

The book is very much a tale of the days Barbara shared with her fellow alpinists. Above all, as she stresses, she and Les enjoyed climbing together;

the spring ski-touring and summer Alpine seasons year after year were an integral part of their married life. The graduation to climbing long, serious and demanding classic routes such as the North Ridge of the Weisshorn, as a rope of two with Les, was a very special milestone for her. However, it is clear that she also treasured the days with the firm and trusted friends who often joined the Swindin rope. This Foreword should have been written by Pete Fleming, who was on so many of the climbs with Barbara and Les, but sadly illness took him first. My recent week in the Lake District for Barbara's birthday brought home to me the great fondness which Les and Barbara's friends have for the two of them. To quote Barbara in talking about her mountain friends, 'We had such fun and shared so much magic.' I was fortunate indeed to have shared many good days in the Alps as part of the Swindin ski-touring teams. Rupert and I were particularly pleased that they joined our party for a week on Mull in 2008, to climb my 'last Munro'.

This book might easily have been written by Barbara as the first British woman to have climbed all Collomb's list of 4000-metre peaks in the Alps. The fact that such an objective was only seriously considered in the last few years of Barbara's Alpine climbing career, and then just not quite managed, does not in any way detract from the pleasure of the book. The sense of achievement and elation shines out during and after so many of the individual ascents, whether the Täsch-Dom traverse or the last ascent of the Alphubel. These and so many other routes were climbed at the peak of Barbara's fitness and one can truly feel what a vital part mountaineering played in her life, her marriage and her friendships. For Barbara, lists and heights really were not at all what mattered most: after a very good day on the Corda Molla of Monte Disgrazia (only 3678m) she notes that it was one of the most splendid days in her whole mountaineering career.

All But One is much more than an account of succeeding alpine seasons. Great interest is added by historical perspectives and parallels drawn with some earlier women mountaineers who wrote or feature in well-known classic works of Alpine literature from the late 19th and early 20th centuries. In addition, interspersed throughout the book, there are short pieces on thought-provoking alpine topics such as weather, fear and fatigue. Barbara also provides perceptive discussion of the need for a mountaineer to control her mental attitude towards the venture to come and be self-aware of the need to do so. She demonstrates how the struggle to keep a positive attitude was often rewarded by the resulting satisfaction of the achievement. Doubts often had to be firmly put to one side in a deliberate manner.

As I turned the pages with pleasure and curiosity, I became convinced that this book could become a classic of its genre. It is truly a story of a devoted and committed couple enjoying all that the European Alps have to offer in terms of challenging classic routes, many of which have great historical resonance for British mountaineers and are a wonderful mountain playground to go to in the company of lifelong friends.

J A TURNER
Former President of the Eagle Ski Club and member of the Pinnacle Club
August 2012

PREFACE

A few years after making my second attempt to climb the final summit on my list of Alpine Fourthousanders, I began to write this book. At the time, I was trying to come to terms with the fact that, because of ill health, I might never have another chance to attain my goal. Eventually I accepted the situation, and abandoned the book, but recently friends have encouraged me to complete the story.

It has been interesting, nearly twenty years later, to examine my Alpine career more objectively than I could have done in the days when I still hoped to pick up again where I had left off. In those days, I imagined I could have one more attempt to reach the summit of the Aiguille Blanche de Peuterey, and thus become the first British woman to have climbed all the Fourthousanders.

You may ask why anyone would write a book about a project that was not completed. It is not, however, the first time a climber has published an account of what might be considered an unsuccessful adventure. Indeed, the first mountaineering book I ever picked up off a shelf in my childhood home was Hugh Ruttledge's story of the 1933 attempt on Everest.[1] Although I had not yet learned to read or write – the scribbles on a few pages are a testimony to that – the black and white photographs of tents pitched on glaciers and mountaineers climbing ladders registered in my young mind. The expedition didn't succeed in its objective, but Ruttledge's record is still a worthy document in the history of Himalayan climbing. My own account is not just about success and failure. It is a celebration of the mountains and recognition of the impact that mountaineering has had throughout such a long period of my life. It is also a tribute to all those who helped me to achieve what I did, to those who encouraged me and to those who waited anxiously at home whilst I was indulging in what is essentially a selfish pursuit. I am deeply grateful for the patience and tolerance of all concerned.

Whilst I was actively engaged in the climbing world, I rarely thought about the fact that I was a female mountaineer. Climbers were climbers. Whether they were men or women was of no more importance to me than whether they were from the working classes or the aristocracy, or from one

---

1   *Everest 1933* by Hugh Ruttledge, Hodder & Stoughton, 1934

part of the world or another. We all shared the same passion for the mountains. While writing this book, however, I have become increasingly conscious of issues, both trivial and serious, that concern women climbers in particular, and, at the same time, awed by the achievements of the early female pioneers. The names of some of these women are well known in climbing circles, but others are not. I have mentioned just a few, chosen to illustrate a point about a particular route or situation. No offence is intended to the many fine women climbers I haven't included. This is a personal account of the climbs I have undertaken, and was never meant to be a history of British women climbers.

Above all, I tell my story very much from a woman's perspective, both my mountaineering career and my professional life having taken place in a distinctly male-dominated community. Gradually, from the mid-1960s to the mid-1990s, the period when I was an active member of the mountaineering world, there was an increase in the overall number of female climbers, and this has continued into the 21st century. At the same time, in my profession, the imbalance between the number of men and women who reached higher positions on the career ladder has to some extent been redressed.

Many people have a natural instinct to leave something tangible behind for posterity. In 1976, after the birth of my sister's children, I recognised this desire in myself and started to write up in a private journal as much as I could remember about my early climbs in the Alps. I then continued year after year to record every Alpine route I climbed and every ski-tour I went on. That journal, as well as the recollections of my husband and friends, has been the main source of information upon which the descriptions of my climbing experiences are based.

I am indebted not only to all the people who climbed with me, both in the Alps and in Britain, but also, above all, to my husband, Les Swindin, who helped me learn to climb, and who, at one time or another, stood with me on the summit of all but one of the major Fourthousanders. Without Pete Fleming, however, it is unlikely that I would ever have risen to the challenge of climbing all fifty-two peaks and I am indebted to him for his encouragement and faith in my abilities. I thank his wife, Margaret, too, for her friendship and all the support she gave us in pursuing our objectives, often enduring a lonely vigil as she waited for us to return from the mountains. All three have helped me at many stages during the writing of this tale. Richard Heery read an early draft and gave me invaluable advice, and I am indebted to him for the title of *All But One*.

Barbara Swindin – August 2012

AUSTRIA

RHINE

INN

ENGADINE

ST MORITZ
BERNINA • • PONTRESINA
ALPS
Piz ▲ ▲ Piz Palü
Bernina
▲
Monte
Disgrazia
•
SONDRIO

Lake
Como

Lake
Lugano

Lake
Maggiore

LECCO

MILAN

ITALY

Ye are bound for the mountains?
Ah! with you let me go,
Where yon cold distant barrier
The vast range of snow
Through its loose clouds lifts dimly
Its white peaks in air:
How deep is the stillness:
Ah! would I were there.

– MATTHEW ARNOLD

INTRODUCTION

No sagacity could have foretold that anything of the kind could occur
and no precautions could have forestalled or met it.
– DOROTHY PILLEY[1]

The Aiguille Verte and the Droites

1 *Climbing Days* by Dorothy Pilley

INTRODUCTION

CHANCE

Suddenly the snow-step collapsed. A surge of adrenalin spurred me into action and I rammed my ice axe into the firmer layer of snow beneath the surface, quickly regaining my equilibrium. 'Careful, B!' I thought. This was no place to fall. One serious slip here could have sent the three of us sliding down, down, down, hundreds of metres to oblivion. I rapidly picked myself up to continue the descent.

Earlier that morning in August 1990, Pete, Les and I had sat happily on the summit of Les Droites, the last French peak I needed to climb in order to complete my list of Alpine Fourthousanders. I had already climbed all the Swiss mountains on that list, and there remained just one more peak to do in Italy: the Aiguille Blanche de Peuterey. From the Droites, I had stared at the sharp outline of this final target, dwarfed by the adjacent white dome of Mont Blanc.

Now we were descending a snow-covered rib from the summit crest to reach the slopes of the glacier below but, at ten o'clock in the morning, the sun was already playing its part in our lives. However careful we were, it was all too easy to slip in the softening snow. I need not have panicked, though. This had just been a minor incident, such as happens to most mountaineers at one time or another, but it was a warning. As experienced alpinists, we were aware of the risk and we were on our guard. Nothing, however, could have led us to expect what happened a little while later.

We continued downwards, even more cautiously and, after abseiling down a short cliff to a wide snow slope, pressed on as fast as we could, traversing to the far side before descending steeply, facing inwards on the front points of our crampons. Then we reached an easier gradient and turned outwards to walk normally. My mouth felt parched in the heat and I silently implored the men to stop, so that we could have a drink. I knew there was no point in voicing that wish aloud; we were all aware that we needed to hurry. As the day wore on, the snow would become more dangerous in the sun and, even though we had by then reached what is called a Normal Route, one taken by the majority of alpinists descending from the nearby summit of the Courtes, we were on a south-facing slope.

High above us, something moved. Hearing a distant sound of rumbling, Les looked up. Then, to his utter horror, he witnessed the collapse of a substantial portion of the cliff at the top of the slope we had just crossed. As it hit the ground, it began to bounce down over the snow 700 metres or so above us. How many seconds would it take to descend to our level? Not only was this great chunk of rock falling, but it was also disintegrating: huge boulders were flying down on both sides of it and it continued to split into a myriad of fragments. All the debris was fanning out as the rock fell, and the wider it spread, the more likely we were to be in its fall line.

Roped together as we were, we all started to run, Pete leading the way. He was heading across the slope now, away from the line of the rockfall and towards the only shelter we could see: a vertical outcrop of rock nearer the edge of this vast snow slope. Just as Pete reached the foot of the outcrop, Les shouted at us to stop because he thought we were about to pull him over. Lying on the ground, he would have been defenceless against the onslaught.

So I came to a standstill and, unable to join Pete, flattened myself against the side of the rock. I was not in a position to look up. I must have been so vulnerable, yet I clung there hugging the rock, willing it to save me. Les, meanwhile, remained out on the slope, dodging the debris. The slightest splinter of stone touching the rope, or brushing against one of us, would be enough to dislodge us, if not obliterate us at a stroke.

A wave of snow two metres high came down just to one side of us, across the path we had taken a few moments before. With my head beneath my helmet and my face turned to the rock wall, I could see nothing, but I heard it all. For several minutes, great boulders, small stones and tiny splinters of rock came thundering past us. The noise was deafening and images of the battlefields of Northern France in the First World War flashed through my mind. Eventually the sounds died down.

'Are you all right, B?' I heard Les say.

'Yes, I'm still alive, I'm not hurt … Are you?'

He too was untouched. What about Pete? The silence filled me with dread so I shouted his name. There was no reply.

BEGINNINGS

'We always said you were a mountain goat.'

My parents repeated this many times over the years. As a child, I was always a fidget. I am told that even in my cot I would never lie still. As soon as I had learned to walk, I wanted to climb. On the way to the shops with my mother and my baby sister, I would walk along the top of the roadside wall rather than use the pavement. Then I wanted to climb the oak tree at the bottom of the garden, but my mother drew the line at that: 'If you fall off, you'll hurt yourself!'

Perhaps that was the moment when I began to learn fear and, as I grew up, my instinctive impulses to live dangerously gradually ebbed away – an inauspicious start for someone who would one day aspire to climb all the Alpine peaks over 4000m. Yet I had always had that urge, right from the beginning, to stand higher than the world around me.

By the time I was in my early teens, scrambling on bouldery seashores in the summer holidays, I had already become cautious, wary of the drop below me. All the same, those rocks occupied me for hours. I loved the feel of them, the intricate game of finding handholds and footholds, and the anxious pleasure of manoeuvring from one boulder to the next, crossing gaps and scaling little walls. It was a solitary pleasure, stimulating my imagination and a longing for something beyond my reach.

I loved to be outdoors. My experience as a girl guide confirmed how much more exciting camping and hiking were than learning the traditional homemaking crafts that girls in those days were expected to master: cooking, needlework and childcare. It was fun to light a wood fire outdoors and brew a billycan of tea. We learned how to tie knots in a rope and lasso a tree branch, to recognise the stars and read a map, using a compass. All these activities appealed to me so much more than trying to prove that I was a potential housewife. If only I could have been a boy scout.

Barbara at two years old.   Photo: The Family Collection.

4

There were few opportunities for girls growing up in the 1950s to undertake serious athletic training and, even if any had come my way, I probably wouldn't have taken them, as I was by nature shy of pushing myself forward. I was – and am – slightly built and my adolescent years did not prepare me physically for the lifestyle I was to adopt from my mid-twenties onwards. No doubt my lack of training during those years was partly responsible for the way my musculo-skeletal system responded to the violence of the twists and falls and overstretching which I inflicted upon it in the early years of my mountaineering career. With hindsight, it is easy to believe this. At the time, I would hear none of it and scoffed at those who hinted at the dangers. I would not be discouraged and, with the resilience of youth, bounced back every time after a setback.

Although, as a girl, my gymnastic ability never developed very far and was not accompanied by any acquisition of physical strength, hills and mountains had always featured in my life. My parents first met on a walking holiday in Switzerland just before the Second World War and their reminiscences kindled my interest in the Alps. My father's eldest sister used to send us postcards from Austria and Switzerland, where she loved to spend her holidays walking and scrambling in the mountains, and the chocolate box images fed my imagination with romantic ideas of snow-covered peaks. In my ignorance, I thought that real mountains were covered with snow all year round. We lived in Gloucestershire, where the hills of the Severn Vale and the Cotswolds are green and nothing exceeds 350m above sea-level. I adored the snow, but in the 1940s and 1950s, a home-made sledge was my only introduction to winter sports. It was almost unheard of for ordinary people to go skiing.

It was not until I was at university that I first had an opportunity to do some serious hill walking. I was with a group formed for that purpose and one of the first mountains we ascended was Snowdon, via the sharp ridge from Crib Goch to Crib-y-ddysgl. This was my introduction to rock scrambling and, despite my apprehensiveness, I thought that February day had given me one of the best experiences I had ever had. Whenever, on many occasions since, I have seen coachloads of students on that ridge, the memory of my first ascent has flashed back. There must have been at least twenty of us. We were perilously ignorant of the potential dangers, especially in winter, but were fortunate to have dry rock and only the tiniest evidence of previous snow. At least I was shod in a proper pair of bendy leather walking boots but, apart from that, I had no specialised outdoor clothing at all.

Even the craggy approach to the East Summit of Crib Goch from the col on the Pyg Track gave me some interesting moments and I have often wondered which line we actually took. When I reached the top of the East Ridge, I looked with astonishment at the way ahead. If you stumble here, you could fall a long way down the steep, stony flank of the mountain on one side or the other. You would be horribly injured and very likely die. But, determined not to show my timidity, I followed the crowd very carefully along the narrow crest until we reached slightly less daunting ground. We wove our way without incident over and around the various pinnacles and, as we progressed, I felt more and more pleased that I had put myself into this exhilarating situation. It wasn't the potential danger that I enjoyed, it was the sense of elevation high above the valleys that gave me an irrational thrill, an intense feeling of satisfaction. Here we were in a place where, for all its popularity with hill-goers, relatively few human beings tread. It was also a relief to know that I had been able to overcome the nervousness I felt at the tremendous exposure of this route. The innate fear of heights I had acquired since my early childhood was not unconquerable.

It was, however, already my last year as a student and I had never considered joining the apparently male-dominated university climbing club. If only I'd had the ability, determination and previous climbing experience of an eighteen year old girl such as Janet Cox, and known she'd been a member of that very club a few years before, when she was also a student at Birmingham University. That might have inspired me to join. Until then, however, I hadn't really thought out what course my life should take and I wasn't involved in any active sport at all. I had been brought up to anticipate a future akin to the lives of the women I had known since childhood: marriage, children, the usual pattern. It would be wrong to imagine I had already abandoned these assumptions, but from then on it was the yearning to be active, to reach high summits, to live outdoors, to envelop myself in the mountain world, that was to assume a greater and greater place in my aspirations. It was to become my raison d'être.

My first passion had been foreign languages. For several years I devoted most of my spare time to learning to speak at least one language as fluently as a native. Because of my somewhat disrupted secondary education, when my hope of starting a second foreign language was dashed by a sudden change of school, my ambition centred upon French and, at sixteen, I fell in love with France. Despite the problems at school, I was offered a place at university to study French and German. I was most fortunate, as few girls were privileged to go on to higher education in the early 1960s.

After university, I started a career in the business world, before returning to Gloucestershire, where I eventually took up teaching in Further Education in my mid-twenties. Strange coincidences sometimes happen. On a walking holiday in Scotland with my sister in the summer of 1966, I met someone who had recently lived in Gloucestershire. Noting my enthusiasm for rocky ridges and high places, she thought I might be interested in joining my local mountaineering club and gave me the name of a key member. It was in the Gloucestershire Mountaineering Club (GMC) that, for the first time since leaving university, I found a group of like-minded people. Shortly after that, I met the man I married and with whom I have shared a passion for the Alps that has lasted ever since. Whether I would have graduated to Alpine climbing without Les Swindin is anyone's guess.

Les had recently taken up a post as a Chemistry Lecturer at the local Technical College, having spent many years working in industry. Tall, lean and extremely fit, he had been a competitive sportsman since his early childhood, following, as an amateur, in the footsteps of his father, George Swindin, who was a professional footballer. George spent most of his career as goalkeeper for Arsenal Football Club. By the time Les met me, however, he was completely devoted to mountaineeering. Already a good rock climber, having had his introduction to this activity in the Black Cuillin on the Isle of Skye (the fiercest baptism anyone could have in Britain) he also had some Alpine experience. His first season was in the summer of 1965, the centenary of the first ascent of the Matterhorn, when he spent two weeks in Zermatt. Two of his companions already had a little Alpine experience but Les and three others were total novices. Guideless, the six young men climbed the Rimpfischhorn, Les's first Fourthousander. Within the following week, he and one of the other novices, Alan Bevitt, also climbed the Zinalrothorn and the Matterhorn. Not a bad start!

By the summer of 1970, Les and I had enjoyed three years together, mountain climbing in England, Wales and Scotland, in all weathers and all seasons. The snow and ice conditions in those late 1960s winters were supreme and, thanks to low temperatures, the 'white stuff' lasted several months in the mountain areas, so I served a useful apprenticeship. Despite frozen eyelashes, numbed fingers and bitterly cold toes cramped into close-fitting leather boots, I was in my element on snow. Rock climbing was another matter. Right from the start I was very nervous. Where had the fearless little girl of my childhood gone? It took several years before I acquired a good technique and, even then, I could rarely bring myself to lead.

Libby Peter's recent article in the magazine *Climber*[2] describes how Jacky McMahon had rock climbed for over thirty years before deciding in her mid-forties that she wanted to lead. She had begun climbing as a child in

---

2 *'Jacky's Indian Summer'* by Libby Peter, *Climber*, May 2012

the 1980s and, over time, had learned to control her fears, becoming a very competent second, but she had felt no urge to lead until now, the second decade of the 21st century. It was her love of the hills and mountains that sustained her. Like Jacky, I had been no natural rock climber either, but my passion for the mountain environment drove me on. I was neither as bold as such early pioneers as Katy Richardson or Dorothy Pilley, nor did I have the innate ability to flow up the moves on a rock face as Nea Morin had done before me. In my case, climbing had to be learned.

To a large extent, my earlier rock climbs were a means to an end. I was spurred on by the need to be a competent second, if not a leader, in order to scale the more difficult mountains, wherever they might be. Eventually I learned the pleasures of rock climbing for its own sake. I began to enjoy the feeling that ascending a steep crag is a little like a vertical jigsaw puzzle where you make decision after decision as you move from one handhold or foothold to the next, finding the most appropriate solution for your height, strength and flexibility as you move upwards. I have even been known to enthuse about the delights of warm, sunny crags and a wide range of classic rock routes. But, above all, I simply loved the mountains and felt so inspired by them that I was determined to climb to the summit of as many Alpine peaks as opportunity permitted.

WOMEN AND MOUNTAINEERING: EARLY DAYS

When I started mountaineering, I had heard of men who had climbed in the Himalaya, men I had noticed in my father's books: Mallory and Irvine, and Tilman and their contemporaries in the 1920s and 1930s. I was also aware of the first ascent of Everest by Edmund Hillary and Sherpa Tenzing in 1953 – a year that stood out in my mind more on account of the coronation of Queen Elizabeth than for the mountaineering achievement which coincided with it. I had, however, never seen any pictures nor read any stories about female mountaineers, and knew nothing about the history of Alpine mountaineering. The words 'alpinism' and 'alpinist' didn't feature in my vocabulary. I hadn't heard of the golden age of mountain climbing in the 19th century, and I had no idea that a number of women had also climbed in those days. It was only after my own early adventures, when I progressed from easy rock climbs to harder ones, taking advantage of the 'modern' clothing and equipment available in the 1970s, that I began to appreciate how skilled my predecessors had been, with their ladylike outfits and primitive gear.

They were also courageous and determined, those first lady alpinists who defied convention in the Victorian Age. One of the earliest British women to climb was Lucy Walker, who ascended the Strahlhorn in 1860 and attempted the Jungfrau that same year. By the time she climbed the Matterhorn in 1871, the first woman to do so, she had already been to the summit of at least eighteen other Fourthousanders. As on all her Alpine expeditions, she was wearing a long dress.

Miss Walker was probably one of the first female alpinists to be spurred on by a competitive urge: upon learning that an American, Miss Meta Brevoort, was intending to climb the Matterhorn, she set out immediately and succeeded in reaching the summit several days before her contemporary. Although Lucy Walker was the first, several other women soon followed in her footsteps. Miss Brevoort not only climbed to the summit from Zermatt, but also descended via the Italian Ridge to Breuil, or Cervinia, as we call it today. Two British sisters, the Misses Pigeon, made the same traverse the following year.

The Walker family with friends and guides, including Lucy Walker and her guide, Melchior Anderegg, back row R, Chamonix, France, July 1870. © The Alpine Club Photo Library, London.

This was the era when social conventions decreed that ladies should be chaperoned when in the company of a mountain guide. When Miss Walker was climbing with her trusted guide and friend, Melchior Anderegg from Zermatt, she was accompanied at all times by either her father or her brother. She came from a wealthy family, as did most of the women who followed her precedent over the next two decades. Today, it is difficult to imagine just how they coped with the hardships of scaling rock and snow, and living in primitive conditions at high altitude. How was it that they were physically strong enough to reach Alpine summits, when they had none of the advantages of training that young climbers have nowadays? The truth is that, before the age of the motor car, the majority of men and

Mrs. Aubrey (Elizabeth) Le Blond, 1861-1934, first president of the Ladies' Alpine Club 1907-12 (also 1932-34), on a Norwegian peak in 1899. Photo: Joseph Imboden. © The Alpine Club Photo Library, London.

women were far more physically active in their daily lives than the average person is today. Consequently, these pioneering women may not have been so very unfit for the task of walking long distances uphill in the Alps. Lucy Walker, when she started to climb in her early twenties, also had the advantage of two obvious role models for the physical requirements of mountaineering: her more experienced father and brother.

Elizabeth Hawkins-Whitshed, born in 1860, started climbing in the Alps in the 1880s. She had been brought up in a very wealthy, aristocratic family with the expectation of life as the wife of a member of the upper classes and, after making her début in high society, she married Frederick Burnaby, a Guards Officer twice her age and said to be a member of the Prince of Wales' social set.[3] She was only eighteen years old. In 1880, about five years before her husband was killed in battle, she bore him a son, Harry. Although she was recorded in the April 1881 Census as living in a household in Kensington, with a valet, butler and four other servants, Mrs. Burnaby did not stay in London for very long. Advised to go out to Switzerland for health reasons, she lived mainly there for many years from 1882.

It was in the Engadine, from St. Moritz, that she discovered mountain climbing. Before that first visit to Switzerland, she had not been at all interested in mountains but a trip to the Diavolezza Pass near Pontresina completely transformed her ideas. From then on, her health improved and, the following year, despite being a young mother, she embarked upon a

Mrs. Aubrey (Elizabeth) Le Blond, wearing face mask, self-portrait on Durmaalstind, Norway, c.1900. © *The Alpine Club Photo Library, London.*

3 *Women on the Rope* by Cicely Williams

twenty-year career of climbing in the Alps. By the end of 1882, she had ascended both Mont Blanc and the Grandes Jorasses, being benighted on the latter, an experience that she thoroughly enjoyed.[4] Her son was a delicate child, as his mother had been, and spent his early years in Ireland in the care of his maternal grandmother.

After Fred Burnaby's death, the young widow remarried, becoming Mrs. Main, only to be widowed a second time. In 1900, 'Lizzie', as she was known to her friends, married for the third time, but had no more children. Her third husband, Mr. Le Blond, gave her the name by which she is best known today, and it was as Mrs. Aubrey Le Blond that she became the first President of the Ladies' Alpine Club in 1907.

Mrs. Le Blond was so fit and determined that she once cycled all the way from St. Moritz to Rome. According to her obituary, she had to carry her bicycle, laden with luggage, along parts of the path beside Lake Como, as there was no road there at that time. During her marriage with Aubrey Le Blond, the couple travelled a great deal in Asia. Lizzie Le Blond died in 1934 with a fine Alpine record to her name. She was a remarkable woman. Not only did she climb mountains in the summertime, but she was also one of the first women to make Alpine ascents in winter and, unlike Lucy Walker, she was prepared to climb 'manless' – or, rather, she climbed alone with her male guides, dispensing with a chaperone. Colonel Strutt of the Alpine Club described her thus:

She was a highly skilful climber and, in her best days, was certainly rivalled in performance by Miss Richardson alone. Her chief characteristic was her extraordinary judgment. In the writer's opinion … this judgment has never been surpassed by any mountaineer, professional or amateur, of the so-called stronger sex.[5]

Katy Richardson also climbed in the Alps in the 1880s. She was a petite, dainty woman, six years older than Mrs. Le Blond. Whereas Mrs. Le Blond would climb in breeches, only putting a skirt on again when she reached a village, Katy Richardson always wore a skirt when she climbed, just as Lucy Walker had done. Her diet on the mountains was similar to Miss Walker's too, though in Miss Richardson's case, bread, butter and honey were substituted for sponge cake, and tea for champagne. In that respect, my own diet on Monte Disgrazia in 1988 was not dissimilar to Miss Richardson's! Despite the inconveniences of her stature and clothing,

4 ibid
5 Ladies Alpine Club Yearbook, 1935; Colonel Strutt's words from the Alpine Journal vol. XLVI, quoted in obituary

she was a very determined, energetic alpinist and is known for having made six first ascents and fourteen first ascents by a woman.

Her first visit to the Alps seems to have been in 1871, when she was in Zermatt.[6] That same year she also discovered the Engadine, where she made ascents of a number of low mountains, but it was not until the following year that she started to climb the high peaks. Over eleven summer seasons, she made a total of 116 *grandes courses* or major routes, and sixty *ascensions secondaires*.[7] She is remarkable on account of her stamina on exceptionally long, arduous expeditions, as well as her athletic climbing ability. Leaving the hamlet of La Bérarde, at an altitude of approximately 1700m in the Dauphiné, at 9.00 pm on 23rd August 1888, she made the first female ascent of the Grand Pic of the Meije, 3982m, and was back in La Bérarde by 5.30 pm the following afternoon. Two days later she set out for the Ecrins, the only Fourthousander in the region, traversed the mountain from south to north, and returned via the Col des Ecrins to La Bérarde within fifteen hours. She may have been small, but she was strong and very agile. In Chamonix, after traversing the Aiguilles du Dru, one of her guides described her as being able to 'slide over the rocks like a lizard'.[8]

'Katy' was born Sarah K. Richardson near Doncaster in 1854, the second of five daughters of a clergyman, the Reverend George Richardson, and his wife, Isabel Nussey. The Reverend Richardson became vicar of Kilburn in Yorkshire and it was there that a German governess, Pauline Bau(e)rmeister, born in Bassel (sic), was living with the family at the time of the 1871 Census. Perhaps this was the connection that had led Miss Richardson to travel to Zermatt the previous year. The Richardson family certainly did not appear to be without financial means. At both their earlier residence and in Kilburn they had two or three servants, suggesting that the vicar had not only his stipend but also a supplementary income. Somehow or other, his daughter was able to spend several summer vacations over the following years climbing in the Alps, visiting the Engadine in south-eastern Switzerland, and the Dauphiné in France, as well as the Pennine Alps in the vicinity of Zermatt. In addition to transport, she had to pay for hotel accommodation and guides. When she died in 1927, Miss Richardson's estate was estimated at £6624 3s 5d,[9] a not inconsiderable sum in those days. By comparison, the originally wealthy Mrs. Le Blond, who had inherited an estate in Ireland from her father, as well as marrying

6 *La Montagne* vol. XXIII, CAF Paris, 1927: article by Mary Paillon
7 ibid
8 ibid
9 *Dictionary of National Biography*, Oxford University Press, 2011
10 ibid

the apparently well-to-do Frederick Burnaby, left an estate worth only £4410 14s 6d[10] when she died in 1934.

Another noteworthy British female climber of the Victorian era was Gertrude Bell, born in 1868. She too was of diminutive stature, a mere 4 feet 10 inches tall, yet possessed the qualities of a truly élite mountaineer. During the brief six-year period that she spent climbing in the Alps at the turn of the century when she was already over thirty, Miss Bell climbed a number of the highest peaks in the Pennine Alps, Mont Blanc Massif and the Dauphiné but, as far as mountaineering is concerned, she is best known for her participation in an attempt on the North-East Face of the Finster-aarhorn in the Bernese Oberland. Of course, the name of Gertrude Bell is much more widely associated with her political and administrative acti-vities in the Middle East, where she was a negotiator on behalf of the British government. A first-class honours graduate of Oxford University, she was a historian, archaeologist and linguist, a quite outstanding woman of her time. She was fluent in Arabic and Persian, as well as French and German, and, like Mrs. Le Blond, she came from the upper echelons of British society. Her grandfather had been an industrialist and Liberal Member of Parliament, and her father, a 2nd baronet, held prestigious political positions in County Durham and North Yorkshire. Gertrude Bell was passionate about her various interests, energetic and determined, and had a great love of travel and exploration.

Non-climbers might imagine that physical stature is a guide to a climber's ability. A tall, well-built woman might appear to have the advantage over one who is shorter and more slightly built but, although the former may have greater strength and a longer stride, the latter is often just as capable, if not more so, of climbing neatly and efficiently – and thereby just as quickly. Gertrude Bell and Katy Richardson are two such examples. When women are 'taken up' routes, as the Victorians were and as many of us have been since, the lack of bodyweight is a great advantage on many occasions, especially when the guide is inclined to aid his client by physically 'hauling' her up a steep step. In this record of my own Alpine ascents, I have rarely needed to confess to being helped by any such tactic and the aforemen-tioned determined Victorian ladies probably needed little, if any, assistance of that kind either. (Towards the end of my mountaineering career, there was, however, one occasion near the summit of the Dent du Géant when I certainly benefited from just such a tug on the rope.) My own slightness of stature and lack of weight contributed to the ease with which I was able to move up steep rock, but only after I had learned to rely on these natural advantages and not try to use muscle strength I simply did not possess.

Today's young women, with their opportunities to train in gyms and on climbing walls, doubtless acquire much greater physical strength than their predecessors, leading to greater achievements than would have been thought possible in years gone by.

One advantage the Victorian ladies had over the modern climber was the fact that they rarely had to carry very much, if anything at all. They not only had guides, whose rucksacks accommodated the client's food, clothing and other items as well as their own, but also porters, whose task was to assist the guides with their burdens. However, once female climbers began to climb guideless, and particularly when they climbed on women-only ropes, they had no choice but to carry on their own backs everything they needed for the expedition, and they could no longer rely upon the superior strength of a man to haul them up a difficult step. Having climbed exclusively with men in the Alps, I was never in that totally independent situation. When my husband accompanied me, he usually carried a heavier pack than I did, particularly on the walks up to the huts.

Any activity involving risk casts a shadow over the people close to the participant. Climbing is potentially dangerous, so the family and friends of climbers bear a degree of anxiety. The climber may acknowledge this, yet continues to climb. Those who wish to climb at the same time as raising a family have a serious dilemma. Society has traditionally viewed mothers, in particular, as indispensable to their children, and has frequently been quick to condemn women climbers for their 'irresponsibility' and 'selfishness'. Women themselves often find it undesirable to put their own lives at risk when they have young children, and thus they quit climbing, either temporarily or permanently.

Lucy Walker, Katy Richardson and Gertrude Bell remained single all their lives and had no children, so the issues of being a wife and mother never impinged upon their climbing careers. Mrs. Le Blond solved the problem of any potential conflict by leaving her only child chiefly in the care of his grandmother whilst she lived and climbed in the Alps. One unexpected result of the First World War, which brought a halt to alpinism for several years, was that the huge loss of a generation of young men – leaving many girls with little prospect of marrying and having children – meant that some of these young women were free to pursue their mountaineering ambitions without the ties of a family.

Between 1914 and 1918, while the world was at war, many members of the Ladies' Alpine Club devoted their energies to voluntary work. In July 1914, Mrs. Le Blond and her son, who had joined her in Switzerland on account of his own health problems, just managed to return to England as war broke out. Nevertheless, this did not deter Mrs. Le Blond from spending a considerable period of time in France and Italy with the Red Cross. She was renowned for her 'Motor Kitchen', and described this work, saying that she was involved in 'making comforts for the Alpini':

We can only wonder how any human beings could drag heavy guns up those mountains.[11]

In 1888, immediately after making the first female ascent of the Meije in the Dauphiné Alps, Katy Richardson met a French climber, Mary Paillon. They became climbing partners and were such close friends that Miss Richardson eventually moved to France, becoming a permanent resident at the Paillon family home in Oullins, near Lyon. In the article Mary Paillon wrote for the *La Montagne* after Miss Richardson's death, she described the Englishwoman as 'almost a sister'. The two friends are reported as helping the war effort:

Mademoiselle Paillon et Miss K. Richardson ont continué à s'occuper spéciale-ment de vêtir les réfugiés et les repatriés.[12]

For LAC members between 1914 and 1918, Miss Maud Meyer, wartime President, aptly summed up the situation:

Most of us seem metaphorically, to have converted our ice-axes into knitting needles and our ropes into wool or into bandages, and the high mountains have been only things to dream of, not to see.[13]

Although some of the LAC women did climb again after the war, for others the period of domesticity became permanent. For me, it wouldn't be a war that threatened the termination of my climbing activities, only my preconceived ideas about the role of a mother. Should I start a family?

---

11 Annual Report, LAC, 1916
12 Annual Report, LAC, 1917
13 Annual Report, LAC, 1916

PART ONE
FIRST STEPS IN THE ALPS

I felt in a trance, already tasting that mixture of ecstasy and weariness and discomfort
that from the beginning to the end is the basic quality of the Alpine experience.
– DOROTHY PILLEY[1]

The Matterhorn

1

First Alpine Season:
Pennine Alps

'Congratulations, Barbara. You've just climbed your first 4000m peak!'

With that remark, our friend, Geoff Causey, first drew my attention to this magic figure, but it was to be many years before I realised that some mountaineers deliberately 'collect' Alpine Fourthousanders in order to complete a 'list'. Although I had heard of the Welsh Threethousands and the Scottish Munros, I knew nothing of Karl Blodig's Alpine List, compiled at least seventy years previously. I did know that Robin Collomb was the editor of the Alpine Club guidebooks we were using, but his List of Fourthousanders wasn't published until the following year. It was early August 1970 and Geoff, Les and I were on top of the Lagginhorn, admiring the vast panorama of snow-covered peaks and glaciers set out all around us. The two men had already climbed a number of other Fourthousanders but this was my début and I didn't really understand the significance of my achievement in reaching this summit. That day I was simply happy to be there.

It was my first season mountaineering in the Alps and the Lagginhorn was the fourth Alpine peak I had climbed. I had trained seriously during the preceding months. Just before we set out for our trip, Les and I had even regularly carried heavy rucksacks up and down the little hill behind our house on the outskirts of Gloucester. The previous year, even though I was teaching until half-past eight every Friday evening and we could never get away early, we had spent almost half our weekends walking and climbing in North Wales and the Lake District. It is amazing to look back and realise that, despite the fact that the motorways were still unlinked between the north and south of Birmingham and the M5 only started north of Tewkesbury, we could drive from Gloucester to Great Langdale on a Friday night at least as quickly as we can decades later. The roads were simply not as busy.

My training period culminated with a grand finale in Wales. I thought that if I was capable of walking round the Welsh Threethousands, the fourteen peaks over 3000 feet high in Snowdonia, in a single day, then I would be fit enough to accompany Les and the other members of our party on Alpine routes. One Friday night in June we duly arrived with three friends from Gloucestershire at the Pen-y-Gwryd hotel in time to down a couple of beers before closing time (half-past ten in those days). Then we set off for Snowdon via the Miners' Track. At four in the morning, after a few hours of fitful sleep on the concrete path outside the Snowdon Summit café, I started out with my friend, Di, leaving Les, Di's husband, Tony, and their climbing partner, Alan, to take our bivouac kit back down with them. They were going to spend the day climbing on Clogwyn Du'r Arddu, one of Snowdonia's most impressive crags, whilst Di and I sweated our way over the mountains in a heatwave. Some thirteen hours later, I staggered down the stony track towards Aber Falls, where Les was waiting for me in his little green MGB sports car. The soles of my feet felt as if they were treading on hot nails but I had made it. From then on, I was confident that I had the stamina to cope with the Alps.

As soon as the end of the summer term came, we were off. Because we worked in a Technical College, our holidays started earlier than those of our schoolteacher friend, Geoff, so we were able to slip in a week of acclimatisation before he and our other friends arrived. Les took me to Zinal in the Swiss canton of Valais for my initiation. We were blessed with a week of perfect weather and spent every day out on the mountains. At first we walked but, towards the end of the week, Les declared me ready for my first climb. It was to be Lo Besso, a relatively low, but spectacularly shaped rock peak at the head of the Val d'Anniviers.

We set out well-laden up the track past the Petit Mountet Hut and continued for hours up the narrow, eroded path on the left bank of the glacier. (Years later a new route was constructed high above the right bank and the path that we took in 1970 fell into disuse.) It took me at least the six hours indicated in the guidebook to reach the hut but the walkers we met along the way were friendly and helped to break the tedium. Eventually we arrived at the glacier-crossing point and there followed a seemingly endless moraine before we reached the real sting in the tail: a short, sharp, rocky slope leading up to the Mountet Hut.

There I sat down wearily at a table and Les revived me with the bowls of lemon tea I had been assured were a ritual on arrival at a hut. I already knew what to expect with the overnight accommodation – all the guests lying in long rows on wide communal bunks called *matratzenlager* – and I counted myself fortunate to have a bed space in a not too overcrowded dormitory. It was a relief that the hut was not overfull. I had heard all too many tales about having to sleep on floors, tables and even window-ledges in the preceding few years. In 1970, it was quite usual for climbers to turn up unannounced at a hut at any time of day or night and tradition decreed that they would not be turned away.

Once recovered from the arduous walk, I relaxed and enjoyed our situation. The Mountet Hut occupies one of the most delightful spots in the Alps and has always remained one of my favourite places. It was an immaculate blue-sky day and from the hut we could see a glorious cirque of peaks towering above us in a wide arc on the far side of the glacier system. Three Fourthousanders, the Dent Blanche, the Obergabelhorn and the Zinalrothorn, are all there and the gaps between and beyond are filled with lower peaks, no less beautiful, the Trifthorn and Wellenkuppe, Mont Durand and the Pointe de Zinal, and, at the far end, the Grand Cornier. I was enraptured; I had never been anywhere like this before. The perfect symmetry of the Obergabelhorn with its sparkling white North Face, flanked on each side by a distinctive ridge, particularly appealed to me.

However, my night was spent in a state of turmoil. I lay awake for hours, nerves on edge, listening to the creaks and groans of the glacier and the sound of stones falling. Tales about overcrowded huts were not the only stories I had heard. My friends had frequently recounted with great hilarity an anecdote from two years before when one of their companions had fallen into a crevasse. The prospect of the two of us crossing the glacier alone to the foot of the Besso had filled me with dread, so, in the course of the evening at the hut, Les and I had agreed to join forces with two English boys to traverse the ice and snow, before going our separate ways to climb.

I need not have worried. The following morning we had no problems on the glacier and I was soon engaged in some delightful climbing on an easy rock ridge where tiny Alpine flowers blossomed in every conceivable crevice. The colours were stunning and I found it difficult to believe that such apparently delicate plants could grow in this inhospitable terrain. Then, at last, I stood on top of the Besso: my Alpine climbing career had begun.

A few days later, we were in Arolla, in the upper reaches of the Val d'Hérens, meeting up with four friends. The first of these was Pat Nind, a member of the Gloucestershire Mountaineering Club, who had been brought up with her two brothers on a farm in the Cotswolds. Now in her early twenties, Pat, despite her slight stature, was much stronger than me and already had a reputation as a fit, fast hill walker and capable rock climber. From the day we first met, Pat had encouraged me to improve my walking speed in the mountains and to take every opportunity to learn to climb. She was always very determined and enthusiastic herself, just the female role model I needed. Having gained some Alpine experience in Austria, she had then spent a couple of weeks climbing in Switzerland in the summer of 1969. With her on that trip were the same three men who joined us now.

Geoff Causey, a tall, lanky, rugby-playing, sports-loving man, originally from Lancashire, was in his late twenties. A couple of years before, he had taken a post teaching Maths at Kendal Grammar School. He had been an active member of his university climbing club, so, by 1970, he had been rock climbing for ten years. Like Les, he had also done a number of classic routes in the Alps. Not only did Geoff's climbing skills inspire confidence but, with his sense of humour and ability to entertain, he could also be relied upon to be the life and soul of the party.

Geoff's Alpine partner that summer was John Oaks, a strongly built young man from Lincolnshire who, at 5 feet 6 inches, was no taller than me. Despite his lack of height, John was perfectly capable of walking just as fast as the long-legged Geoff and Les. I once asked him how he kept up with them. He replied that it was simply a matter of sheer determination: 'You just have to trot along taking twice as many steps as the others.'

I tried to emulate him, but it didn't work for me.

John had been a plumber since he left school and his trade had done just as much for his physique as any training at the gym. He was the youngest of the men in the party and in those days apparently used to consider himself the 'apprentice' alongside his relatively experienced climbing friends.

The fourth member of our group was Andrew Reynolds, an engineer from Lincoln. He and Pat were to be married later that year. Like Geoff, Andrew had a great sense of humour and was, moreover, a master of repartee. I was also most impressed by his ability to walk and climb all day wearing the same combination of clothes that he had put on in the middle of a cold Alpine night, even when we were traipsing back across a snow-covered glacier under a broiling sun. I, on the other hand, stopped frequently to adjust my own attire, no doubt much to the irritation of my climbing partners.

Andrew had climbed in the Alps several times before, initially on a course with the Austrian Alpine Club and then, for his first independent trip, teaming up with Geoff in 1967 in Switzerland. As far as Alpine climbing was concerned, Geoff was a complete novice that year. The tale of their minor epic on the 4158m Jungfrau, the first Alpine peak that Geoff ever climbed, lives on in the folklore of the Lincoln Mountaineering Club to which they belonged. With only a basic knowledge of German, they set about translating a page of the guidebook they had purchased when they arrived in the Bernese Oberland. It took them so long to decipher the first route they read that they decided not to waste any more time looking for an alternative.

Without further delay, and totally unacclimatised, these two fit young Englishmen set off from Stechelberg in the Lauterbrunnen Valley for the Rottal Hut.

They hadn't bargained on such a gruelling approach to their mountain and by the time they had reached the unmanned hut, lit a fire and fed themselves, they were quite weary. After a sleepless night, Geoff persuaded Andrew to rise at 2.00 am for an even earlier start than they had planned. It took them almost twelve hours to reach the summit of the Jungfrau via the Inner Rottal route. This was double the time quoted in the guidebook. Everything seemed to militate against speed: tricky route finding (thanks mainly to the lack of information they had gleaned from the guidebook), soft snow once the fierce heat of the day was upon them, and lack of acclimatisation. Despite all that, the enthusiastic, inexperienced pair succeeded in getting to the top of the mountain and in making their escape, not without considerable difficulty, especially as they had no money with them. They hadn't expected to need to take the mountain railway back down to the valley from the Jungfraujoch.

This extraordinary tale gave me reason to be wary of their tactics. However, by the time we all met in the Alps that summer, both Andrew and Geoff had made a considerable number of much more efficient ascents than on that first occasion. With Les and John they had had a successful Alpine climbing trip in 1968, and then with Pat and John in 1969. Thus, the whole group was quite experienced compared with me, the Alpine novice.

Athough fighting fit by my own standards, I was apprehensive. All my companions were normally much faster on the hill than I was and they all knew how it felt to climb at 4000m above sea-level. I was aware that at that altitude some people suffer from headaches or nausea, or simply a feeling of sluggishness. Fortunately, my week's acclimatisation paid off. By the time we met our friends, my body had adjusted to the altitude and I was able to put on a reasonably good show of stamina and speed. That boosted my morale enormously and the season of 1970 remains one of the most memorable in my climbing career. How happy I was! I felt full of energy, the novelty of each experience was marvellously stimulating: never before had I set out in the darkness of night to walk up a glacier, roped to my companions and surrounded by the silence of the high mountains, broken only by the creaking of the ice and the crunch of crampons on the snow. Sometimes dawn would bring a spectacular show of colour to the sky, the mountains and all the surrounding snowfields. I had to learn how to climb rock in crampons, leap over crevasses and move at a steady pace hour after hour. Then would come the joy of climbing to the summit, rewarded by the vast panorama of range after range of mountains as far as the horizon. Every climb offered me a new and different experience.

In addition to all that, we had so much fun. Alpine climbing was a serious matter, but there were many relaxed moments when we joked and laughed together. This lightened the tension created by difficult decisions and the ever-present underlying apprehension about potential dangers, and was an important part of the close relationships that we built with our fellow climbers.

As countless other mountaineers have discovered, the Arolla area is very suitable as an introduction to alpinism. Back in 1924, Dorothy Thompson was recommended by her guide to get experience there before heading to Mont Blanc.[2] Over the following decade, she climbed prolifically in the Mont Blanc Massif and in the Pennine Alps, becoming one of the highest achieving female alpinists of that period. Numerous training courses for beginners have been based in Arolla. There are several huts within comfortable walking distance from the valley, and the surrounding peaks, no higher than 3900m, provide routes at grades suitable for the novice climber.

That July in 1970, during our first week as a team of six, we climbed on the lesser peaks and ridges above Arolla. I was gaining experience in moving over glaciers, balancing along exposed rock ridges and climbing roped together using the minimum number of belays. It never occurred to me to lead. I was simply happy to follow where Les led and to descend with him securing me from above when the going became tricky. I had complete faith in our companions. They gave me no reason to think otherwise. They were competent and confident, but also cautious. But however careful you are, unforeseeable things can happen and we were indeed blessed by good fortune – something we came to realise on the Matterhorn in the last week of our holiday together.

Before that, however, after a short stormy period, we moved a few miles from Arolla to the Saas Valley, where we camped on a little site behind a hotel in the centre of Saas Grund. The following day was 1st August, Swiss National Day, and in the afternoon we watched a procession of villagers in traditional costume riding by on colourful floats to the accompaniment of the local brass band. In the evening we went up to the main square of Saas Fee, where local dignitaries were making lengthy speeches in Swiss-German dialect. Try as I might, I could not understand more than the occasional word. The language was so different from the German I had learned. High up on the mountainsides, lights shone from chalets and huts; bonfires

---

2 *Climbing with Joseph Georges* by Dorothy E. Thompson

were lit and fireworks let off into the cool Alpine night. Reasoning that the huts would be full, we had postponed our climbing plans until there was a better chance of a comfortable night at a refuge.

For our next expedition, we walked up to the Weissmies Hut above Saas Grund. In those days we tended to dismiss cable cars in favour of the cheaper and, as we thought, fitness-enhancing hut walks all the way up from the valley bottom. At the time, too, we were only allowed to take £50 per person per annum out of the UK, plus a small car allowance, so we saved our precious money and ignored the existence of a somewhat rudimentary mechanical lift, the predecessor of the modern gondola which was built some years later to open up the Hohsaas skiing area.

On the first morning of our stay at the Weissmies Hut, all six of us traversed the Jägigrat. This was not a choice I would have made for myself but I didn't object to going along with the others. The route was entirely on rock and, as on the Aiguilles Rouges d'Arolla the week before, I found it somewhat nerve-racking and strenuous. Rock climbing, especially on exposed ridges, was simply not my forte. The Jägigrat was also my introduction to the looseness of so much Alpine rock and that certainly didn't endear it to me. Neither did the fact that we were obliged to do some abseiling – but at least that was good practice for the future.

Having climbed the Jägigrat, we turned our thoughts to higher mountains and the following morning five of us set out before dawn to traverse the Fletschhorn and Lagginhorn. Pat, feeling unwell, had decided to stay at the hut. In fact, when we arrived at the roping-up point on the edge of the glacier, both Andrew and John also declared themselves unwell and decided to come no further. This was decision time. At that stage, not only did Geoff probably have little faith in my Alpine abilities, but his experience on the Jungfrau three years before had undoubtedly made him more cautious. Now, on the glacier in the fading darkness just before daybreak, he had to decide whether or not to accompany Les and me on what, for us, at the time, seemed a serious expedition. Les himself was probably doubtful about taking me on the route alone without the safety valve of another competent companion. After some hesitation, Geoff decided to rope up with us and that was how we tackled my first 4000m peak.

It was a perfect Alpine day, with crisp, cold conditions that ensured an easy ascent up the snow face of the Fletschhorn, one of those mountains that falls just short of 4000m. There were few other parties around and we had the easy descent down to the col on the other side to ourselves. From there, the nature of our route changed radically, as we embarked on the short, rocky North Ridge up the Lagginhorn.

Probably, by then, I was beginning to feel the altitude, and maybe this was why I slowed down. At one point, I stood looking upwards, wondering however I was going to pull myself up the next rocky step, when I heard Geoff's voice from behind me.

'Can I give you a bunk-up, Barbara? It might be the quickest way,' he suggested.

Slightly embarrassed about my ineptitude and, worse still, having to accept assistance, I was nevertheless grateful to be given a helpful shove from below as I made the strenuous move up the steep little corner. On numerous, subsequent occasions I remembered that incident and wished that this friendly companion was behind me, just giving me that reassuring little push to help me reach the next handhold with the minimum amount of effort. A little cheating here and there seems justified when speed ultimately means safety. None of us wanted to be late descending from the mountain. In any case, I had no wish to have Les hassling me again, as he had done the week before on the Aiguilles Rouges d'Arolla. At nine o'clock in the morning, much to the amusement of our climbing companion, John Oaks, Les was heard chivvying me on with the words:

'For goodness sake, B, hurry up. You'll get us benighted!'

A few days later, however, Les's concern was justified. On any high mountain route it is advisable to climb efficiently in order to avoid delay that could lead to an unintentional bivouac. Two British alpinists were, in fact, caught out that very week by their slowness on the route we had climbed and had to endure not one, but two nights out on that long rock ridge.

From the summit of the Lagginhorn, the Alps were spread out around us but I was still too much of a novice to know the names of many mountains. There they all were, the other 4000m peaks of the Pennine Alps, the Mont Blanc Massif and the southern flanks of the Bernese Oberland, surrounded by their lesser neighbours. In due course they were to attain in my mind the status of friends, treacherous friends some of them indeed, but objects one and all of my affection. Many a time I would stand on an Alpine summit on a clear day and eye them all with a feeling of elation, memories of other splendid days flooding my mind, but that day in 1970 I was still unaware what the future held in store. So, whilst my leaders pointed out the peaks they recognised, I just sat there, soaking up the view, relaxing after my hard work and enjoying the satisfaction of having reached the top.

After a quick bite to eat, we turned our attention to the descent and that is when I began to quake. Although we had spent two winters using crampons in the snows of England, Wales and Scotland, I had never before descended such an exposed, steep, icy slope as this. The conditions were treacherous for the first thirty or forty metres and the drop from the ridge seemed positively alarming. I teetered downwards with a little encouragement from my leaders, heaving a huge sigh of relief as the gradient eased off and the ground became less frozen. After another hour of careful descent down the West Ridge, we began the hot trek across the midday glacier snows to the Weissmies Hut. It had been a fine day out on the mountain. Pat, Andrew and John were by now sufficiently fit to go back down to the valley, so we all returned to our tents in Saas Grund.

Our goal a few days later was the Matterhorn. Apart from Les, none of the party had done it before. On this occasion we had no compunction about taking the cable car from Zermatt up to Schwarzsee, as we were now fully acclimatised and wanted to conserve our energies for the climb itself. It may have been an expensive item in our slender budget but it was certainly worth any sacrifice we had to make. As the cable car rose, the Matterhorn seemed to grow in stature and its steepness increased as we approached. It really is the 'jewel of the Alps'.

From Schwarzsee we walked up to the Hörnli Hut where, despite not having booked in advance, we obtained dormitory places. Quenching our thirst, however, proved more difficult. This was the first hut where I experienced the problem of an insufficient water supply and we were unable to obtain the wherewithal to make the customary lemon tea. In the middle of the afternoon, all we could purchase, at huge expense, was a bottle of melted snow water laced with lemonade crystals. It was also here that I encountered the only guardian in the whole of the next quarter of a century who refused to allow me the privilege of spending the night there at the reduced rate normally charged to a wife accompanying a member of the Swiss Alpine Club. Les and Geoff had both joined the association earlier that year and we were thus somewhat put out at the guardian's attitude. Not even my ability to speak German could move him but perhaps he harboured some kind of Swiss-German prejudice against *Hochdeutsch*.[3] More likely, he had no need of our custom, being guardian of such a busy hut.

Indeed, the hut was heaving with people. We were lucky to get our food cooked at an early hour. In those days we carried simple food up to the huts and it was standard practice for the guardian or one of his assistants to cook it for us. This saved us a great deal of money over the years but was a habit we eventually abandoned, as our financial situation improved and our bodies aged. Buying meals at the hut lightens the load considerably.

---

3 *Hochdeutsch:* the official version of the German language generally taught to foreigners

In the late afternoon Les and the others spent some time scrambling about looking at the start of the route. Les knew from his previous experience that it would be tricky in the dark to keep to the best line on the lower slopes of the Hörnli Ridge. I stood outside the hut in a state of fascination, overwhelmed by awe. The mountain soared above me. It seemed so steep and precipitous that I could not imagine myself capable of climbing it. I knew, however, that on most fine days in the summer there was a constant stream of climbers on this ridge. My companions joked that old ladies, children and even cows had climbed there. This last suggestion must surely be a figment of the imagination but I did learn later that the first female ascent of the Hörnli Ridge, in 1871, was made by Lucy Walker, probably clad in a long, white, print frock, such as she wore throughout her Alpine career. Presumably she sustained herself with her usual climbing diet of champagne and sponge cake. At least, 99 years later, Pat and I had the advantage of wearing breeches and feeding on the more substantial fare of tinned sardines, dried fruit, nuts and chocolate.

By now I was becoming accustomed to Alpine starts. The routes we were doing that summer generally required us to get up at about 3.00 am in order to be on our way long before the sun came up. The main reason for such early rising is the effect the sun has on the snow. When the snow softens, glacier crossings not only become unpleasant but can also be dangerous, as snow bridges across crevasses may give way. On steep slopes under the hot sun, blocks of ice and rock are more likely to part company from the mountain and come crashing down, obliterating anyone in their path. Here on the Hörnli Ridge of the Matterhorn, these were not the issues that required us to rise at such an early hour. It was more a question of the large number of people climbing the same, quite long route on this serious mountain, and then descending by exactly the same line to return to the hut afterwards. The guides and their clients were given top priority to enable them to make as efficient a climb as possible, unhampered by the tourists. We, the tourists, were then allowed to breakfast and depart in the wake of the guided parties. At that time of night, breakfast is always an unappetising affair. Chewing dry bread and swilling it down with coffee or tea whitened with powdered milk is never easy.

We made as prompt a departure as possible at 4.00 am despite the crowds, but even though the men had reconnoitred the route the day before, we still managed to lose our way on the lower slopes, as did many other parties. After some time weaving about in torchlight, looking for the best line, we eventually found ourselves gaining height at a reasonable rate.

Daylight came and the difficulty of route finding was behind us. We were roped together in three pairs: Geoff and John, Pat and Andrew, Les and I. By now I was going really well and perhaps that's why the following incident, some two or three hours after leaving the hut, didn't bother me unduly – at the time, at least. We were carefully ascending the zigzag route up the East Face when suddenly, from somewhere above us, possibly kicked down by the solo climber ahead, a large boulder came rocketing down. It just bounced over Pat and Andy's rope, almost brushing it as it passed by, and hurtled on down the mountain. Nobody was hit, neither our party nor any other, and we carried on, but our friends were not so sure of the wisdom of climbing the Hörnli Ridge after that. (Later, back in the valley, we agreed that the route, although worthy of ascent on historical grounds, is nevertheless a 'heap of choss'. I vowed to myself that I would never climb it again, as I felt that my luck might run out. Even so, I know that if I had climbed the mountain by any other route, the Italian Ridge perhaps, or even the Zmuttgrat, I would probably have risked my life by descending the Hörnli again. In 1970, however, I had no idea that I would ever consider climbing the Matterhorn a second time. It was enough to be there just that once.)

The Moseley Slabs, which we reached soon afterwards, were sheer enjoyment. It was a pleasure to be doing some real climbing on solid rock. By now I was looking forward to a break and a nibble at the Solvay Refuge but when we arrived, we were disinclined to linger. The stench of urine and excrement was absolutely vile. So, after only the briefest of pauses, we carried on up the rocks to the Shoulder.

The ridge continues in fine style towards the fixed ropes on the step below the summit. I deliberately blotted from my mind any thoughts of the accident that befell the first ascensionists, Edward Whymper and his party in 1865;[4] they avoided this section by taking a line further right on the North Face. By now I was aware of the altitude and busy gathering together enough strength to heave myself heavenwards on those massively thick gymnasium-style ropes. At the same time, guided parties were already beginning to descend and there was no time for dawdling.

Above the fixed ropes we needed crampons for the final, icy slope and then, at last, we reached the top. To my utter astonishment, I was standing on the summit of the Matterhorn! I could scarcely believe that I was there, perched above the long, sharp drop to the world below. It was a relief to be

---

4 *Scrambles amongst the Alps* by Edward Whymper. Of the party of seven who climbed the Matterhorn on its first ascent, only three survived the accident on the descent.

free from our toil, even for only a few moments. The buildings of the village of Zermatt looked like little dots on a sunken carpet and it was strange to imagine the inhabitants going about their daily chores whilst we gazed down from our precarious stance. Our friends were content to stay on the Swiss peak, savouring their achievement and snatching a few moments of relaxation, but Les and I had had a private joke about going to Italy for our holidays that year, so we traversed the narrow snow arête and visited the slightly lower Italian summit too. Gently easing my way across that exposed crest, I relished the feeling of elevation, though it was tempered by a slight sense of disappointment. The mountains immediately around us seemed somewhat dwarfed, and therefore less impressive than I had imagined they would look. Immediately after the climb, when I looked at the map, I reasoned that the 4477m Matterhorn stands a little apart from the neighbouring peaks, and its closest neighbour, the Dent d'Hérens, at 4171m, is considerably lower. Thinking about it now, I suspect that these other peaks, being unknown to me at the time, held less significance for me than they would have done if I had made the ascent of the Matterhorn later on in my climbing career.

The joy and sense of relief I experienced at completing the ascent was transitory. Unlike the young Eileen Jackson in 1925, aged only fifteen and 'the fastest climber the young Bernard Biner, Zermatt guide, had ever had on his rope',[5] who retraced her steps down the Hörnli Ridge in a mere one hour, forty-five minutes, it took me six hours to descend to the hut again. Without doubt, the Matterhorn took the initial toll on my now irritable knees. Indeed, the following day I could barely straighten my legs. Nevertheless, the satisfaction I had experienced on reaching the summit returned once the agony of the descent was over and, even as we were winging our way back down to Zermatt in the cable car, my heart was brimming over with emotion. My nose pressed to the cabin window, I could not have enough of that sight: that giant, that incredible wedge of rock, with its summer remnants of snow and ice – I had climbed it! I had been right to the top.

It was a fitting climax to my first Alpine season. From then on I was hooked.

---

5 *Women on the Rope* by Cicely Williams

2

APPRENTICESHIP

How do people learn to climb? How do they learn to climb safely? Today, many commercial Alpine mountaineering courses exist and some aspiring climbers choose that way to build up their confidence. Perhaps this is the modern equivalent of hiring a guide, as earlier generations of alpinists did. Certainly, in the first few decades of the 20th century, as well as in the pioneering days of the 19th, that was the common practice. Most amateur alpinists in those days came from a wealthy background. The European guides were strong local men who had grown up in alpine villages, having spent their formative years working at manual trades and moving about in the harsh environment. They were tough, knowledgeable and very capable. They knew how to move on rock, how to walk and climb on ice and snow, and how to protect themselves from danger. They understood the climate and the snow, and they passed on this knowledge and these skills to the amateur climbers of their day. These amateurs, mainly men but, as we have seen, some women too, were often extremely gifted rock climbers and possessed great stamina for the long days out in the mountains. They needed it: before the advent of mass tourism, there were few mechanical means of being transported from the villages to a higher altitude. Alpinists usually had to walk far longer distances than they do today to reach the start of the climbs.

In the 1960s and 1970s, many people learned to climb, as I did, by joining local mountaineering clubs and meeting like-minded amateurs with a little more experience than themselves. In my case, it was the Gloucestershire Mountaineering Club, founded in 1955 after a public film show had been held in Cheltenham, sponsored by the Central Council for Physical Recreation (CCPR), the Mountaineering Association (MA), the Ramblers' Association (RA), the Holiday Fellowship and the Cooperative Holidays Association. A number of the founder members already knew each other through two local branches of the RA and were keen to extend their walking activities into more adventurous terrain by branching out into the realms of scrambling and roped climbing.

As the club members wanted to visit the mountains of North Wales on a regular basis, it wasn't long before they purchased a couple of derelict semi-detached cottages on the outskirts of a village in Snowdonia. This became the GMC Hut and it was here that a dozen or more members would meet once a month. Despite the need to spend a considerable amount of time renovating the cottages to make them into more habitable, if fairly spartan, accommodation, members still found plenty of time to walk and climb in the nearby mountains.

The Club also satisfied the needs of the more impecunious members by providing communal transport at shared expense between Gloucestershire and North Wales, or any other venue chosen for a meet. The Wye Valley, Brecon Beacons and Black Mountains were all within easy range of home, and occasionally trips were also made to the Peak District and the Lake District, or elsewhere. When I first joined the GMC, I was delighted to learn that some members also explored mountain areas abroad. The annual slide shows were fascinating and, during my first year or so of membership, I encountered people who had recently walked, scrambled and climbed in Corsica, the Dolomites and the Alps. It was all very inspiring.

On my first weekend with the GMC, I was introduced to easy rock climbing and abseiling in South Wales and, soon after that, I was taken to crags not far from home, in the Avon Gorge and at Wintour's Leap, overlooking the River Wye. I felt considerable trepidation but I coped, although I much preferred mountain scrambles and walks in Snowdonia. My 'teachers' were simply other club members, with varying degrees of experience, but to me, the total novice, they appeared – and were – very competent. They showed me how to tie on to the rope by clipping a karabiner to my waist-length, a long piece of cord wrapped several times around my waist. This was the era just before the advent of the first commercially made waist-harnesses such as the 'Whillans'.[1]

As far as the actual climbing was concerned, the general advice was to keep three points of contact with the rock at all times, moving only one foot or hand whilst the others were firmly placed and, at all costs, to avoid falling off. There was also a good deal of talk about the new nylon ropes which were replacing the now outdated hemp, and new forms of protection were being developed. Some climbers made their own metal chockstones and Les found the college welding shop particularly useful for this purpose. However, by the end of the 1960s, nuts and wedges were appearing on the shelves of climbing shops. All this new equipment helped to make learning

---

1 A harness named after the climber Don Whillans

to climb a much safer enterprise than it had been hitherto. We nearly always climbed multi-pitch routes at about Diff or V Diff standard and beginners usually wore walking boots. Only those who habitually did harder climbs wore PAs or RDs,[2] the specialist rock-climbing shoes of the time.

It wasn't long before I came across members of two other clubs. These organisations, the Lincoln MC and the Wellingborough MC, were run on similar lines to the GMC and had frequent meets in the same areas as us. They also had a fairly mixed membership of men and women of all ages. Most people would try the majority of the activities on the programme, only a few members being dedicated rock climbers at that time. Les and I made friends in all three clubs and many of those friendships have lasted ever since. There is no doubt that such clubs played a considerable role in the development of climbing from the 1950s onwards. Other societies, those with a national membership, had been established many years previously and often had a higher entry qualification, such as proven mountain-walking ability or rock-climbing experience, but the local clubs were usually open to all, giving the novice a starting-point. Without the GMC, I would probably never have become a mountaineer. It was not until a number of years later that I joined two of the more prestigious associations: the Alpine Club and the Fell & Rock Climbing Club (F&RCC).

A few rock-climbing courses did exist in those days, mostly at the well-known Outdoor Pursuits centres such as Plas-y-Brenin in Snowdonia, but attendance at a course meant spending money and, as that was in rather short supply at the time, I never went on one. Climbing walls barely existed and it was at least the mid-1970s before we first had access to an indoor wall in our home area. Even then, it was only the existing wall of a school gymnasium, with handholds and footholds made of protruding bricks and concrete slabs. I found these walls so unnatural that they gave me a much greater sense of vertigo than any of the traditional rock routes I climbed. So I learned only on outdoor crags with a number of people from local clubs, who are to be commended for their patience with my lack of natural ability and my nervousness.

In those years, I not only started to learn to rock climb and acquired considerable stamina by walking great distances in the mountains but, in the winter months of the late 1960s, I was also introduced to climbing in snow up some of the easier gullies on the mountains of Snowdonia and the Lake District. I acquired my first pair of heavy, leather climbing boots, as well as an ice axe with a long wooden shaft, crampons complete with

---

2 Shoes named after the French climbers Pierre Allain and René Desmaisons

long nylon straps, and a luxurious, bright red Terray duvet jacket. This latter purchase seemed very spendthrift at the time but it proved its worth on many a cold morning in the Alps, as well as keeping me cosy in the open-topped MGB that carried Les and me everywhere we went. We visited the snow-covered hills of Scotland together and it was on the descent from Buachaille Etive Mòr, on the edge of Rannoch Moor at the head of Glencoe, that I first practised walking downhill with the brand new spikes attached to the soles of my boots. It was quite terrifying that first time, trying to concentrate on splaying my feet out to avoid tripping over the unaccustomed metalwork and the long nylon straps. I had hitherto felt much safer simply in my boots, an illusion that I abandoned as soon as I became familiar with the feel of crampons on hard snow. Icy slopes can be lethal in Vibram soles. The nailed boots our predecessors wore must have been less dangerous in such conditions. Then I turned to alpinism, and eventually I became proficient at climbing on icy rock in crampons too.

1970 was my first summer in the Alps on snow-covered peaks and I had never before crossed a crevasse-ridden glacier or climbed beneath overhanging séracs. Les issued me with a couple of prusik loops and explained how to use them to climb up a rope out of a crevasse. Throughout my climbing career, I always carried them whenever I was in glaciated terrain but, luckily, in all those years I never had to use them, as I never fell into a crevasse and neither did Les.

That first summer climbing together in Switzerland, I experienced a variety of rock climbing at high altitude and, as on the Matterhorn, discovered that some Alpine rock is notoriously loose. In the UK, we had always climbed on solid rock and rarely had to worry about handholds that moved as soon as you touched them, or stones falling from above. Neither did we often have to worry about accidentally kicking loose rocks down upon the climbers below. Fortunately, scrambling down scree-strewn slopes and ascending snow gullies at home had already taught me to take the greatest care about these things. It was a surprise to find that, on a number of occasions, our European counterparts weren't always as careful as we tried to be.

Glaciers occasionally present the climber with interesting problems. One of these is the *bergschrund*, or gap between the ice and the mountain itself. The terrain leading up to the *bergschrund* is solid ice, often with a substantial covering of snow, and the terrain above the void is generally snow covered too. Where the *bergschrund* lies directly below a steep mountain slope, it can be difficult to cross. Sometimes you immediately see a solid bridge of snow that you can use to reach the terrain above, but at other times it is more tricky and your search for an access point may result in some technical climbing, or even combined tactics, where one person physically assists another to reach a foothold from which the leader can continue to a safe stance. There the leader either uses an ice axe or ice screw for a belay, depending on the state of the snow. The leader is thus able to secure both climbers as the second climbs over the *bergschrund* and up the slope. Before ice screws became available, the alternative might have been to cut a small bollard in the ice if it was too hard to push an axe handle through the surface, but I don't recall this ever being necessary on any route I climbed.

During our early years of Alpine climbing, we rarely had a problem in ascent but later on we occasionally had to abandon a route because we couldn't cross the *bergschrund*. Our first attempt at the Whymper Couloir on the Aiguille Verte in the Mont Blanc Massif was just such a case. Back in 1971, however, it was on the descent of a mountain that I first encountered the *bergschrund* question. On our way up Piz Glüschaint in the Engadine in the darkness of early morning, four of us had taken a tortuous course through an icefall where car-sized blocks of ice, or séracs, overhung our route. Now we were descending on the far side of the mountain and came to the edge of the snow slope above the *bergschrund*. The upper lip of the deep, gaping hole didn't protrude very far, so, belayed from above, we had to jump outwards and a couple of metres downwards to avoid falling in. This was the first of a number of occasions throughout my climbing years that we had to perform a similar athletic feat in exciting circumstances. The last person in the party had to relinquish the belay and trust that someone below was firmly anchored whilst he or she jumped.

By 1974 I had built up enough confidence to tackle a wide variety of Alpine climbing at easy grades up to and including *Assez Difficile* (AD). The *Facile* (F) snow plods were simply a matter of willpower and keeping a watchful eye open for hidden crevasses. On *Peu Difficile* (PD) routes, there was never any rock climbing at a standard that I couldn't handle, although sometimes I lacked the strength to make a strenuous move upwards as quickly as my companions desired. Then came the next grade of AD, with its occasional technicalities on rock and steeper, icier terrain than I had climbed before. The approach to the Forbes Arête on the Aiguille du Chardonnet in the Mont Blanc Massif was my first taste of a 53° ice slope. In fact, there was no problem at all, as huge 'bucket' steps had been cut in the slope and the only danger came from the climbers above us, who insisted on trying to make the steps even larger, showering us with a continuous stream of fragments of ice in the process. This route confirmed my breakthrough into the next grade of Alpine climbing. It was the type of route I always enjoyed the most: mixed terrain, with a variety of snow, ice and fairly straightforward rock climbing. Moreover, Les and I traversed the Forbes Arête with no other companions, something we had rarely done at that stage. This breakthrough reassured me that the two of us had become a self-sufficient team, even for a slightly more challenging route than usual.

Speed is of paramount importance for safety in the Alps. In Scotland in winter we had already learned to be efficient with our time, as there are so few daylight hours. We were always determined to avoid being caught out in the dark, as an unplanned night in freezing temperatures would be extremely unpleasant, if not life-threatening. The same is true of the Alps, even in summer, as the night-time temperatures are usually well below 0°C. Once the sun goes down, alpinists generally retreat inside their bivouac tents or, in most cases, into the mountain huts, as we did. Out on the terrace, the air quickly takes on a chill but, in the late morning, the converse is the problem. The warmth of the sun starts to melt the snow and ice, and dangerous conditions can result. So I was encouraged right from the start not to spend any more time than necessary getting ready at the beginning of the day and, once we were out, to move as quickly as I comfortably could. It was, however, important not to try to move too fast, rather to keep a steady pace and avoid stopping. All this was none too easy to achieve. I also found it difficult to be as efficient as my companions at getting ready to set out on the route in the morning. Often in cramped and crowded conditions, by the light of your head-torch, you had to find your boots and ice axe amongst the many others in the racks provided at the hut entrance, squeeze your warm feet into cold leather and fumble with laces in the semi-dark. You also often had to queue to use the only latrine, which might be perched upon the edge of a cliff some distance from the hut door. Then you would put on your harness or, back in 1970, a waist-belt with loops for suspending such necessary gear as spare karabiners, prusik loops and other items for your intended route.

Learning to live in an Alpine hut wasn't too taxing for someone already accustomed to the fairly primitive nature of the mountaineering club huts in the UK in the 1960s and 1970s. Not every British hut at that time had indoor flush toilets. We often spent the weekends at the LMC Hut in the Lake District. This was a loft above an old sawmill by the river in Elterwater, where we had to go out into the yard to reach an old-fashioned earth closet in a tiny wooden 'sentry box'. So the facilities provided high up on the mountainsides of the European Alps held few surprises. Colleagues at work might not have felt so envious if they had really understood how we lived.

It was obvious from their comments that they imagined that every time we went to the mountains, we stayed in the kind of accommodation they would require themselves, if only they could afford the time or the money, or weren't tied down by family commitments. Our accommodation was, however, strictly below even the budget end of the market. There were no cosy double rooms with en-suite facilities; instead we snuggled down into our sleeping bags in a large room open to the rafters and next to whichever man or woman decided to take the adjacent bunk. In the Alps there were rarely separate bunks: most huts had one or more *matratzenlager*, where you were usually allocated a bed space by the guardian, regardless of gender. Often, however, if you arrived early enough at the hut, before the mass of climbers, and you had several companions in your own party, you would be given a space large enough to divide between you as you wished. That's how I frequently contrived to be at the end of the line beside the wall, guaranteeing me only one neighbour, Les. However, this wasn't always very comfortable as the mattress often tilted a little in that position, resulting in an awkward incline to one side.

Various problems arise in crowded hut dormitories. In his book about the Fourthousanders, Will McLewin wrote that he 'rarely slept well and the inevitable snorer meant that the nights were not even restful'.[3] He preferred to bivouac. Nevertheless, over a period of 25 years we persisted in using the huts wherever possible, though not without some memorable disturbances. Worst of all was the night we spent in the Topali Hut above the Mattertal in 1976, when a German schoolteacher in charge of a group of youngsters dropped off to sleep the minute his head hit the pillow and treated us to an endless succession of eruptions that sounded like a donkey in deep distress. No amount of kicking, shaking or pillow-throwing had any effect upon this cacophony. Another serious annoyance to a climber needing to set out very early for a long route is the occasional group of late-evening revellers or the presence of a group of over-excited children. In the Tracuit Hut above Zinal in the Pennine Alps, our attempt to rest before setting out at 2.00 am on the traverse of the Weisshorn was greatly hampered by a large number of youngsters chattering and giggling in the dormitory, whilst a simultaneous musical evening was taking place in the living room just below. No wonder many climbers prefer to bivouac.

For me, the very worst aspect of dormitory life in Alpine huts was the heat and smell generated by many sweaty bodies lying together in one room, wrapped in dusty hut blankets. The stench and stuffiness could be

3 *In Monte Viso's Horizon* by Will McLewin

overwhelming. What wouldn't I have given at such moments to swap my surroundings for the almost equally unpleasant experience of being chilled to the bone in a perishing cold dormitory, like the one in the Hollandia Hut in the Bernese Oberland in July 1973? The most memorable experience that my friends ever had of my frustration at being in an airless dormitory was at the Tschierva Hut in the Engadine in 1971. The incident stood me in good stead for many years to come and I was always careful after that to keep my misery as much to myself as possible. The dormitory was extremely hot and greatly overcrowded. I felt as if I could scarcely breathe. I moaned and groaned for what obviously seemed an age to everyone else, and finally I threatened to die.

'I wish you would,' piped up some English-speaking wit from the opposite bunk.

That silenced me! But it transpired that I was by no means the only person who found it difficult to breathe. Someone went to the window to open it. An almighty crash followed as the entire window-frame caved in. After that I dozed, but nobody could have been happier than I was to rise at some god-forsaken hour to go down to breakfast and set off into the icy darkness well before the first red streaks of dawn appeared in the sky. To my constant astonishment, my friends have patiently tolerated my often grumpy nature on more occasions than I care to mention, but that night in the Tschierva Hut I really got my comeuppance. I was never allowed to forget it.

Will McLewin also justified his decision to bivouac rather than use the Alpine huts by writing that 'eating usually involved hassle unless you had plenty of money to spend'.[4] That was also our experience in those days, although we usually managed to acquire plentiful hot water to make our own drinks. At the Tschierva Hut, however, the guardian was particularly unwelcoming. When we returned there from our climb the following day, the service wasn't up to the usual standards. Unlike at the Hörnli Hut the year before, where water was at a premium, here there seemed to be an adequate supply. It is quite normal all over the Swiss Alps to buy, or in those days acquire free of charge, a litre or so of hot water with which the guests can make their own tea when coming back to the refuge after a day out. Not so at the Tschierva Hut that day in 1971. When Les asked for hot water, he was told there was none but he persisted in his request, pointing out that, as it was possible to buy a cup of tea, there must be a supply of hot water. His initiative was rewarded and we duly received enough for the two of us to make our own brew.

4 ibid.

It could be embarrassing to be a British tourist in Switzerland at that time. We really felt so poor compared with our European counterparts. In the early 1970s, the British pound had sunk dramatically against the Swiss franc and other currencies, and the British economy was described as sick, suffering from *der britischen Krankheit*, or British disease. So we economised as much as possible. For many years we took simple food up to the huts and asked the guardian to heat it up for us. Ready-cooked sausages and powdered mashed potato were frequently on our menu. Instant soups and instant powdered desserts were also lightweight and required little preparation at the hut. A tin of fruit was a luxury that we might take if the walk up from the valley wasn't too demanding. Many British climbers in the 1970s would take dehydrated meals to the huts and ask the guardian to prepare them. If there were language problems, this could lead to misunderstandings, undercooked, inedible food and delayed meals. With my ability to speak French and German, I soon discovered that the guardians disliked this habit, so we did our best to make life easy for everybody and rarely had trouble getting our food prepared. It was, however, only in Switzerland that you could ask the guardian for his assistance in this way. In France, there was usually a self-caterers' kitchen, where you were allowed to use your own camping gas stove or similar. In Italy, there rarely seemed to be any provision for self-catering, so we simply had to spend money and buy whatever meal we could afford. On one occasion this consisted of spaghetti – without sauce or any other addition!

3

Grand Tour of the Alps: Bernese Oberland, Pennine Alps, Engadine and Mont Blanc

From 1973 onwards, our Alpine climbing continued in earnest over ten successive summers without a break. Some years we would spend five weeks of the long vacation abroad and most of that time was dedicated to the mountains. Usually I was content to use my holidays for this purpose but there were times when I fantasised about relaxing on a sun-drenched beach with the waves of the Mediterranean lapping gently at my feet. Once the toil of hut walks and arduous glacier-crossings was over, however, these wistful longings were always banished to the back of my mind and I would be overcome by the joy of being at high altitude amongst the snowy peaks I loved so much.

In 1973, I had not yet experienced a desire to be anywhere other than where I was at that moment. It was a season which started with rain, and mixed weather dogged our plans all through the holiday, but we were fortunate indeed to be in the right position at the right time at least once every week. That is how Les and I achieved a tally of one route each week out of the five we spent in the Alps that year. The result was that I climbed a total of six more Fourthousanders, two on the same day. It so happened that the Grünhorn, Strahlhorn and Allalinhorn were the most attractive and convenient peaks to climb from the huts where we had based ourselves. Piz Bernina was, however, another matter and we deliberately chose to climb it for the pleasure of traversing it by its most alluring snow ridge, the Biancograt. Then, for our last expedition, we decided to head for the highest point in the Western Alps, something I had coveted the previous summer in Chamonix when, on numerous occasions, I had gazed longingly up at Mont Blanc and its neighbour, Mont Maudit.

That summer, we had driven straight out from England to the Lötschental, an unspoilt valley on the south side of the Bernese Oberland. There was no campsite, so we made do with wild camping near the village of Blatten.

This didn't please one of the local farmers but he allowed us to stay where we were for the first few days whilst waiting for the rain to stop. Then we took down our tent, stowed it in the car, packed our rucksacks and set off on foot for a grand tour of the Bernese Oberland. In the mountains we would be staying at huts overnight, but we did carry an emergency bivouac shelter big enough for the two of us. This was not a tent, but a home-made Zdarski sack, a rudimentary bag large enough for us both to sit inside and keep warmer and drier than we would have been outside in a snow or rain storm. Fortunately we rarely ever needed to use it and I never had to spend a whole night in it.

We were not alone on this expedition in the Bernese Oberland. Geoff Causey had joined us once again; also Richard Heery, a colleague of his at Kendal Grammar School, and his wife, Katherine. We had first met the Heerys' one evening at the pub we used to frequent in Great Langdale. Richard, with his long hair and wild beard, and Katherine, wearing an exotic-looking, full-length 'maxidress', looked like students to me at the time. They were, in fact, in their early twenties, having been at university during the revolutionary era of the late 1960s, and were now both young professionals in their first teaching posts. Richard had only a minimum of Alpine experience and Katherine had none. Geoff and Richard had also brought along two students, Stuart Cooke and Andy Thompson, who had just finished the Sixth Form at Kendal Grammar. For the first time, I was by no means the least experienced alpinist in the party.

As soon as the weather cleared sufficiently, we drove to the roadhead at Fafleralp and left the cars there, walking along the valley bottom until we reached the beginning of the Langgletscher. 'Long glacier' is an appropriate name for this approach to the col at the far end of the Lötschental. Our destination was the Hollandia Hut, situated at an altitude of 3235m, six hours away, and for most of this time our objective was a clearly visible dot on the horizon at the far end of the glacier. The refuge was just above the Lötschenlücke, the col directly ahead. We were more or less on our knees by the time we reached the head of the glacier, wading through deep, soft snow with heavy packs on our backs. The packs contained provisions for three full days and three half days, and we intended to buy two or three hut meals towards the end of our six-day expedition. My tiny old canvas Pinnacle rucksack was full to bursting, but probably only weighed about a third of what Les and the other men were carrying. Although I had to carry an ice axe, crampons, harness and a few other small pieces of climbing equipment, Les's rucksack was loaded with the rope and other bulkier gear, and our food. This arrangement continued over the many years we climbed together and I rarely ever questioned it. As Les was always so much faster on the hut walks, regardless of what he carried, I could see no point in insisting on taking any more of the load than he allocated to me.

As far as personal possessions are concerned, an alpinist tries to keep the load to the minimum. Everything has to be carried on your back and, in the case of this expedition, we were planning to move from hut to hut, so only the bare essentials were allowed. Extra weight is exhausting and I, for one, would need every ounce of strength to spend five or six days up in the high mountains. I did, however, carry a few spare clothes to replace damp sweaty ones at the end of a long day, but it was a question of putting the used shirt and vest back on for the next route, regardless of the number of days they had been worn. There was also the matter of underwear. Boots the Chemists sold some rather handy paper knickers at that time, but these were of no use when they became drenched in perspiration, because the owner was left wearing nothing but a string of elastic round her waist. Even worse, on a trip to the outdoor thunderbox, the flimsy item could simply be ripped away in the draught. So it was a mistake to compromise too much on the really necessary items of clothing. Toothbrushes could be chopped down, soap was dispensable because there would be no water to wash in, and other toiletries were kept to the absolute minimum. I did, however, usually contrive to take one small luxury to help me pass the time when resting in the afternoons after a long morning out on the hill. Sometimes this might be a book, or even half a book, a paperback chopped up to avoid carrying the part already read, and later, when my interest in art developed, I would take a tiny sketchpad and a pencil.

Arriving at the Hollandia Hut, we quickly discovered that there was no guardian in residence and the only occupants were a small group of Germans. The temperature in the dormitory was probably the lowest I ever experienced inside a mountain hut, even in the winter season. Les and I huddled together under as many of the heavy, 'Army-style' blankets as we could bear, but even then I shivered half the night.

The living quarters were much better, with the luxury of a wood-burning stove, and we spent many hours chatting in a mixture of English and German, playing cards and otherwise entertaining ourselves. Not long after we arrived, the cloud came down and it began to snow. And it continued to snow all through the night and the following day, giving us no choice but to stay where we were. During the daytime, we all, including the Germans, sat in the kitchen, where we kept the stove burning, not only to keep ourselves warm but also to ensure a constant supply of drinking water. To obtain snow to use as melt-water, we went through an outside door in the corridor into what looked like a snow cave. Previous residents had carved lumps out of the mound that had built up against the exterior wall, so we did the same.

Our plans to climb the nearby peaks, the Ebnefluh or the Kranzberg, were abandoned. We set our sights on getting to the Konkordia Hut if we could, but travelling down the long, highly crevassed Grosser Aletschfirn was far too hazardous whilst snow was still falling.

On the second day, to our astonishment, we heard a voice on the slope below the hut. By some miracle, a French-speaking Swiss had walked up alone from Fafleralp in whiteout conditions without accident.

On the third day there was a sufficient break in the weather for us to leave for the Konkordia Hut. We all tied together in a rope of seven to protect ourselves against falling into hidden crevasses. Then we set off in the fresh snow. By the time we reached Konkordiaplatz, the broad, flat hub of the glacier system, it was about midday and the snow on the surface had turned to water. We had to wade ankle-deep in places over the bare ice as we crossed this vast, glacial desert. Arriving from the Lötschenlücke, we could see the hut perched high on a rocky promontory on the far side.

Reaching it was our next challenge. We had arrived at the foot of the ladders (in 1973, the modern metal staircase had not been built). Climbing what was left of the old wooden ladders was quite a nerve-racking business, and here and there we had to negotiate our way carefully over the exposed rock face with only a piece of cable to help prevent a fall. Half-way up the 100m cliff, one of Katherine's boots jammed in a crack. This wasn't very amusing at all! It took quite some time for her to get it free and I was beginning to wonder if she would have to take her foot out of her boot and leave the recalcitrant object behind.

This was to be the first of several visits Les and I made to the Konkordia Hut. Back then, there were two huts, one a few metres higher up the cliff than the other, and we were given bed spaces in the lower, older one. Konkordia is at the very heart of the Bernese Oberland and on good days the view from the terrace outside the refuge is quite stunning. You look straight out towards the 4000m Aletschhorn and up the long Grosser Aletschfirn, the glacier we had just descended. Great peaks rise up all around you above the swathes of ice and snow that constitute one of the largest glacier systems in Western Europe. You experience the rawness of nature here. On bad days, however, the feeling of isolation is even greater, when the wind is howling and the cliff is covered in snow. Then I really began to feel like a pioneer, away from civilisation, at the mercy of the elements. In reality, when the hut has a guardian, as it does at almost every conceivable opportunity, the guests are cocooned in a well-provisioned, comfortable world, with the latest technological communications and well-organised, welcoming hospitality.

The Konkordiaplatz at the foot of the cliff is a vast area. It is the meeting point of five glaciers: the Jungfraufirn, which descends from the Jungfraujoch, where the trains from Kleiner Scheidegg disgorge their passengers, many of whom in spring ski down to Konkordia on their way through this wonderland of snow-capped peaks; the Ewigschneefeld, to the east of the Jungfraufirn, and the much shorter Grüneggfirn, which descends from the Grünhornlücke over which one has to pass on the way to the Finsteraarhorn Hut. The fourth glacier, the Grosser Aletschfirn, descends from the Lötschenlücke to the west to Konkordiaplatz, and there all the glaciers form one great tongue of ice known as the Grosser Aletschgletscher, the longest glacier in the whole of the Alps. In spring we have followed it all the way down on ski, eventually coming to the Rhône Valley. On a hot day in summer on the intermittent bare ice and moraine, or under a scorching sun in spring snow, the ascent of the Aletsch Glacier can seem an interminable torture.

By the following morning the weather had improved sufficiently for us to make an attempt on a big mountain, and everyone except Katherine set out for the Gross Grünhorn. This Fourthousander straddles the ridge between the Ewigschneefeld and the Fiescher Glacier. We took the route up the Grüneggfirn, blazing a trail in the fresh snow. It seemed a never-ending ascent up the slopes towards the Grünegghorn, the smaller peak just to the south-west of the Grünhorn. At first I was moving fairly well but, as the slopes steepened, I thought I would never reach the col on the ridge above. Then, having attained that goal, the easy snow arête rose unremittingly in front of us and I swear that, for every two steps forward, I took one step back. I certainly felt very weak indeed and very sorry for holding up Andy, who had roped up with Les and me. At last we reached the summit of the Grünegghorn and descended the ridge on the far side, where Geoff and the rest of the party had been waiting for us for ages.

At this point we reassembled in three ropes of two, as opposed to the two ropes of three that we had chosen for safety in the crevassed terrain below. For climbing up the rocky ridge to the summit of the Gross Grünhorn, we would be quicker in pairs, and if I really was too exhausted to go as far as that, at least Les and I could turn back without spoiling anyone else's chance of getting to the top. As it happened, quite low down on the ridge, whilst Geoff and his partner kept to the crest, Les and I followed an easier line up the flank and overtook them. As I later wrote in my journal:

From then on I became aware of a new flow of energy. On we went, now in front, to reach the summit well ahead of the others. Talk about adding insult to injury – I was the last person who deserved to reach the summit first having held everybody up all day.

From the top I experienced my first view of the Finsteraarhorn, 'Monarch of the Bernese Alps'. This splendid peak has a quite distinctive shape and is always recognisable towering above the glaciers of the Oberland. I have also spotted the Finsteraarhorn from many summits in the Pennine Alps on a clear day. The Finsteraarhorn is the mountain where, in 1902, Gertrude Bell and her guides made an attempt on the unclimbed North-East Face. The party was besieged by a ferocious storm with blizzards and freezing temperatures and spent 57 hours out, including 53 roped together. Their attempt was defeated but the guide, Ulrich Fuhrer, paid tribute to Miss Bell's outstanding calmness and bravery. As I stood on top of the Grünhorn that day in 1973, I looked at the Finsteraarhorn, glistening in the sun beneath its mantle of fresh snow, and thought how splendid it would be to climb that jagged mountain one day.

We really were rewarded for our patience at the Hollandia Hut and for our perseverance in climbing in somewhat arduous conditions. Unfortunately, the weather broke again the next day and there seemed little point in sitting it out any longer, as our provisions were getting low. We all seven, therefore, left the Konkordia Hut and traipsed back up the glacier to the Lötschenlücke, then all the way down to Fafleralp. We did not pitch camp again in the Lötschental but drove off together to the Pennine Alps and Saas Grund, where we were due to meet some more friends, Pat and Andrew Reynolds, John Oaks and Andy Hodges. Andy, a young man from the Gloucestershire Mountaineering Club, was a naturally gifted rock climber but not a very experienced alpinist at that time. He would accompany us on many future holidays, both in the Alps and in Scotland.

Here in the Pennine Alps, the weather was no more settled than in the Bernese Oberland and during the ten days or so that we were based in Saas Grund, the only hut I visited was the Britannia, spending a total of four nights there and climbing just two routes. The first week saw us there for two nights. On the first morning, we went out quite early to try to climb the Egginer, the little mountain near the refuge, but the conditions were so poor that we turned back. By seven in the morning we were all in the living room, playing cards. We spent the rest of the day amusing ourselves at shove ha'penny and table soccer, making use of precious Swiss coins on the dining tables.

The following day was fine and we set out for the Strahlhorn, which entailed a long snow plod up to the Adler Pass, followed by a short ridge to the summit of this easy Fourthousander. There were seven of us again, the same group as in the Bernese Oberland the previous week. Our other friends were acclimatising on lower routes. The first hour or so was pleasant enough but, as we progressed up the glacier, the snow became softer and softer and we sank in at every step. As we headed up the final slope to the Adler Pass, long-limbed Geoff, who was in front, was disappearing in up to his thighs – or so he said afterwards. From the Pass, the going was much easier and we were blessed with sunshine as we sat at the top of the Strahl-horn, admiring the impressive faces of Monte Rosa just in front of us. Later, descending the glacier, we passed an elderly couple who were climbing up on ski, much more suitable footwear for the occasion than our mountain-eering boots. This incident stayed at the back of my mind for several years and I thought how pleasant it must be to *schuss* down that glacier, so much easier than trudging along on foot. (In fact, when I did get the opportunity to ski down it from the Adler Pass on the High Level Route in 1979, the glacier trail was a solid rut of ice and we had a most unpleasant descent. At that time we were still rather inexperienced ski-tourers.)

Our return trek that day from the Strahlhorn to the Britannia Hut was not without incident. Somewhere towards the end of the Allalin Glacier, we were having to leap over wide-open crevasses. On one occasion Katherine, the shortest person in the party, landed on the far side in such a way that she toppled backwards and fell into the void below. It was an enormous hole and we had quite a performance pulling her out again. Fortunately, there were plenty of us to haul and no physical harm was done, but Katherine never forgot the sensation of dangling in that huge ice cavern. She said it reminded her of the interior of a cathedral.

A number of us returned to the Britannia Hut the following week, hoping for another break in the unsettled weather, but then too we only had one fine day. Once again we spent the first day waiting for the mist to clear. On the second day, long before dawn, Les was up inspecting the sky. It was a cold, crisp night, with some cloud still, but the stars were out. The guardian was most reluctant to get up until Les had persisted in knocking on his door for some time, calling: *Hüttenwirt! Die Sterne scheinen!* ('Guardian! The stars are shining!') At last the man came out of his hidey-hole and agreed to make us some tea-water before we departed for the Allalinhorn. There were eight of us in the party. Katherine had stayed in the valley to meet a non-climbing friend and John Oaks and Andy Hodges were climbing elsewhere, but Pat and Andrew Reynolds had joined the rest of us.

This was to be the first of my three ascents of the Allalinhorn, each by a different route. On this occasion we climbed the Hohlaubgrat, by far the most interesting of the three. It was just an easy snow ascent for most of the way but when we came within 100m of the summit, a rock barrier presented the one 'bad step' on the ridge, giving us considerable entertainment. During the approach, I had gradually sunk to my usual position at the rear of the party and consequently had to stand for an hour and a quarter on the snow ridge waiting for the others to surmount the obstacle. By the time I at last started to climb, my feet were numb and the pitch exhausted me. The last few metres to the summit were intolerable and when I finally joined our friends on the top, I sat on the ground writhing in agony as the blood rushed through my feet and my toes came back to life. 'Hot aches' were not infrequently a feature of my climbing days in that particular pair of close-fitting leather boots, but this ranked high on the list of painful experiences.

The descent from the Allalinhorn down the Normal Route on to the Fee Glacier was easy and I remember watching ice avalanching off the séracs hanging on the right-hand wall as we passed, but the glacier is wide and we did not appear to be in any danger.

The large group of friends broke up after that, some of us deciding to quit the Pennine Alps and go in search of better weather down in south-east Switzerland. Back to the Engadine again! And this time we were pleased to find that a new and much more hospitable guardian had taken on the Tschierva Hut. I was in any case under oath not to make a commotion in the dormitory if the sleeping conditions happened to be as unpleasant as on our previous visit.

Our objective that year was much more serious than before: we had decided to climb Piz Bernina by the Biancograt. Just six of us set out to do this memorable route: Geoff Causey and Andy Reynolds, John Oaks and Andy Hodges, Les and myself, the others opting for an ascent of Piz Morteratsch. We were quite keyed up about the Biancograt, imagining from what we had read and heard that it was a very serious expedition. For me, indeed, it was one of the few routes graded higher than PD that I had climbed to date. The Biancograt is classified as AD, just one grade harder.

The weather and snow conditions that night were perfect. Because there is quite a long approach to the mountain across moraine and then up a glacier, we made an early start in order to reach the col at dawn. That meant we would be in daylight climbing on the ridge itself. The name Biancograt, or white ridge, really only applies to one permanently snow-covered stretch of the north ridge of Piz Bianco, the foresummit of Piz Bernina, as the rest of the ridge comprises many rock steps. We needed to see what we were doing and we were not keen to climb up there by torchlight.

For the first section from the hut to the glacier, it was still dark, so torches were indispensable, and it was there on those scree-covered slopes that Geoff had a moment of panic. His torch battery failed. Fortunately we persuaded him to continue with us, otherwise he would have missed one of the most superb days out in the mountains we had ever had, and we would have been the poorer without his company. Having said that, once we did get on the glacier, in order to keep well ahead of the various guided parties from the hut, who had taken a different route to reach this point, Geoff and Andy Reynolds suddenly increased their pace considerably and I simply couldn't keep up. However, John took pity on me and he and his partner, Andy Hodges, stayed just ahead of us all the way to the col, thus preventing me, the weakest person in this strong group, from becoming demoralised. Unfortunately I was just a bit too slow arriving at the col in time to see the sunrise at its zenith and I felt particularly guilty that I had inadvertently deprived my three companions too. However, as my journal records, what we did see was quite spectacular all the same:

Far away on the horizon the sun had just emerged, and, that morning, it appeared like a huge, red disc casting a pink light over the extensive snows of the peaks and glaciers all around. It was breathtaking.

Indeed it was. It was one of those moments in the high Alps when you realise just how privileged you are to be there.

After that unforgettable halt at the col, we started the climb up the rocky ridge above us. I was in the seventh heaven of delight because I was so sure that, having reached the col in good time, the summit was 'in the bag'. The climbing was straightforward and the snow arête beyond, the Biancograt itself, was aesthetically unsurpassable and the ridge, whilst being wide enough for comfort, gave me a glorious sense of elevation. One glance downwards revealed the glaciers and valleys hundreds of metres almost directly below.

We reached the summit in good time, where we found Geoff and Andy who had already been there a while. Our spirits were high and, whilst we consumed our well-deserved rations, they burst into song to the tune of 'Waltzing Matilda':

Climbing the Eiger, climbing the Eiger,
Who'll come a-climbing the Eiger with me?
I can't find a guide to take me up the Eigerwand,
Who'll come a-climbing the Eiger with me?

A fairly inappropriate climbing song so far from the Bernese Oberland! But we had reason to be cheerful: we had had the route virtually to ourselves. Apart from a soloist in front of us, all the other parties who had set out from the Tschierva Hut were now well behind us. I didn't then realise just what bliss this was: twelve years later, on our second ascent, Les and I had a very different experience.

We didn't stay any longer on the summit than necessary, however, as we were concerned about the dangers of the long descent of the Morteratsch Glacier in the midday sun. We were to take a particularly intricate route through the 'Buuch', wending our way directly beneath some perilously threatening séracs. At the time, this was the usual descent route from the head of the glacier but later it became impassable and when we returned to Piz Bernina in 1985, we did not consider it, taking instead a line across the Bellavista Terrace and then a route down the Fortezza Ridge.

After Piz Bernina, anything else in the area would have seemed an anticlimax to me, so I lazed about for a few days, enjoying the sun. It was only when most of our friends had gone home that Les and I turned our thoughts towards one last route that season. It was by then our fifth week in the Alps.

Accompanied by John Oaks and Andy Hodges, we drove all the way back through Switzerland to Martigny in the Valais and then branched off over the Col du Forclaz to Chamonix. Mont Blanc was calling us, a fitting end to our splendid holiday. The four of us took the cable car from Les Houches up to Bellevue and, from there, the mountain railway to its terminus at the Nid d'Aigle. Walking up the steep rocky slopes to the Goûter Hut, I was somewhat nervous at the thought of crossing the notorious couloir *en route*, knowing that there had been numerous fatalities there over the years. To my relief, we encountered no stonefall and I was glad that we were not planning to come back the same way.

The Goûter Hut is perched just below the top of the Aiguille of the same name and there is little more in front of it than a small terrace above a precipitous drop of six or seven hundred metres to the glacier below. The walk out to the one and only extremely primitive and evil-smelling latrine is etched forever on my mind. It was quite obvious that the male guests didn't always bother to walk that far, but we females had less choice in the matter. At least this vulgar male practice did have the compensation that I didn't have to stand and freeze whilst queuing on the narrow, icy platform quite as long as I might otherwise have done. Such were the joys of living at high altitude. From 2013, however, alpinists staying at the Goûter Hut should have a very different experience from ours. A new, eco-friendly building is currently being constructed a few metres away from the old one and its 1990 extension, so 21st-century climbers will be assured of electricity generated by solar panels and wind turbines, as well as modern toilet facilities using the latest suction devices and an efficient system of recycled water from the kitchen.

Prior booking has been obligatory for many years now but in 1973 this was not the case, so we made sure that we arrived in good time to secure bed spaces. This we duly did, though there was no question of a whole space each. For the first and only time in my Alpine experience, we were each officially allotted – as was every other guest in our dormitory – exactly half a bed space each on the upper tier of a long communal *matratzenlager*. There was no question of lying other than head to toe all the way along the mattress. It was a room which would normally have housed about a dozen people on both the upper and the lower bunk, but we must have been double that.

During what remained of the afternoon, I put this situation out of my mind and the evening brought a delight that more than compensated for the drawbacks of the night to come. Located at the extreme north-western tip of the Mont Blanc Massif, at an altitude of 3817m, the Goûter Hut offers an uninterrupted skyscape over the hills and valleys of France and is an ideal place to view the sunset. That evening, when the sun went down, the whole world seemed to be aglow. There was a mass of cloud swirling about, suffused with an ever-changing range of lemon and gold, rose pink, deep carmine and purple. It was indescribably beautiful.

At approximately eight in the evening, we went to lie down for the night. We were due to rise at two. There was no question of trying to sleep: I simply lay there, as still as I could, not moaning or groaning – I had learnt my lesson – but just counting the hours away one by one. When I was not congratulating myself on my survival, I was planning an escape route out of the hut in case of suffocation. I was aware that it was not just the dormitories that were overfull, but that there were also guests lying in the corridors and all over the living room.

Two o'clock came at last and we went down to the breakfast room, where we managed to secure four places, despite the fact that there were already people standing, sitting and lying everywhere. Les came close to being injured when someone accidentally poured scalding water over our table. Fortunately he wasn't hurt. At three o'clock we stepped out into the night: it was brilliant moonlight, crystal clear. There was no need to use torches. Neither did we rope up.

There was an obvious trail all the way and, to my delight, the crowds thinned as we progressed, so I soon forgot that almost every occupant of the hut was on the route as well. Our progress was good and it didn't seem long before we reached the Vallot Refuge on the far side of the Dôme du Goûter, where we stopped for a few moments to eat some chocolate. We peered over the eastern side of the mountain here, but it was still in shadow and, in any case, it was too early to expect a trail of climbers ascending from the Grands Mulets Hut.

Still unroped, we pressed on up the Bosses Ridge. Now at an altitude of over 4500m, I was just beginning to feel the lack of oxygen and slowed down a little, but underfoot the conditions were perfect and it was quite easy to plod on safely, crampons crunching reassuringly into the firm surface of the snow. Although we were soloing, we stayed more or less together as we climbed silently on in single file.

By six o'clock we were approaching the summit up the final, sharp, snow ridge. It was very cold but there was no wind and, with my duvet jacket covering my upper body and long johns under thick trousers, I felt just fine. The sun was beginning to rise as I slowly ascended that last crest and, way down below on the clouds, the shadow of Mont Blanc was forming. At 4807m, we may only have been standing at the highest point in Western Europe but it felt to me as if we were on top of the world.

The summit of Mont Blanc is a broad plateau and it didn't feel over-crowded that morning, despite the presence of a few other parties. The main mass of climbers was behind us, lower down on the approach. We spent a good half-hour savouring our achievement and the loftiness of our position and, as the sun gradually rose, John suddenly exclaimed:

'Look! Just down there! Have you seen that?'

Our shadows were cast upon the clouds below us with a faint aura of rainbow colours. Our achievement had been rewarded by that occasional natural phenomenon: a Brocken spectre. We waved our arms to convince ourselves that this was no illusion and the shadows waved back. Up there on the summit, I was feeling so very happy that I could hardly bear to leave.

But leave one must and, having decided to traverse the mountain to the Aiguille du Midi cable car station, we descended to the Col de la Brenva, where we roped up as the crevasses looked rather threatening. From there, we had no difficulty at all in climbing our next Fourthousander, Mont Maudit. From its summit there was a magnificent view of the rock spires of the Chamonix Aiguilles below. The only awkward part of the whole expedition was the steep descent from Mont Maudit, including one enormous crevasse that we had to leap across. That was where I stubbed one of my big toes very badly as I landed and, once I got back to the valley, I found that I was condemned for a while to wear only sandals. Eventually the nail fell away but luckily I hadn't broken the bone.

The summer had given us a really satisfying series of climbs, despite the poor weather between expeditions. All the routes we had done were the type I preferred: mainly snow, with some relatively short rock sections. I was completely within my comfort zone as far as the technical difficulties were concerned and therefore thoroughly enjoyed the climbing. Of course, there were moments when the conditions made the going tough, such as the fresh snow on our way to the Grünhorn, or the unpleasantly cold stance near the top of the Allalinhorn, but these were just passing moments of discomfort, and the overall impression of the ascents we made was one of great joy and satisfaction. We had climbed in several areas of outstanding beauty, high above the world we normally inhabited; we had snatched the opportunities between rainstorms and succeeded in reaching our objectives. Moreover, we had enjoyed the company of many friends, with whom we had shared these pleasures. I recall no discord, only the harmony of like minds and a general atmosphere of fun, particularly during the periods when we were confined to Alpine huts because the conditions outside were so inhospitable. The only times I was aware of any tension were when I, usually the slowest member of the party, occasionally held the quickest members up for longer than they may have wished. Most of the time, my team mates seemed to tolerate this weakness very patiently and, occasionally, someone would suggest a slightly slower speed or longer rest on my behalf.

For me, there were two highlights of this summer season. The first was our ascent of the Biancograt on Piz Bernina (a route I had feared might be beyond my capabilities) with one of the most memorable sunrises I ever saw in the Alps. The second was the traverse of Mont Blanc; above all, because it is the highest point in Western Europe but also because we had the good fortune to be able to walk from the Goûter Hut to the summit unroped, each moving at our own pace, bright moonlight shining down upon our route.

4

A Brief Interlude
at Snell's

The 1973 season was so remarkable that it would be easy to forget the previous summer, but that had been memorable in a completely different way. In May 1972 I had turned thirty. Looking back, I believe that this was more of a landmark than I realised at the time. Les and I had been married for three years and it began to seem appropriate to consider whether or not we might start a family. If we decided, as we did, to postpone the decision a little longer, then I knew I had to take some immediate action about my teaching career. At that point, although Alpine climbing was already very important to me, I was prepared to sacrifice some time to another strand of my life. I enjoyed teaching but was greatly frustrated by the lowly position I had been in for three years at the college and was beginning to wonder if I should apply elsewhere for a higher grade post. Before I did so, I was keen to upgrade my profile and, as a linguist, was conscious of the need to keep my languages fluent and up-to-date.

To this end I obtained a summer job working in Snell Sports, a climbing shop in Chamonix. There I would be able to speak French all day, six days a week, and meet Les and our climbing friends whenever I was not working. What energy I had! It was not until the end of that summer that I realised just how much teachers really did need a long summer break. Having worked in industry before I started teaching, I was used to an annual leave of only three weeks and the lengthy vacation allowed by the teaching profession still seemed unnecessarily long. 1972 was the last year I felt like that and I vowed that I would never sacrifice my summer break again.

During that summer in Chamonix, Les took every opportunity to climb and, as the weather was mainly very stable through July, he gained a wide variety of experience and did several of the great classic routes in the Mont Blanc Massif. It was fortunate that my motivation to work at my French was so great and that I enjoyed the work in the shop so much, as I might otherwise have realised what gems I was missing: the Rochefort Arête amongst other things. I was, however, perfectly happy as long as I could keep fit by swimming in the magnificent open-air pool and then, on my one day off each week, either walk or climb.

A chat with the owner of a climbing shop in the Lake District one weekend in early 1972 had resulted in an introduction to Donald Snell in Chamonix. Snell, like his father before him, was renowned for taking a great interest in the élite British climbers who frequented this Mecca of the French Alps, so I was very pleased to be offered work in his smart shop in the centre of the town, just down the street from the Bar National. This bar was famous as a haunt of British climbers.

I negotiated an extra week's summer leave from the college, enabling me to make the most of this vocational opportunity, and also reserved a couple of weeks for a holiday at the end of the summer. Having arranged to travel out to Chamonix with two of our climbing friends, I squeezed myself and my luggage into John Oaks' already loaded Mini. With Norman Smithers, another Lincoln Mountaineering Club member, squashed into the back seat with rucksacks and camping gear, and me in the front passenger seat, hugging a primus stove between my knees, we set off at the beginning of July, a week before Les was due to come out for his climbing trip. Somewhere in the middle of the French countryside, a stone was thrown up from the road, shattering our windscreen, and we drove on another 20km or so, wearing our Alpine climbing goggles as a windshield. These were the days before windscreens were made from layers of toughened glass and the A26 motorway with its smooth, pebble-free surface did not yet exist.

Fortunately, I had updated my French since my university course, which was heavily biased towards literary language, and I was able to persuade a French garage owner in the nearest town to fit a new windscreen, even though it was almost lunchtime, that sacrosanct period of rest when most businesses closed for at least two hours.

That evening we arrived in Chamonix and my friends dropped me off at Snell Sports before making their way to a campsite. Donald Snell was waiting at the shop and immediately whisked me away to his house, where his wife treated me to a family dinner. This cosy introduction to the home life of a small group of Chamoniards was quite a contrast to the bed-sitter Monsieur Snell had acquired for me at the top of a dilapidated building in the centre of Chamonix. My spirits sank as we climbed the gloomy staircase at the rear of some smart cafés and shops on one of the main squares. It reminded me all too starkly of the house where I had lived in Bordeaux in the early 1960s. The room itself was sparsely furnished and, although there was hot and cold running water in the sink, you had to go along a corridor past some other rooms inhabited by unknown people to reach the WC, a veritable throne room, with the lavatory perched upon a plinth. This was, of course, luxury compared with an Alpine hut but my morale hit a low point just then. Late evening now, it was dark and I had no idea what sort of view to expect from my garret window. I peered out over the rooftops but the sky was devoid of stars. All I could see was thick cloud, just as I had experienced on my first brief visit with Les in 1969, when it poured with rain for several days. Now, weary after the long journey and previous night, when the only sleep I had had was a brief doze on the car ferry from Dover to Calais, I scarcely had time to wonder what the next day would bring before I fell asleep.

For the next seven weeks I worked at the shop from 8.30 in the morning until 7.30 in the evening, with a couple of hours' break in the middle of the day. Snell's was open every day of the week throughout the summer season and the staff were only entitled to one day off each week. Wednesday was my free day and I always made the most of it, either walking or climbing in the mountains. At lunchtimes I would often swim in a nearby hotel pool with some of the other shop girls, or use the municipal pool, a magnificent 50m strip of water outdoors. On a sunny summer's day it was a delight to float on one's back, gazing up at the snow-covered skyline of the Goûter Ridge on Mont Blanc.

On my first day at Snell's, I was assigned to Danielle, a local girl with a great sense of fun and a salesgirl of considerable experience. Our counter was situated on the ground floor, opposite the main entrance, and from there we sold a wide variety of casual clothes, as well as sportswear and light-weight walking boots. The climbing equipment and specialised footwear were in the basement and therefore not part of our domain. Danielle introduced me to the art of folding shirts and sweaters, and hanging trousers neatly after browsing customers had disturbed them. She also taught me the various words used to describe the many different types of headgear on display. This specific vocabulary was completely new to me but became an essential element of my sales repertoire. To my immense relief, I learned that I didn't have to handle money at all. Whenever we sold an item, we simply had to write out a chit and the financial transaction was finalised at the *caisse*. That saved me from having to rely on my rusty arithmetical skills. I had never been destined to be a mathematician.

Evening came at last, and I retreated to my solitary 'eagle's nest', high above the streets of Chamonix. I cooked myself a very simple meal on the little camping-gas stove that Monsieur Snell had provided for me and then, before I had time to feel lonely, a knock on the door announced the arrival of John and Norman, who had strolled into town from their campsite. The Lincoln Mountaineering Club 50th Anniversary Journal quotes an article written by John Oaks after the 1972 Alpine trip:

We were invited to Barbara Swindin's apartment that evening and given an elaborate plan to ensure our safe arrival (after a litre of vin rouge anything could happen). B. was busy with 'domestic chores', so Norman and I clambered out over the radiator and on to the flat roof to view all the peaks: from the Dru to the Midi Norman named the tops and faces of the Chamonix Aiguilles.

Like John, I was quite overwhelmed by the view. Until then, I had been too busy to notice that the clouds had lifted. There before us, pointing high into the sky, two or three thousand metres above the town, was the spikiest range of rock pinnacles and ridges I had ever seen. So my miserable garret had its advantages after all.

The following weekend Les and another friend arrived and, in between their days away in the mountains, I would meet the group after work and enjoy their company. After Les's climbing companions had returned to England, we would spend Wednesdays together and this gave me the opportunity to enjoy some Alpine climbing too. However, I only did two Alpine routes that summer before deciding that the effort involved on top of working six days a week was simply too great for me. Both routes were worthwhile. The first was a traverse of the Midi-Plan Arête, an airy crest of rock and snow perched high above the Chamonix Valley. That was perhaps my most exciting route to date. For the second, we returned to the Aiguille du Midi, this time taking the last téléphérique of the day, Donald Snell having kindly allowed me to leave the shop early. We spent a very pleasant, convivial evening at the Cosmiques Hut and set off early next morning for Mont Blanc du Tacul. I was very pleased to have this opportunity to climb one of the great outliers of Mont Blanc itself and I thought, wrongly, that as the Tacul only reaches 4248m, I wouldn't find the altitude too arduous.

On this occasion we were accompanied by John Parry, a climbing partner Les had got to know on one of his visits to Snell's Field, an unofficial campsite on the edge of Chamonix where you could often find a nucleus of unattached British climbers.

It was a bitterly cold morning when we set out for Mont Blanc du Tacul by its Normal Route. We had also intended to go to the adjacent peak, Mont Maudit, if I proved fit enough, but the chilly breeze sapped too much of my strength that day and my general lack of acclimatisation became apparent once we were above the 4000m mark. Worse still, I was not very well clad, having only brought out to France the minimum of mountaineering clothing. Fortunately, however, whilst my legs froze, I was at least able to shelter my upper body in my cosy Terray duvet jacket.

It was an uneventful, straightforward climb, really just a simple snow-plod on a firm surface, but the higher we climbed, the harsher the wind became. As I wrote in my journal:

It was as much as I could do to get to the summit of the Tacul and the wind was too unpleasant for us to spend much time there. I think Les really was worried that I might suffer from exposure.

There was no sense of elation here. I was suffering too much from the freezing temperature and the chilly bite of the wind, so we turned back without attempting to continue to Mont Maudit. Later, on the lower slopes, we came into the sun. Warmer now, I found the descent through the sérac barriers most enjoyable. Yet, by the time we reached the final, wearisome plod up the steep snow ridge to the Aiguille du Midi, the sun was beating down relentlessly and it was a pleasure to step inside the cool tunnel leading to the cable car station. Such are the contrasts of heat and cold on a day out on the glaciers of the high Alps.

Back in the shop, I continued to work with enthusiasm until the middle of August. By then trade was beginning to dwindle as the number of tourists gradually declined towards the end of the main season. I began to hanker after my freedom and arranged to leave at the end of the third week of the month. Throughout my time at the shop, Monsieur Snell, hidden in his office behind a two-way mirror, had had many opportunities to survey what was happening on the ground floor where we worked. It was some time before I realised that I was being observed but, fortunately, the boss was pleased with my apparent skill as a saleswoman, my competence in the French language and my ability to act as interpreter when necessary.

One day I was called down to the basement, where a group of Russian climbers were engaged in a bartering exercise. They were trying to exchange some products they had brought with them for some French climbing equipment. As they spoke neither French nor English, they were attempting to communicate in German but none of the sales staff could understand what they were saying. I therefore had the entertaining job of interpreting the Russians' German into French. The negotiations concluded satisfactorily for all concerned.

Despite encouragement from Donald Snell to return the following summer for another stint, I decided that I had no desire to sacrifice another long vacation. I had convinced myself that my language skills were sufficiently honed for my career purposes and I wanted to make Alpine climbing my priority between mid-July and mid-August for the foreseeable future.

PART TWO

CONSOLIDATION

I wanted to extend my skill, so that on my next Alpine climb
I should be less of a passenger and more of a partner.
– JANET ADAM SMITH[1]

The Dent du Géant and the Rochefort Arête

1 *Mountain Holidays* by Janet Adam Smith

1

NEW ALPINE PARTNERS

Following the magnificent 1973 grand tour of the Alps with our GMC and LMC friends, we were joined in Switzerland the next summer, not by the usual faces, but by Colin and Sue Wornham, whom we had known for several years. Les had first met them on a meet with the Wellingborough Mountaineering Club in the mid-1960s, before he came to live in Gloucestershire. Colin was, by 1974, an experienced mountaineer and later qualified as a mountain guide; Sue was a strong hill walker, having done many Munros in Scotland, but she didn't do a great deal of rock climbing. During the period when I knew her, her activities in the Alps focused more on ski-mountaineering than on summer climbing. Sadly, she died of cancer before the end of the following decade.

In 1974, Colin and Sue both worked in secondary schools so, once again, because of the shorter summer term at college, Les and I were able to travel out to Switzerland a week before our companions. This time, however, the weather proved most unkind and we did no acclimatisation at all before moving to Arolla to meet them. It so happened that there was also a meet of the Association of British Members of the Swiss Alpine Club in Arolla that year and we had some good fun at the huts with the participants. Sometimes with Sue, and sometimes without her, we did several routes at relatively low altitude before setting our sights higher. Then we were ready to climb the Dent Blanche.

At 4356m, the Dent Blanche is over 100m lower than the Matterhorn but it is, nevertheless, 'one of the most magnificent of all the Valais 4000 metre peaks and a majestic piece of mountain architecture', as Lindsay Griffin describes it in his guidebook.[2] As far as the Normal Route from the Rossier Hut is concerned, he goes on to say:

---

2 *Valais Alps West* by Lindsay Griffin

Unlike many of the Normal Routes on the big Valais peaks, the South Ridge is no push-over and in bad conditions can be quite taxing. It is worth bearing in mind that this is a big mountain with no short or straightforward descent, so all routes to the summit are serious and committing propositions.

There was certainly no question of our party trying any of the other ridges. Unfortunately, I must have eaten something that disagreed with me, as on the six-hour walk up to the hut from Ferpècle I began to feel quite weak and unwell. By the time we were wading through the midday snow on the Glacier des Manzettes, the two men were, needless to say, way ahead. Thank goodness for Sue, who kindly lent me her long-handled ice axe and carried some of my load. Otherwise I might not have reached the hut until much later. Once there, I rested as much as possible but, although I tried to get some food inside me, eating was a struggle. At 3507m, the Rossier Hut is one of the highest in Switzerland, so it may be that the altitude was also affecting me. That evening, in compensation, we witnessed a sunset just as beautiful as the one we had seen the year before from the Goûter Hut.

Bed that night was yet another crowded *matratzenlager* up in the attic but I slept nevertheless. A strange phenomenon occurred. I often had vivid dreams at high altitude and on that occasion, in the very early hours of 30th July, I dreamt that someone was holding up a little baby for me to see. Now, I was not at all in the habit of having dreams about children, and certainly not about babies, but my only sister was expecting her first child some six weeks later. A few days after this, when we were in Chamonix, I went to Donald Snell's sports shop to see if there was any mail for me. To my astonishment, there was a telegram informing me that my niece had been born six weeks prematurely on the very day that I was climbing the Dent Blanche. Thirty-six years later, in 2010, another odd event occurred. I was in the foothills of the French Pyrenees and, for the second time in my life, I dreamt about a baby. This time the child was lying on a scrap of bubble wrap. I woke up in a state of shock but tried to convince myself that this was pure coincidence. It so happened that my niece herself was expecting her first child, though not for another two months. Exactly two weeks later, she unexpectedly gave birth to her own tiny daughter, seven weeks before the due date.

Since the rainstorms that greeted our arrival in the Alps, the Valais had had a period of fairly stable, sunny weather. The South Ridge of the Dent Blanche was in good condition and, despite my weakness the previous afternoon, I had no trouble at all on the climb. At one point, as I wrote in my journal, we took a hazardous traverse and notorious couloir to avoid the Grand Gendarme:

Once we started on the ridge proper, the abruptness became quite awe-inspiring, somewhat reminiscent of the Matterhorn, but there was no real difficulty and here most of the rock was solid. The Dent Blanche stands alone, apart from other peaks, and this gives the climber a sense of isolation. Avoiding the Grand Gendarme involved us in ascending some ice, but there were various belay stakes and bucket steps between. The slopes beneath you are so precipitous, that there is a great feeling of exposure, but most of the rock climbing on the upper part of the ridge is provided with good holds. It was interesting both in ascent and descent. Having recently completed the traverse of the long, rocky Cuillin Ridge in Skye, I had no difficulty here on this relatively short, delightful climb.

The exhilaration I experienced when I reached the top may only have been surpassed by the intrepid Dorothy Pilley Richards. She and her husband, Ivor Richards (I.A.R., as she generally called him), and their guides summitted after making the first ascent of the much more serious North-North-West Ridge (TD[3]) in the summer of 1928. This particular route, also called the North Ridge, had first enticed I.A.R. in 1921 and Dorothy Pilley refers to the mountain as a 'Witch'. For them, the Dent Blanche evidently assumed the *bête noire* status that the Aiguille Blanche had for me many decades later. When they did reach the summit, it was already five o'clock in the afternoon, the route having taken almost eleven hours from the Col de la Dent Blanche. They probably did not have time, therefore, to enjoy the view of the Matterhorn as much as I did. On the summit of the Dent Blanche I had a strong sensation that I could put out a hand and touch the summit of the Matterhorn. It seemed so near, and yet it was 7km away. Eight years later, on the summit of the Dent d'Hérens, a mere 3km on the far side of the Matterhorn, I experienced exactly the same feeling for the second time, so compelling is that peak.

Colin and Sue didn't stay out in the Alps as long as we did and after they had gone home, Les and I drove to the Dauphiné Alps. We camped at Ailefroide, a dismal place when the weather is poor, and once again it rained, so I was glad to leave it when the next sunny spell arrived. We walked up the Glacier Blanc to the Caron Hut (now called the Ecrins Hut) and spent a cramped night there with hordes of other climbers. The early morning rising was noted for its regimentation. Les had managed to slip out of the room before the general alarm went off, but I always took longer to get myself ready and when I tried to leave the room, I was forcibly prevented from doing so by one of the hut staff. I had to wait until the appointed time.

---

3 TD: très difficile, one of the hardest climbing grades

Our day's goal was the Barre des Ecrins. We set off at high speed up the glacier to try to beat the crowds, as we knew that the summit ridge is very narrow and we didn't want to be held up by slower parties. What we hadn't realised was that the vast majority of climbers were not going to the Barre at all, but would settle for the Dôme des Ecrins, the lower summit, also over 4000m, which we did not intend to do.

However fast I walked, it was impossible for us to be first to reach the lower slopes of the north face. 'North Face' is a name associated with some very grand routes in the Alps but, on the Ecrins, the Normal Route ascends the lower part of the north face before traversing rightwards to the Brèche Lory, the gap between the snow-covered Dôme and the long rock ridge called the Barre. The angle is easy all the way but, although we were able to keep moving without having to stop and wait for anybody, my feet were numb and I had to take my crampons off before we reached the Brèche in order to thaw out my toes. This proved to be a mistake, as we then had to make our way up an ice pitch to reach the rock ridge above. The climb to the summit of the Barre des Ecrins itself is very pleasant indeed, rather like a very long version of the exposed Crib Goch ridge on Snowdon that I had climbed for the first time ten years previously.

The ascent marked the end of our 1974 summer holiday and, from the summit, we had a magnificent view of Mont Blanc. This was the first time I had seen it from the south, and I was most impressed by the way in which it towers majestically above the intervening ground, standing apart from the main bulk of the Alps away to the east.

A year later, Les and I arranged to meet Colin Wornham in the Alps again. Sue had decided not to join us that summer. As so often in previous seasons, the weather scotched our plans to slip in a couple of easy routes for acclimatisation before our rendezvous with Colin but the three of us met up in Chamonix and did a little training together. First, on the Aiguille de l'Index, a fine rock climb high on the mountainside on the northern side of the Chamonix Valley with a magnificent view of the Mont Blanc Massif. Then, a brief, unmemorable sortie on the Aiguille d'Argentière, which I recall only for the lethal nature of the icy descent. I was too busy keeping warm to enjoy the lovely panorama from the summit. After that we were ready for greater things.

Back in 1972, one of Les's climbing partners, Reg Monks, had talked about the airy East Ridge of the Aiguille de Bionnassay. I believe that when he climbed it, the snow crest was so narrow that he and his party had to descend it *à cheval*, one leg on each side of the ridge. As Colin, Les and I were now contemplating climbing the Bionnassay, this recollection disturbed me.

It was a British woman, Katy Richardson, who made the first descent of the East Ridge in 1888, when she traversed the mountain with her guides, but I doubt that knowing this would have made any difference to me. I hid my apprehension as best I could, knowing I would be with two very competent climbers.

Our objective was to ascend the mountain by the Original Route on its 1000m North-West Face. Then we planned to traverse the knife-edge arête down to the Col de Bionnassay and thence climb a further three or four hundred metres up to and over the Col du Dôme de Goûter in order to descend the Grands Mulets Glacier on our way back to Chamonix.

We took the funicular railway, as we had in 1973 on our way to Mont Blanc. This time, the walk from the terminus at the Nid d'Aigle to our destination was easy and without any danger of rockfall. It was a delight to spend the afternoon and evening at the Tête Rousse Hut, admiring the spectacular snow face we intended to climb in the early hours of the following day, though the prospect of wending our way up through the awe-inspiring array of séracs was somewhat daunting. I banished this image from my mind and snatched a few hours sleep before the earliest-yet wakening time of one o'clock in the morning. Conditions were excellent. It was a fine, cold night. The glacier was firmly frozen and our route promised to be as safe as such routes ever can be.

Before two o'clock the three of us were roped together, swiftly traversing the Bionnassay Glacier towards the icy heaps of avalanche debris which lay at the bottom of the North-West Face. This broken field of devastation was not only awkward to cross but also reminded us all too clearly of the seriousness of our route. We began to climb and the effort and interest in what we were doing chased away any doubts in my mind. Then Colin slipped. As I wrote later:

The adrenalin pumped round my body in that sudden spurt just as it does when we pull up sharply on a motorway. We all dug in instinctively with our axes and mercifully he stopped. After that we were even more careful.

If only it had not been so dark, it must have been very beautiful. We made our way gradually up past enormous ice towers, round sérac barriers and along terraces. Eventually, as dawn approached, we arrived at the summit ridge. This was quite icy and made an appropriate finish to a splendid climb but it was cold on the summit, so we didn't stay long. In any case we still had a very long way to go.

We moved off down the famous East Ridge. To my relief, it was not that day anything like as narrow as I had been led to believe. It really wasn't a knife-edge at all:

There was just enough room to walk along the snow crest in comfort and feel the elation of striding aloft above the near vertical slopes leading down to the glaciers six or seven hundred metres below on each side.

Naïvely, I imagined that Reg had been exaggerating the difficulties. It was not for many years, until my ascent of the same ridge in 1993, that I could really appreciate what he had meant. On that second occasion, the snow crest was a very different proposition.

We arrived in good spirits at the Col de Bionnassay and set off on the exhausting plod up to the Col du Dôme de Goûter. I began to feel very tired: we were now at a height of well over 4000m. The weather was very fine and there was no need to hurry at this (still fairly early) hour of the morning, so the men paused to take photographs whilst I regained my strength. When we reached the col, I felt quite exhilarated and memories of our moonlight stroll to Mont Blanc flooded back. I was not at all disappointed to omit the summit of Mont Blanc from our route on this occasion, however, as the ascent of the North-West Face of the Aiguille de Bionnassay was such an achievement in itself. We embarked upon the long descent to Chamonix and, by the time we reached the glacier area of la Jonction below the Grands Mulets Hut, where we had to weave in and out of a labyrinth of huge crevasses, I was beginning to feel like a robot. It was with a huge sense of relief that I finally reached the Plan l'Aiguille cable car station to take a well-earned ride down to the Chamonix Valley. We had been on the go for twelve hours. What a day! This really rated as one of the very best.

After our excellent week in Chamonix, we moved over the border into Switzerland and met up with John Oaks, that year accompanied by John Parker and Myles Plant from the Lincoln Mountaineering Club. Our base was the campsite just beyond the village of Zinal in the Val d'Anniviers, where Les and I had spent the initial week of my first alpine season. Here we were well placed for some of the loveliest peaks of the Pennine Alps and a return visit to my old favourite, the Mountet Hut. We were still obliged to take the same track to get there as on our previous visit, but once that was behind us, we could sit and contemplate the delights to come. Again, we had perfect weather, so the following morning Les and Colin went off together to climb the North Face of the Obergabelhorn, whilst I accompanied the others on an easier route to the Pointe de Zinal. This was the first time I had ever climbed in the Alps without Les in my party and I felt that I was taking quite a significant psychological step forward, even though John Oaks was most definitely the leader of my rope.

Not being in the least concerned about 4000m peak-bagging at that time, I was not at all perturbed about missing out on the Obergabelhorn. I simply accepted that the North Face route was too hard for me, and was glad that Les could enjoy a more serious route whilst I was doing something more appropriate to my own level of alpinism. It was an enjoyable day, after which we all turned our thoughts towards the Zinalrothorn.

For Les, this would be a celebration, his fiftieth Alpine route. He wanted to do something special to mark the occasion and, although he had previously climbed the Zinalrothorn from the Zermatt Valley, he was keen to tackle its North Ridge. He and I set off to do this on our own. Fortunately I didn't realise in advance just how vertiginous the North Ridge would prove to be. Whilst John Parker took a rest day at the hut, Colin, John Oaks and Myles chose a longer route, the complete traverse of the mountain by ascending from the south on the Rothorngrat and then descending the North Ridge. This could all be done quite easily in a day from the Mountet Hut.

It was quite warm when Les and I set off up the moraine and when we arrived at the foot of the Arête du Blanc, the snow crest leading up to the point where the rock scrambling starts, we were able to continue without putting on our crampons. As the snow crest narrowed, I began to panic slightly in case I slipped. I really disliked being without the security of my metal spikes. How I had changed since the early days when crampons used to make me feel wobbly and uncomfortable. Les insisted that it was quite unnecessary to put them on and I didn't argue, but continued to climb somewhat gingerly. We reached the start of the rocks safely and had a short rest before moving on.

To begin with, the climbing was pleasant and easy enough, but the ridge gradually narrows and becomes extremely exposed. Then we came to the thinnest flake I had ever seen, the Rasoir. This airy blade well deserves its name. I found it quite difficult to ascend to its crest, as I had to balance on very tiny holds and then, having gained height, I launched out to the right and teetered across the face of the 'razor blade', my hands on the upper edge, my feet upon the most minuscule of holds. One look down between my legs revealed the abyss below. Having reached the other end of the short traverse, I descended the edge *à cheval*, secured by the rope which was hooked over the top of the blade. With relief, I arrived at the gap beyond but, from then on, I was plagued with the thought of the return trip.

After the Rasoir, the rest of the rock climbing was nothing, not even the Bourrique, which is described as a hand-traverse, first on one side and then the other. Only when I came to the final obstacle, the Bosse, did I become overawed again. The Bosse is a steep, impressive tower, but it was equipped with pitons and when we later came back down it from the summit, I was pleased to find it extremely easy. Even the Rasoir proved less difficult on the return journey.

Once on the summit of the Zinalrothorn, the tension in my nervous system released and I relaxed in the sunshine. We could already see our friends approaching from the ridge on the other side of the mountain and I was looking forward to their company on the descent. As planned, we reversed the North Ridge, now as a party of five, but still as two ropes, and returned to the Mountet Hut. There, as so often afterwards, once the occasional frightening moments had receded into the recesses of my mind, I was able to sit back and revel in the feeling that we had had a very satisfactory expedition. It was only sometime later that afternoon, when we were relaxing at the hut and contemplating whether we could afford to celebrate by buying dinner and a bottle of wine, that Les realised we had inadvertently left most of our cash in the valley! This wasn't as serious as when Geoff Causey and Andrew Reynolds had left their money in Stechelberg before climbing the Jungfrau in 1967. Here, not only did we have no need to catch an expensive train back to the valley, but we were also with friends who would have been able to supplement our hut fees. Buying a hut meal was, however, too much of an expense to subsidise as well as buying their own food, so Les, Colin and I had no choice but to leave the others to enjoy another night at the Mountet Hut, whilst we carried on back down that long, long track to Zinal.

2

WOMEN AND MOUNTAINEERING: GREAT STRIDES FORWARD

It wasn't until the 1920s that new developments in the history of women's climbing started to occur. Meanwhile, Dorothy Pilley, born in 1893 and filled with notions about mountains gleaned from childhood fiction, was discovering the reality of the mountain environment for the first time. She was in her late teens on a family holiday in Beddgelert, near the foot of Snowdon, and was immediately captivated by the rugged landscape. She returned the following year with a school-friend and together they set off on exciting walking expeditions. During the course of one, they met Herbert Carr, who had already embarked upon his own climbing career. It was he who invited the two friends to climb on Tryfan, 'the only Welsh mountain that cannot be climbed without using hands'.[1] From then onwards, Dorothy Pilley became a passionate rock climber and 'mountain madness had her now for ever in its grasp'.[2] In 1918, she joined the F&RCC, helping to found the London Section in 1920, and in 1921 became a Founder Member of the women-only Pinnacle Club.

The difference between Dorothy Pilley's natural aptitude and enthusiasm for rock climbing and my own fears and lack of immediate talent some fifty years later is immeasurable. What I believe we shared, however, was an innate enthusiasm for the mountains, an overwhelming sense of joy and wonder at the stark, rocky environment of Snowdonia, the delight in the Lakeland hills and their many crags, and the bleak, wild roughness of the Black Cuillin on the Isle of Skye. We also shared the same practice grounds before we started Alpine climbing but, unlike my predecessor, I didn't feel obliged to wear a skirt over a pair of tweed knickerbockers when walking around Beddgelert. Thus I never had to worry, as she did, about forgetting to bring that skirt back from the foot of the route where she had left it. She never forgot that her own predecessor, Mrs. Le Blond, once had the misfortune to leave her skirt at the top of the Zinalrothorn. It was so vital

1 *Climbing Days* by Dorothy Pilley
2 ibid.

that she didn't return to the Alpine village without wearing it, that she and her guide went all the way back up this 4000m peak to retrieve it.

As for myself, from the 1960s onwards, I was only too glad to abandon feminine clothes, although I enjoyed wearing them for my social life and at my place of work. In my spare time, I revelled in the freedom of trousers and walking boots. This was the lifestyle I truly wanted to adopt. It allowed me to feel completely free from the remaining social constraints on women at that time. The mountain environment, too, gave me an overwhelming sense of peace that I rarely experienced elsewhere. At last I had escaped from the exceptionally sheltered background of my childhood where my sister and I had been imbued with attitudes that dated back to the beginning of the twentieth century.

Dorothy Pilley, English mountain climber, climbing on the Calyn Face. © *The Alpine Club Photo Library, London.*

Dorothy Pilley met her husband early in her climbing career, just as I met mine, but she was much bolder and more independent than me when she took her first steps to learn to climb. By the time she and I.A.R. became a permanent climbing partnership, she didn't need him to teach her what to do. She was already an experienced lead rock climber and had made a good number of alpine ascents. The Richardses formed a relationship with the guide, Joseph Georges, and he accompanied them on many routes, including the first ascent of the North Ridge of the Dent Blanche in 1928. Although a car accident injured her badly thirty years later, irretrievably damaging her hip, Dorothy Pilley Richards continued to be as active in the mountains as her disability allowed. Her climbing days were finally over by the end of the 1960s but it seems that nothing could destroy her enthusiasm for mountains and mountaineering. Having no children of her own, she took a great deal of interest in the exploits of her friends' children and grandchildren, just as I like to do. Even at the end of her long life, she was still spending time at mountain huts and enjoying the social life which accompanies so much of climbing. She died in 1986.

Such partnerships as the Richardses' are not unusual in alpine climbing. In the course of my own story I mention two other married couples: John Kemsley and his wife, Freda, who acted as my Proposer when I applied to join the Alpine Club in 1976, and Robin and Hazel Costello, members of the F&RCC, whom we met in the Mattertal many years later. Long before

'Cordée féminine' – Micheline Morin, Nea Morin with Alice Damesme at the Aigle Hut after Meije traverse, 1933. © The Alpine Club Photo Library, London.

any of us were born, however, there were the newly married Mr. and Mrs. A. F. Mummery, who climbed the Täschhorn on their honeymoon in 1887. Much later on, there were the Morins, Nea and her husband, Jean, a leading French climber from Paris. From the late 1920s until the outbreak of the Second World War, they also climbed together in the Alps, but not exclusively. One of the greatest women climbers of all, Nea (née Barnard) was a great advocate of guideless women's ropes and, with her sister-in-law and a woman friend, frequently climbed without men. A considerable number of their climbs were first ascents in the Chamonix Aiguilles. As Jean was killed on a mission during the war, the Morins' climbing partnership was of fairly short duration compared with Nea's own climbing career, which, despite arthritis, continued until just a few years before she died in 1986. These are just a few instances and, doubtless, in the future when historians look back at the present era, there will be examples not only of married couples, but also of unmarried heterosexual and gay partnerships.

Different generations of the same family have often climbed together and some of these partnerships prove that motherhood doesn't always signal a halt to a woman's climbing days. It was only to be expected that Nea Morin, who had been encouraged to climb as a little girl by her father, would bring up her own children to climb. She and her daughter, Denise, made a formidable women's rope and did many routes together. Like both her parents, Denise became a member of the élite French mountaineering society, the Groupe de Haute Montagne (GHM). In 1986, Denise, by then Lady Evans, was the first female President of the Alpine Club. Nea Morin also belonged to the Pinnacle Club, which was particularly well placed to form a base from which mothers could introduce their sons and daughters to climbing. Cicely Williams wrote about 'mother and daughter' relationships and family climbing thus:

The dominant theme is the sharing of deep and very personal experiences with those whom one loves in a world of incomparable beauty.[3]

This also applies to any other kind of partnership, whether intimate or not. The regular hiring of the same guide by a client is one example. Close relationships were formed as a result of mutual trust, and friendship developed. Such was the situation between Lucy Walker and Melchior Anderegg, who kept in contact for the rest of their lives. Asked why she never married, Lucy Walker replied that she 'loved the mountains and loved Melchior and

3 *Women on the Rope* by Cicely Williams

he was already married'.[4] Katy Richardson frequently hired Emile Rey as her guide, and once she met Mary Paillon, the two ladies were inseparable. Dorothy Pilley and her husband frequently climbed with Joseph Georges and, when they left Europe for a life overseas, Dorothy Thompson 'inherited' him as her one and only guide.

Dorothy Thompson, a photograph taken in the thirties by Mrs. Elaine Feibusch Lowry. © The Alpine Club Photo Library, London.

4 ibid.

The 1920s and 1930s are notable for several great achievements by women climbers. Already a member of the Pinnacle Club, and a close friend of Dorothy Pilley, Dorothy Thompson was an exceptional alpinist. Born in 1888, she only started to climb in the Alps after the First World War. When she reached the summit of the Zinalrothorn in 1923, her first season, she was immediately captivated by the idea of climbing all the peaks she could see. She was not as wealthy as many of her predecessors and wondered how she could afford to achieve such an ambition:

I was debating … how, without a larger purse than was at my command, I was ever to think of climbing them.[5]

By the time Dorothy Thompson had climbed the Dent Blanche in 1924, Joseph Georges was so impressed by her abilities that he praised her achievements to other guides in Zermatt. She joined the LAC the same year and, from then on, climbed a great many of the major routes in the Dauphiné, Mont Blanc Massif and the Pennine Alps. Her enthusiasm for Alpine climbing continued throughout the following decade and, in 1929, she became the first woman to be 'taken up' the Brouillard Arête on the Italian side of Mont Blanc. It wasn't, however, until she reached the top, that her guide informed her of this fact. Not in the least competitive, she was astonished, as she had only climbed the route to satisfy her own desire. She simply loved to be in the high mountains surrounded by 'steep rock columns and … the tumbled, chaotic beginnings of one vast glacier from the piled-up snow-masses of another', as she wrote after standing on the Col Eccles, 'one of the superb vantage points of the Alps'.[6]

Joseph Georges encouraged Dorothy Thompson to take an interest in climbing the Peuterey Ridge on Mont Blanc. This would include the Aiguille Blanche – and no woman had yet climbed the whole ridge. Her reaction to her guide's suggestion was similar to my own when, in 1989, Pete and Les encouraged me to climb the Aiguille Blanche in order to complete Collomb's List of Fourthousanders, not just because it would be satisfying to do so, but also because no British woman had yet climbed all the peaks on that list. An unexpected element of competition crept into my climbing ambitions, an element that had never been there before. I had very much the same feelings as those expressed by Dorothy Thompson about the possibility of climbing a considerably lengthier version of the same route:

---

5 *Climbing with Joseph Georges* by Dorothy E. Thompson
6 ibid.

I was not ignorant about the Peuteret [sic]. I had read of it with awe as 'the finest, longest and most difficult ridge in the Alps' … I knew well that at that time only a few men and as yet no woman had climbed the Peuteret Arête. Up till that moment competition had not entered into climbing ambitions. It was still as antithetic to me as it had been in the 1929 season when climbing the Brouillard Arête. But to become the first woman to climb the Peuteret! How completely the ambition altered one's horizons.[7]

She was, in fact, beaten to this goal by one week. Although, in 1933, she was the first woman to descend the Peuterey Ridge, two years later, in 1935, Una Cameron became the first woman to climb it.

Not only did Dorothy Thompson climb many great alpine routes with Joseph Georges, but she also climbed guideless, particularly on rock routes at lower altitude. In the UK, she climbed in the Lake District and on the Isle of Skye. There is another reason for my own empathy with her – the fact that she also did many alpine ski-tours. The Second World War put an end to her Alpine activities and she died in 1961.

Una Cameron is the other British female alpinist I associate particularly with the Aiguille Blanche. Born in 1904, she was of a completely different

Una Cameron. © The Alpine Club Photo Library, London.

7 ibid.

stature from some of the aforementioned women climbers. Rather than being slight and neat, she was well built and strong, and considered her heaviness an advantage, particularly in a gale-force wind. She was from a very wealthy Scottish family, and had the means to have a house built near Courmayeur, on the south side of the Mont Blanc Massif. She never married, and her habits must have surprised the local community at the time, as she wore trousers not only on the mountains, but off the mountains too. She smoked a pipe and, later, cigars. Fluent in French and Italian, she integrated with the native inhabitants of the area and was evidently 'a great character', as Janet Adam Smith wrote in an obituary for the Alpine Journal. Una Cameron, like Dorothy Thompson with Joseph Georges, had a long and friendly association with her two guides, Edouard Bareux and Elisée Croux of Courmayeur. With them she climbed all the great ridges on the Italian side of Mont Blanc: the Brouillard, Innominata, Peuterey and Brenva, as well as classic routes such as the Red Sentinel (D+) and Route Major (TD-). This is a list to which I could not possibly have aspired. She was one of the élite.

Not only do I admire Una Cameron's climbing abilities and tenacity but I also find her of great interest because she was a talented artist. I, too, often feel a strong urge to sketch when I am in the Alps. Miss Cameron trained at the Central School of Arts and Crafts in London, and specialised in woodcuts. The LAC Yearbooks of her time are illustrated with many of her exquisite images. She was not alone among women alpinists in being creative as well as a climber. Mrs. Aubrey Le Blond was a very skilled photographer who made many well-received animated films of winter sports in the Engadine. She was probably the first mountain filmmaker in the world and certainly one of the first female filmmakers. Artistic talent and creativity are widespread amongst mountaineers, as the many exhibitions of the LAC women demonstrated, just as the collections and shows of the Alpine Club have always done, and still do today. The artistic, creative mountaineer cannot fail to notice the aesthetic qualities of the mountain environment, the shapes and lines of rock and ice and of the mountains themselves, and the colours – white is not a single colour: snow may appear to be white but, if you look carefully, you see blues and greens, greys and many shades of violet. Rock, too, is multi-coloured and multi-faceted. Sunlight and shadow, depth of tone from the lightest light to the darkest dark, all play their part in building the images before our eyes. Other aesthetic qualities, the sound of water, thunderstorms, creaking ice and falling stones, the feel of the rock, rough and smooth, the intangible sense of eeriness in the mist or the warm sensual touch of the sun on the skin, all these play a part in the mind of a creative person. It is not surprising that mountains feature in both art and music.

3

THE YEAR OF THE HUTS

In my journal I wrote that 1976 was the year of the huts, rather than of the mountains. At home in England, that summer was glorious, with drought from June until October, and when we returned from the Alps at the end of August, we were confronted with scorched, brown lawns and dried-up plants. Yet in the Alpine areas we visited, we had more than our normal share of rain, even of snow, and not just at high altitude. We experienced storms too, not only in the relative safety of the campsite, but also up on the mountains. This was for me a new and exciting, but not particularly pleasant, dimension of mountaineering.

Our season started in the way it was to continue. Les and I had driven out on our own to Switzerland and based ourselves at a pleasant little campsite in Sembrancher, a tiny village on the road from Martigny to the Grand St. Bernard Pass, where we stayed on several subsequent occasions. We decided to make Mont Vélan our training route that year, whilst we awaited the arrival of Andy Hodges and John Oaks. From Bourg St. Pierre we walked up to the Vélan Hut on a hot day and spent a very pleasant evening with only the guardian for company. Perhaps all the other climbers in the area had more accurate information about the weather than we did. Before we retired for the night, we spent some time watching the unusual cloud formations and no sooner had we settled down to sleep than the first clap of thunder could be heard. According to my journal:

In no time at all the storm was right overhead and the whole sky was lit up by lightning. The hut seemed to tremble in the thunder. I thought of the story I had read of a hut, part of which was swept down the mountain, some of the occupants with it and others left lying in the matratzenlager with the void below. After that I must have slept.

Although we were able to set out for the route up the mountain the following morning, the clouds simply would not shift in time and we retreated from the Col de la Gouille, as the glacier we had to cross on the other side was completely invisible in the gloom.

Having returned to Sembrancher, we waited for our two friends to arrive and then we all set off together for an attempt to acclimatise. We drove up to Champex, a pretty resort beside a little lake near the border between Switzerland and France. It is possible to ski in spring or walk in summer over the glaciers and passes from Argentière in the Chamonix Valley to Champex on the well-known High Level Route. From Champex, we took a chairlift up the immediate hillside and headed for the Trient Hut. Although we had fair weather on most of the walk, by the time we arrived it was evident that the 'meteorological gods' were not going to be friendly.

The following day we had no choice but to sit it out and wait for better visibility. Andy and I whiled away the time playing a makeshift game of draughts with tiny pieces of cardboard wrapper from a sardine tin, moving them about on an area of the chequered dining table. When we emerged from the hut the next morning, the sky was clear enough to tempt us to do a short rock route. We crossed the Trient Glacier and climbed the South Ridge of the Aiguille Purtscheller, only to be cheated of the summit when an electric storm took us by surprise, hitting our little peak. We made a hasty retreat.

As the weather did not improve, we decided to drive all the way through Switzerland again in the hope of finding better conditions in the Engadine. We did not. Even on the journey over the Julier Pass it was obvious from the amount of fresh snow on the roadside that the weather was actually worse in the east than it had been in the Valais. So we headed south-west through Northern Italy, intending to go to the Maritime Alps in France, but changed our minds and detoured to the Dauphiné instead. There the sun came out and encouraged us on to the mountains again. From the summit of Le Râteau above the little village of La Grave, we had a perfect view of Mont Blanc. This lured us back to the area where we had started out a week or so before. We returned to the Swiss canton of Valais to pick up the threads of our original plans but, once again, the weather would get the better of us.

We had set our sights on climbing the Grand Combin, the most westerly Fourthousander in Switzerland. From Bourg St. Pierre we headed for the Valsorey Hut, on the opposite side of the valley to the Vélan Hut that Les and I had visited two weeks before. Even before we reached the hut, the weather had taken a turn for the worse and I arrived only after I had had a good soaking. The hut was quite small and the guardian, a very old man, sat in the same room as his guests, attending to the stove. During the afternoon we caught occasional glimpses of the surrounding mountains but the old man was not optimistic. Only if you could see Mont Blanc, he said, would the weather be fine enough for our proposed ascent of the Grand Combin. The weather did not improve. The following morning, when we stepped outside, we saw several inches of fresh snow on the terrace. We never did see Mont Blanc that day.

A few years later, I read somewhere that the old man had died in an avalanche near his hut. For him, too, the epitaph for some local men, including a former guardian of the Vélan Hut, which we read on a plaque on the way up the other side of this same valley, came true:

Les montagnes qu'ils aimaient tant les ont rendus à Dieu.
(The mountains they loved so much have given them back to God.)

At last, a day or so later, we were granted a break in the weather and this time our expedition included a 4000m peak: the Bishorn. Although 4153m high, this mountain is a mere outlier of the imposing Weisshorn, that rises another 200m above it. Between the snowcap of the Bishorn and the pyramid of the Weisshorn, with its rock faces on the western and south-eastern sides and its snow face to the north, lies the lengthy North Ridge, recognisable from far and wide by its huge gendarme. For many climbers, the Bishorn is a little bonus, ticked off their list of Fourthousanders when making the traverse of the Weisshorn, but for us in 1976 it was an objective in its own right.

The four of us set out from St. Niklaus in the Mattertal, some 20km from Zermatt, to walk up to the Topali Hut. This delightful, small, unguarded hut was, sadly, destroyed by fire twenty years later. To reach it, we took a steep path up wooded cliffs, followed by a pleasant stroll over alpine pastures. As I walked along carrying my heavy load, I wondered how the cows had come up there. The hut was perched on a promontory at the top of a short, steep moraine and had an uninterrupted view of the Mischabel chain: the Nadelgrat, the Dom, the Täschhorn and the Alphubel, all on the other side of the Zermatt Valley.

There is something really agreeable about being self-sufficient in the comfort of a well-appointed, timber-built chalet high on a Swiss mountain-side. By the time I arrived, John had installed himself as 'guardian', lighting the stove and fetching the water with Andy's help. We were very cosy. Then a few other people arrived, including a party of four elderly Germans whose acquaintance we had already made in previous years on the campsite in the middle of Saas Grund. By now, the hut was about half full. Then two Belgians arrived hot-foot. Why were they in such a hurry? Les looked out of the window, and called to us to join him.

'What the … ! However many are there?' I exclaimed, trying to count the figures walking up the path. 'Ten … twelve … fifteen …' I kept counting.

John and Andy were staring out in amazement too. 'There are even more coming! Look!'

In all, there were 22 people, many of them quite short, making their way towards the hut. This was not what we had expected at a quiet unmanned refuge.

Just two schoolmasters appeared to be in charge of this score of German schoolchildren. They had hoped to take full possession of the hut but they were disappointed. Most of the children spent the night downstairs in the living room whilst the schoolmasters managed to find some space in the dormitory, much to our disadvantage. One of them snored so loudly all night that none of us could sleep. How much alcohol he had drunk, or how many sleeping pills he had swallowed, we never knew.

Before dawn next morning, we made our way up the Abberg Glacier, crossed the Bruneggjoch and then continued to the Bisjoch. It was there that our climb up the East Ridge of the Bishorn began. It is a route that was first climbed by Mrs E. Burnaby (later Mrs. Aubrey Le Blond) in 1884. My journal gives my reaction:

This ridge was very fine indeed, with snow, followed by a rock section, then a splendid snow crest and on towards the summit. A thoroughly recommendable, though not difficult, route.

Our descent to the Turtmann Glacier via the North-East Ridge from Point 3549m made a very unpleasant contrast, with loose rock and scree. The long plod down the glacier and round to the Turtmann Hut seemed very irksome too, especially as I knew that we were intending to reascend it the next day. This we duly did, returning to St. Niklaus and taking in the 3590m Brunegghorn on our way.

The Dom was our next objective. In their book, *The High Mountains of the Alps*, Helmut Dumler and Willi Burkhardt explain the name of this, the highest mountain entirely in Switzerland. In translation, it means cathedral:

Its name has less to do with its commanding position or the fact that, seen from the north, it shines like some celestial temple of snow, but because it is said to be named after Canon Berchtold of the cathedral at Sitten, who was the first to survey the area.[1]

---

1 *The High Mountains of the Alps*, Volume One

Before I learned this, I often wondered why the mountain was thus named, as I never felt it was a particularly appropriate description, even though it is a fine mountain with considerable character. It was only the fleeting view I had of it one day from the East-North-East Ridge of the Lenzspitze that made me think the Dom might, after all, deserve the title of cathedral. From that viewpoint, in swirling mist, I did just have a momentary impression of the great rock wall rising like the towers of a cathedral towards the invisible snow-covered cupola above.

With John and Andy that summer we climbed the North-West Ridge of the Dom, or Festigrat as it is known, as it rises from the Festijoch, the col linking the Festi Glacier to the Hohbärg Glacier on the north-western side of the mountain. This was the first time I had ever walked up from the Mattertal to the Dom Hut and I was greatly impressed by the views back towards the Weisshorn and Bishorn. It is a walk I repeated several times, but never with quite that initial sensation of ecstatic fascination, having climbed the Bishorn just a few days before. Those two peaks, with their lengthy, connecting ridge, soar upward high above the narrow valley far below. From the village of Randa, our path wound its way steeply through pinewoods until it reached alpine pastures some five or six hundred metres higher up. Then it climbed on towards cliffs so steep that they were equipped with steps and ladders. As I stepped gingerly up these, I was amazed to be greeted by shaggily bearded mountain goats, intrepid creatures teetering about on ledges near the top. Far sooner than I had imagined, I came upon a welcoming flag which announced my arrival at the hut.

What a situation! From the large terrace encompassing the curiously shaped Dom Hut, there is one of the most stupendous views that any hut can offer. Because of its position on a promontory at an altitude of nearly 3000m, you look out at the Weisshorn and its neighbours on the opposite side of the valley and, even more excitingly, if you turn towards the head of the Mattertal, there is a quite spectacular vista of the Matterhorn rising abruptly from the glaciers above Zermatt, nearly 20km away.

As evening drew in, the rosy hue of the sky rendered those peaks even more delightful to the eye and there were strange, alluring cloud formations to distract one's attention from the glory of the peaks. Oh, that it might remain fine throughout the night! It did.

Climbing the Dom by the Festigrat was quite straightforward. The situation was superb and once again I felt enraptured. Here, there was no feeling of exposure, just the pleasure of being high above the world. It was very satisfying indeed to reach the summit of the Dom and recognise that we were on top of the highest peak entirely in Switzerland. Furthermore, I was impressed by the sight of the route just below me, down the South Ridge to the Domjoch, and then from there up the North Ridge of the Täschhorn. I didn't dream that, three years later, I would have the privilege of taking part in an expedition on those exciting crests of rock, precipitously perched between the Saas Valley to the east and the Mattertal to the west. After a bite to eat, we turned our backs on this entrancing view and returned to the hut down the Normal Route, passing below beautiful séracs that hung menacingly on the north flank of the Dom, I wondered, as I sped by, how long it would be before they came crashing down. Nature creates such elegant weapons of destruction.

John and Andy now made their way homewards and Les and I moved round to the valley on the eastern side of the Dom, where we took a well-earned rest in Saas Grund – but not for long. Soon we responded again to the spell of the mountains and walked up to the Mischabel Hut. Scrambled might be a more accurate description of the ascent of the second half of this extremely steep path, which wends its way up the mountainside directly above the centre of Saas Fee. Saas Fee, one of those typically Swiss places where vegetable plots are tended alongside high street shops and cafés, is a charming old Alpine village which, at that time, still retained much of its original character despite the proliferation of modern tourist developments. It is also relatively pollution-free, as only Saas Fee's own electric vehicles are permitted to drive through the streets.

We had planned to climb two more 4000m peaks: first the Lenzspitze and then, after traversing along part of the Nadelgrat, the Nadelhorn, returning to the hut across the Hohbalm Glacier. This was not to be. Once again, we were no sooner installed in the hut, than the clouds came down and snow began to fall. What rotten luck we were having that year! Meanwhile the drought scorched on in England.

It must have snowed intermittently all night, and at four o'clock in the morning the sky was still veiled in mist. Two hours later, however, Les dragged me out of bed, saying that the clouds were lifting, and after a hasty breakfast we set off in the direction of the Nadelhorn. We crossed the Hohbalm Glacier with care, as so much snow had fallen that hidden crevasses were a danger, but fortunately neither of us fell through the surface. The North-East Ridge is normally an easy route, often used in descent from the Nadelgrat after the traverse from the Lenzspitze, but the fresh snow and swirling mist gave it a more exciting character that morning. By now, there were many parties behind us but we kept at the front with one other, guided, party and a man who was going solo. He must have been quite apprehensive, however, as he could not quite bring himself to lead the way.

It was a very pleasant climb indeed, though short, and the view non-existent. Yet the conditions were eerie and unusual enough to be exciting, and moreover we felt that we had cheated the weather. Sadly that was our last climb this season, as the weather continued to be poor and we had lost our zest for gambling.

Despite the unsettled weather during much of that summer of 1976, we learned many things. I had even climbed another three Fourthousanders and was still enjoying the overall mountain experience to the full. That was the year when I started to write up all my previous Alpine exploits in a private journal.

4

WEATHER

Throughout my journal runs a thread of comments about the weather. The summer of 1976 was simply one of the worst in that regard. Rain, snowfall and storms were just as much a part of an Alpine summer as a heat wave. Snowfall and heat waves were, however, relatively rare; it was more usual for rain to alternate with periods of sunshine and blue skies, the rainy spells often being much shorter than the sunny ones. Those are my personal recollections – but climate change in the years since then may have changed the pattern. By the beginning of the 1990s, consistently higher temperatures, especially at night, became a problem. The freezing level often affected our plans. To climb Fourthousanders safely, you really need the snow and ice to be well frozen at night down to an altitude well below that of the peaks you want to climb. In 1990, it was particularly noticeable that this wasn't happening often enough during the summer, and this caused rockfall and unstable snow, conditions that make climbing very hazardous.

In many previous years, it was persistent rainfall that stopped play. Camping in the rain is dismal at all times but especially so if you have wet climbing clothes and ropes to dry out in difficult circumstances. (None of the campsites we used in the Alps had any drying facilities.) Packing up a wet, soggy tent is even more unpleasant, which was what we had to do on various occasions when we abandoned one area and moved to another in search of more suitable conditions. Sometimes we visited several areas in a single season simply because of the weather. 1976 was, however, the year when we drove the furthest in pursuit of sunshine and stability. It was fortunate that Les enjoyed driving so much, and that we were never tied to any specific accommodation. We camped wherever we went, except when we stayed in mountain huts.

My journal records many occasions when the weather was particularly notable:

Zinal, 1970: A marvellous week doing training walks in perfect weather.

That was a really lucky start. Only in the second and third weeks of our holiday did we have to contend with a few storms, but they were of short duration and we were safe in the valley at the time. It was perhaps as well we were camping that year in places where there were nearby cafés where we could spend time and relieve the discomfort of lying cramped in our tiny tent. During other rest days, when we were taking a breather from our efforts on the hill, we would sunbathe outside our tent, soaking up the ultraviolet rays in the hope of acquiring a good tan to take back to England. We were unaware then that the sun could be harming us. Alpine mountaineering does little for one's beauty. Only the face and hands are likely to be exposed to the sun, but unless you cake them in high factor sun cream, they can burn easily in the glare off the snow. As you also have to wear dark sunglasses with sidepieces to cut out the sun's rays completely from your eyes, you can easily return from the Alps with large round goggle marks, despite the sun cream, or glacier cream, as we called it then. Vanity has to be resisted, as the alternative to such complete eye protection is conjunctivitis. So a vain alpinist needs to do some intermittent sunbathing to fill in the gaps in the suntan. That, at least, was our way of thinking back in the early 1970s, before the medical profession and the media began to give us frequent advice about avoiding skin cancer. Perhaps it was for the best that it often rained.

In our second summer in the Alps together, Les and I had arranged to meet Geoff Causey and John Oaks in Kandersteg in the Bernese Oberland. There we did a couple of short training routes in good weather before our friends arrived, but then:

Rain set in … After several days we packed up and moved to the Bernina [Alps] where the weather was also somewhat mixed, and in between sallies into the higher hills, we spent much time trying to play bridge in a café in St. Moritz Bad. I say 'trying to play bridge', because J.O. and I were more or less complete novices, whilst Les and Geoff were experienced and took their cards very seriously. The ensuing disorder can be imagined!

Some years, the weather was so unsettled that we occasionally had to sit out bad days in the huts, usually because we hoped the storminess would pass, giving us an opportunity to climb the following day. Depending upon the company and the facilities, we would spend the day in the living room of the hut, chatting, playing cards or other makeshift games, reading books or brewing frequent drinks, to pass the time as much as to keep ourselves hydrated. Routes and tactics would be discussed and revised according to

Barbara and Les on the summit of Les Droites with Mont Blanc and the Aiguille Blanche de Peuterey in the background, 1990. Photo: Pete Fleming.

The Fletschhorn (left of centre) and the Lagginhorn (West Face).
Overleaf: The Pennine Alps with the Matterhorn and Monte Rosa in the distance.

Barbara with Geoff Causey climbing the North Ridge of the Lagginhorn, 1970.

The Matterhorn showing the Hörnli Ridge (centre) and the Dent d'Hérens (R).

L to R: Barbara, John Oaks and Geoff Causey (standing) on the summit of the Matterhorn, 1970.

On the summit of the Strahlhorn. L to R: Geoff Causey, Richard Heery, Katherine Heery, Stuart Cooke; front row: Andy Thompson, 1973.
Overleaf: The Aletschfirn with the Lötschenlücke (R) and the Aletschhorn (centre).

Piz Bernina.

The Biancograt on Piz Bernina.

From L to R: Mont Blanc du Tacul, Mont Maudit, Mont Blanc, Dôme du Goûter and Aiguille de Bionnassay (winter). Photo: Barbara Swindin.

John Oaks leaping over a bergschrund on the descent from Mont Maudit, 1973.

Mont Maudit showing our descent route.
Opposite: Sunset from the Goûter Hut the evening before we climbed Mont Blanc, 1973.

Colin Wornham with the Dent Blanche in the background, 1974.

The North Face of Les Ecrins.
Opposite: Barbara traversing the Rasoir on the Zinalrothorn, 1975.
Overleaf: The South Ridge of the Lagginhorn, 1977.

Ascending the Zwillings Glacier in spring, 1979.

Piz Palü.

Paul Luton descending the glacier after climbing Piz Palü, 1980.

Les and Barbara with Paul Luton on the Fiescher Glacier, 1981.
Photo: Jay Turner.

Barbara with Paul Luton climbing the Wannenhorn, 1981.

Jay Turner and Barbara near the Austrian border, 1989.

Richard Heery, Geoff Causey and Barbara on the summit of Sgurr nan Gillean after traversing the Cuillin Ridge on the Isle of Skye, 1974.

The Dom (L) and Täschhorn (R) with the connecting ridges.

The Finsteraarhorn showing the Normal Route from the Hugisattel.

The West Face of the Alphubel showing the Rotgrat (R of centre).

The Rochefort Arête leading to the Aiguille de Rochefort.

Descending the Whymper Couloir, 1980.
Overleaf: Pete Fleming and Barbara on the summit of the Aiguille Verte with Mont Blanc and the Peuterey Ridge in the background, 1980.

The Grand Combin showing our ascent route via the West Ridge and the descent by the steep snow face to its left. Far R – the Col de Meitin.

The North Ridge of the Weisshorn with the Bishorn (R).

the conditions, and sometimes we simply had to turn about the following day and retreat to the valley because our provisions were running out.

In 1974, in the campsite in Fionnay, an isolated hamlet in the Pennine Alps, I remember lying in my sleeping bag most of the day, fully dressed with woolly hat and gloves because it was so cold. Les and I had gone there at the start of our holiday in order to acclimatise, but:

The weather proved most unkind … It rained and rained and rained.

This continued for three long, tedious days, spent trying to read in most uncomfortable circumstances. In mid-July, in the rain, Fionnay was a dismal place, with no entertainment whatsoever and very few other campers.

Generally, we would only ever set out for a hut or for a climb if we had a fairly encouraging weather forecast. We used to trawl through the local newspapers in the cafés, to glean as much information as possible before committing ourselves and expending a great deal of energy in vain. We also discovered a telephone number to call in Switzerland to get a detailed meteorological report, and I was always sent to a phone box to listen to the automated message. French and German were quite easy for me to decipher and report to Les, but the occasional attempt to understand the forecast in an Italian-speaking area defeated me. There, it was much easier to deduce the prognosis from a weather map in the newspaper. Thus we kept ourselves as well informed as possible.

Dense cloud on snow-covered terrain also gives the skier a serious challenge, as we discovered not only on the slopes in a resort, but even more acutely when we took up ski-mountaineering in 1976. Sometimes it is almost impossible to know whether you are moving up or down a slope, or even whether you are moving at all. This is difficult enough on a groomed piste in a resort, but much more tricky, and even downright dangerous, out on unprepared terrain in the mountains and on glaciers, where there is always the possibility of an unseen crevasse that might gobble you up, skis and all. On one occasion on a ski-tour, when we were attempting to locate a mountain hut, low cloud nearly forced us into deciding between an unplanned bivouac in the snow or a lengthy retreat to the valley, if we could find our way there in the whiteout. We eventually located our objective in the gloom, and it was the altimeter that came to our rescue. Today, however, a ski-mountaineer would be able to use his GPS or smart phone, and who knows what future technological devices there will be to help us *in extremis*?

Over the years we had plenty of practice negotiating ski descents in thick cloud and poor snow conditions, but the end of our first tour in the Bernese Oberland in 1977 was especially memorable, as my journal recalls:

Visibility was nil, and I think our party would have succeeded in making a faster and safer descent without all the extra bodies [because of avalanche warnings, everyone who had been staying in the Hollandia Hut had been told to leave at the same time as us, so there were seventeen people in the group, including other British acquaintances and some Swiss folk]. *Poor skiers* [ourselves included], *long, trailing avalanche cords* [this was before the advent of transceivers], *and, above all, a Swiss local with a gammy leg, whom the guardian had insisted we follow, as he had local knowledge. Instead of allowing Les and one of the Swiss boys to remain faithful to their compass bearing, this fellow insisted that we went his way. So for a while, we did as he suggested, but he was proved wrong. We couldn't find the rocks we had been advised to ski to, and started wandering away from our intended route and on to the Anen Glacier in the mist. Les took over at this point. Visibility was still nil, but, trusting to his altimeter and compass, Les led us safely, with the help of the Swiss boys, down the steep slopes back on to the Langgletscher, the main glacier we should have been following all the time.*

It took us nearly six hours in those conditions to ski from the Hollandia Hut to Fafleralp at the bottom of the glacier and, even then, we still had to slide on down to Blatten, as Fafleralp was just a 'deserted hamlet lost beneath the winter snow'.

From there to Blatten one skis down the road, easy enough, but wearying after the excitements of the battle against wind and snow and mist on the glacier. Here the visibility was normal and we could ski right into Blatten, where the postbus seemed to be waiting especially for us.

On many bad-weather occasions like that one, I felt no real fear. It was simply a matter of getting on with the job in hand. There was an irrational excitement at having to pit your wits against the weather and the hostile environment, and in its own way this was just as heart-warming as the joy of reaching a summit. There was, however, one incident in the 1970s when the weather frightened me to the core. I often enjoyed the thrilling, though spine-chilling, experience of sitting in a tent doorway watching an oncoming storm approach from the west towards the great mountains of Chamonix, with dark clouds rolling in across an otherwise light-toned sky, long drawn-out rolls of thunder and fierce sharp thunderclaps, preceded by sparkling zigzags of lightning threatening to destroy any living being it hit. In 1976, however, I felt very differently. We were caught in a thunderstorm on the Aiguille Purtscheller. One moment we were happily climbing up a sheltered chimney on the lee side of the mountain within a few metres of the summit. The next, we noticed snowflakes falling. John Oaks and Andy Hodges were on the pitch above Les and me, and suddenly we all realised that we had to get down off the rock as soon as possible. The Purtscheller is a fairly exposed pinnacle. So we started to descend a nearby gully:

The rocks began to sing around us. We had no choice but to abseil as fast as we could manage directly down to the glacier. Within a few minutes of beginning our descent, there was a deafening crash above us. The lightning must have struck the rocks near the summit not far above us. J.O. and Andy came hurtling down behind us with trembling limbs and tales of electric shocks passing through their arms. All was well, however, as the storm abated sufficiently for us to complete a safe descent and cross the glacier to the hut. The whole way I wondered whether we would all get back alive, and, if we did not, who would perish and who survive. The sound of my ice axe fizzing with electricity was justification enough for my anxiety.

At the end of the 1970s, a journalist asked me to describe the most frightening moment of my mountaineering experiences. At the time, that incident on the Purtscheller immediately sprang to mind. Mountaineers can so easily find themselves at the mercy of the weather. Yet, equally, two contradictory emotions can jostle for your attention when a storm breaks. Frank Smythe's description of being caught in a thunderstorm on the Schreckhorn rings true for me too:

Within ten minutes the storm was upon us. First we heard the bombardment as the storm clouds reached the isolated peak of the Eiger. Without a pause they rushed across to wreak their fury on the Schreckhorn … It was terrible, but it was also magnificent.[1]

---

1 'A Bad Day on the Schreckhorn' by Frank Smythe, 1926; article first published in the Alpine Journal and reproduced in *Peaks, Passes and Glaciers*, ed. Walt Unsworth

5

SEASON OF DOUBTS

Curiously, in 1977, a year after I had started to write a detailed record of my Alpine exploits, I experienced for the first time an inner recognition that I was losing the sense of enjoyment that alpinism had given me.

That summer I was not so happy. Conditions on some routes were excessively difficult and perhaps that is what unsettled, even frightened me. When I returned home from the Alps, I found I needed to put some distance between my experiences and the activity of recording them in my journal. It was not until December that I could bring myself to sit down to the task and, when I did, I found myself wondering whether I really could rediscover such deep contentment in the Alps. Maybe I had simply come down to earth after my seven-year love affair with alpinism.

That summer season had started well enough. We were in Kandersteg once again, in the western part of the Bernese Oberland. As in the previous year, John Oaks and Andy Hodges joined us and the first route we undertook was the traverse of the Weisse Frau and Blümlisalp on a very fine day. It was a pleasant outing, especially for Les and me, as it permitted us to admire the great Fourthousanders of the Bernese Oberland where we had been holed up in snowstorms on a ski-tour only a few months before. We could clearly see the Jungfrau, Mönch and Finsteraarhorn, and also the Eiger, which falls just short of the magic 4000m figure. I was on good form and thoroughly enjoyed the airy climb along the ridge between our two summits that day.

Then the short spell of fine weather broke and we spent several days trying to keep dry in our campsite as the heavens opened and rain poured down incessantly. Snow fell on the mountains above us and we abandoned plans to go to Grindelwald. The Meteorological Office in Geneva said that the weather might be better in the Pennine Alps, so we went to Saas Grund and spent the following two weeks there. The first few days saw us making several futile attempts to go on the mountains, all thwarted by the weather. Then, at last, after sitting out rain- and snowstorms in the valley, we went up to the Weissmies Hut on a glorious day.

All the surrounding peaks were visible in their newfound glory under a mantle of fresh snow. Luckily for us, some parties, who had been at the hut during the bad weather, attempted that morning to walk across the glacier towards the Normal Route on the Weissmies, thus blazing a trail in the deep snow. The following morning, another clear day, we set out for the Lagginjoch, the col that lies between the South Ridge of the Lagginhorn and the North Ridge of the Weissmies. We intended to climb the former but, once we left the ready-made trail, we had to force our way through acres of virgin snow and our progress became so slow and painful that we changed our plan. Instead, we headed up towards a minor ridge that descends from Point 3722m on the North Ridge of the Weissmies. We climbed this spur, covered in loose, fresh snow somewhat reminiscent of outings in the Scottish Highlands in winter. The climbing was, in fact, quite interesting. We didn't keep to the ridge all the way, but veered right-wards towards a lower point on the North Ridge just beyond Point 3722m.

According to the guidebook, from the point where we joined the main ridge it takes at least another two hours to reach the summit of the Weissmies. It took me considerably longer. Our two friends, being excellent rock climbers and both very fit, strode away ahead at their own pace. I trod much more diffidently in the airy situation in which I found myself. The exposure is unrelenting as you progress along this narrow rock crest. I was quite apprehensive and at one point, on a downward move, my new climbing breeches refused to detach themselves easily from the rock where I'd sat in an attempt to lower myself as safely as possible. It was not until the evening that I noticed the damage to my trousers. So much for my climbing technique!

On and on we went, eventually almost catching up John and Andy, when we came to some slabs that looked rather daunting with their cover of fresh snow. We were wearing crampons, so I found the rock climbing extremely clumsy. In those days I didn't yet have a great deal of experience of using crampons on such airy rock routes. Fortunately for our reputation, we didn't need to call on our friends to protect us from above, although I have no doubt that Les was glad that they were there. It must have been a considerable strain on him having to guide me along that route, as I certainly didn't make a great deal of effort to disguise my nervousness.

Our companions sped away in front again. I was by then becoming very weary of the exposure and continuous rock-climbing challenges. This was exactly the type of route that always tested me to the utmost, although, as I had already made successful ascents of such routes as the South Ridge of the Dent Blanche and the crest along the Barre des Ecrins, Les must have been taken a little by surprise at my timidity. In normal summer conditions, I believe I would have coped a great deal better but the recent snowfall made the route much more challenging than it would have been when dry. Luckily, we hadn't had to climb the most serious pitch of all, the 15m-high 'Grande Dalle', a grade IV rock slab, located between the Lagginjoch and Point 3722m, the section we had omitted by taking the variant up the western slopes of the mountain from the glacier.

My journal tells how I felt as I came to the final point of the North Ridge and reached the summit:

Eventually we arrived, much to my relief, at the snow arête. By now the other two were nearly an hour ahead of us and I didn't expect to see them again until we had returned to the hut. The final snow slope looked very steep and tiring, but I didn't find it too exhausting as I was in a state of mental relief by now. The summit was our own and it was warm in the sun. Then we looked over the brow and John and Andy were sitting there sunning themselves whilst they waited for us to catch them up. How kind of them! I really hadn't expected them to wait so long.

After a while we started the descent to the Weissmies Hut down the Normal Route. It was incredibly hot in the glacier basin and I could barely wait to sit down in front of a bowl of tea. It was about three o'clock in the afternoon when I finally got there, having been out some twelve hours. A long day, but not as long as for some parties who had followed us – they didn't return until seven o'clock in the evening. That night, as I lay in the bunk, I ached all over.

Although I was tired and had considerable reservations about my wisdom in participating in the previous day's activities, it never occurred to me to give the next route a miss. As the weather the following day was also fine, we set out once more for our original objective, the long South Ridge of the Lagginhorn – my second ascent of the first Fourthousander I had ever climbed. On this occasion, as I later wrote in my journal, it proved to be 'an ordeal beyond all measure and I nearly reached breaking point'. It was, therefore, a significant event in my climbing career and for that reason alone deserves to be included in this story. I am also conscious of the fact that, without the strength and patience of my three companions, I could not have coped with such difficult conditions.

We left the hut before first light and followed the same trail as the day before, but when we branched off on untrodden ground towards the Lagginjoch, the snow was a little firmer and we made our own trail, or rather the three men did, somewhat laboriously, until we came near to the col. Here the going was so difficult that we chose to climb rightwards above the col and then descend to it from the lowest part of the Weissmies North Ridge, rather than ascend directly from the glacier. The descent was quite tricky, thanks to the covering of fresh snow from the recent storms.

From the col we moved easily up over barer rock and for a time the climbing was very enjoyable. Indeed, it remained quite pleasant until we came to the Grand Gendarme. By then we had been climbing along the ridge for a couple of hours and, although I was happy enough, I was beginning to imagine that the summit was not too far off. How wrong I was. The difficulties had scarcely begun and in the snowy conditions the trickier parts of the ridge were really demanding.

The Grand Gendarme itself filled me with absolute horror and we called to John and Andy, who were in front, to let me tie on to the end of their rope, thus protecting both Les and me. The top of the pinnacle was covered in deep, fresh snow, with a platform about a foot wide to stand on and a huge drop on either side. From there we descended a steep, snow-covered section, where we had to hunt for foot- and handholds. Then at last, with great relief, I reached the safety of the snow shoulder below. The guidebook suggests that the gendarme can be turned on the left side, but in those conditions it was probably much safer to go over the top. We separated again and John and Andy strode off ahead.

A little further on, there was a rock step where the snow cover was so unstable after John and Andy's ascent that Les had to lead it on his knees. I followed as best I could in similar fashion. I was rapidly tiring now and hoping beyond all hope that the summit would be round the next block – but no. On and on the ridge continued, in a style that reminded me once again of Crib Goch in Snowdonia, or the longer Aonach Eagach Ridge in Glencoe. This ridge on the Lagginhorn, however, was not only covered in unstable snow but had more sustained difficulty and exposure than either of those two. It was also considerably longer than the Barre des Ecrins, which we had climbed in good conditions in 1974. On the Lagginhorn, we sometimes had to turn the difficulties by teetering round on the east side of the ridge above the Laggin Glacier. At other times, we had to step boldly forward directly on the crest, as on a kerbstone, but here there was a drop of about 650m to the snow basin below.

I was rapidly descending into the depths of despair. It was at this point that I shouted to Les that I didn't ever want to climb in the Alps again. After all, hadn't I told him that what I wanted was a holiday! At that moment I really meant what I said.

Eventually we reached the summit, where I wanted to sit and eat, but the three men refused to stay there as they preferred to get the awkward part of the descent over and done with before taking a break. Many metres below, where the ridge begins to flatten out, we stopped. I was exhausted and hungry. We sat there for a reasonable time before continuing the descent down the Normal Route to the Weissmies Hut, the route that Les and I had taken with Geoff Causey in my first Alpine season. We arrived back at the hut, as we had done the previous day, twelve hours after leaving it. Many years later, I discussed this route with John Oaks. He was adamant when he said: 'That was the most serious route we ever did … because of the condition it was in at the time.'

It was certainly one of the greatest endurance tests I ever experienced.

Back in the campsite at Saas Grund, I relaxed. I stayed there whilst the men went up to another hut to climb another route, and I enjoyed the company of Geoff Causey and his climbing partner that year, Richard Heery, who had just arrived. By the time Les came back down to the valley, I was no longer feeling fraught. The mountains were calling again, despite my 'traumatic' experiences, and I was ready to set off for another route. It was not to be. Les had injured himself slightly and it was evident that he needed a week's recuperation. We departed for the South of France, where I soon realised that I had no great desire to return too frequently to the Mediterranean beach scene in midsummer.

6

JUST THE TWO OF US

After the somewhat abrupt and unsatisfactory ending to the 1977 summer season, I was no longer sure that I really wanted to continue spending every summer climbing in the Alps. Some of my confidence seemed to have ebbed away. The demanding ascents of airy rock ridges in such unusually snowy conditions had taken their toll on my morale. I also felt that I had been excessively dependent on my companions, especially on the South Ridge of the Lagginhorn. However, the Alps still cast their spell upon me and I agreed to go back in the summer of 1978 to do some more climbing. I had, in any case, continued to travel to the British mountains most weekends throughout the winter and spring, as well as completing our first independent ski-tour at Easter. My love of the hills, mountaineering and the associated social life had certainly not diminished. Mountain walking and climbing continued to be my *raison d'être*.

Unusually, we set out that year without any plans to climb with other parties, our recent Alpine companions all being otherwise engaged. Yet it was precisely because we climbed alone together that I regained my confidence. We climbed only in good conditions and all the routes we chose were well within my competence. Moreover, after a few outings, my morale was further boosted when we accompanied two young novices on their first Fourthousander. Already, Les was beginning to assume the role of advisor to less experienced British climbers. By now, he had spent ten summer holidays Alpine climbing and had built up a fund of knowledge from personal experience. He had become a very competent lead alpinist on documented routes at grades from Facile to Difficile and had always been able to extricate himself from unexpectedly awkward or dangerous situations. His choice of routes was very sound, his understanding of the weather and conditions also, and his abilities were much appreciated by all those who climbed with him. Moreover, he had been my 'unofficial guide' during most of that time. At campsites we would often talk to other climbers and Les loved to share his knowledge and experiences.

Many years later, when we were in the early years of our retirement from Alpine climbing but still holidaying in the Alps, and sometimes still camping, many younger climbers would turn to Les for advice. By then he was well known as the General Editor of the Alpine Club guidebooks produced over the two decades from 1987 to 2007.

That July and August, because we were climbing with only each other for support, we were more cautious than ever about the snow and weather conditions and, although we set out for seven Alpine routes, we only succeeded in summitting four peaks. Two of these were Fourthousanders that neither of us had previously climbed and each one gave a unique experience in our climbing career together. By the end of our summer holiday, my morale had been thoroughly boosted and, once again, I was contented with my choice of lifestyle.

Our first successful climb that summer was above Argentière, near Chamonix. This time, the weather could hardly have been better and I persuaded Les that we should travel all the way up to the Grands Montets in the cable car, cutting short an otherwise gruelling walk to the Argentière Hut. We thus completed the journey with the greatest of ease, as the route from the cable car station simply descends to the glacier below, then takes the gentlest of gradients along the glacier, with the great buttresses, gullies and ice faces of the Aiguille Verte, Les Droites and Les Courtes to divert our attention from any feeling of exertion. It was this last-named mountain that we were planning to scale in the early hours of the following morning by the easiest route on its north-east flank. An early arrival at the hut gave us a whole afternoon to bask in the sun on the rocks behind the building, intermittently gazing at the splendid chain of peaks before our eyes. Already well rested, we retired early to our dormitory, where we were due to rise again at the very first moment of the next day. Breakfast was scheduled for midnight.

As we were standing outside on the terrace beneath the starlit sky, putting on our boots and gaiters at the ungodly hour of zero, two British lads came in from their evening ascent of the Swiss Route on Les Courtes. They had just descended the route we were about to climb. It was comforting to know that the snow face was in good condition.

We plodded rhythmically across the glacier and I soon began to enjoy the clear silence of the night. It is always surprising how so many climbers can slip away into the darkness, leaving the impression that one is almost alone. There had been numerous other people breakfasting at the same time as us, and several parties were in front, heading for the same route, but we began to catch them up as we approached the slopes on the far side of the glacier. There, below the *bergschrund*, we roped up and put on our crampons. Then we moved slowly and steeply over frozen avalanche debris. As we came to the edge of the gaping *bergschrund*, we could see shadowy forms and hear the voices of other parties, evidently having difficulty finding the best place to cross. At the same time there was a party descending. As I later recounted in my journal:

We therefore moved leftwards towards the centre of the face of Les Courtes and there Les found a promising line. We climbed on to the lower lip of the bergschrund and then edged our way gently under the overhanging upper lip until we arrived at the corner of the mouth. There it was simply a question of easing our bodies carefully out on to the face and up to the relative safety of the slope above: a delicate manoeuvre. From then on it was stamina that counted, as we climbed roped together, but without needing to belay. The slope was in easy condition, with the snow firm, but not icy, except for a short stretch, and it was simple enough to kick good steps where these did not already exist. Meanwhile another couple of climbers, unroped, were moving just to our right. They must have been stronger than me, as they reached the top of the snow face a good quarter of an hour ahead of us.

Eventually we too arrived at the summit ridge. It was a pleasure to step out into the moonlight again, as the upper part of the face had been in shadow. The ridge was fairly narrow and led directly to the summit, a few minutes away. There we waited in silence with the other couple for some twenty minutes until the sun began to rise over Switzerland. We were shivering with the cold but were gradually rewarded by the beauty of the slowly changing sky. On the horizon, the dark outlines of the Matterhorn, Dent Blanche and Weisshorn came into view, old familiar friends. I was so glad I hadn't allowed the difficulties of the previous summer's routes to deter me from continuing to climb in the Alps. Time heals, and this feeling of joy was the proof. We turned and looked towards France: Mont Blanc and all its satellites. It seemed as if we had the world to ourselves, yet out there on almost all the mountains we could see, there were probably people making their way towards the summits. By the last quarter of the 20th century, mountaineering in the European Alps was no longer the pastime of the privileged few. In weather like this, most of the well-known huts would be teeming with alpinists and the Normal Routes would be positively crawling with human ants.

It was too cold to stay long on the summit, so we soon started on our way down towards the Col de la Tour des Courtes and the Couvercle Hut.

At the col, I was amazed to see party after party of climbers of various nationalities ascending from the Talèfre Glacier. How pleasant it had been to climb the mountain by a more serious and thus less-frequented route.

Mountaineering is often marked by contrasts. It was becoming very hot indeed when we arrived at the Couvercle Hut. It was the first time I had been there and I was most impressed when I saw the old, original hut, sheltered under the huge rock already familiar from photographs. By now it was a glorious day, though still only nine o'clock in the morning. For a while I sat outside the hut, the newer one, simply gazing awestruck at the Grandes Jorasses. Magnificent! It was amazing to think that people could actually climb those imposing, north-facing buttresses. Such routes, the Walker Spur, the Croz Spur and the other North Face routes were not for me, but perhaps one day I might aspire to the ascent of the Grandes Jorasses by an easier line on the other side of the mountain.

In the meantime, common sense prevailed. We were exhausted from our sleepless night and, having been informed by the guardian that we would need to get up again at midnight if we wanted to climb the Aiguille Verte the following day, we sacrificed the sunshine and the panorama for an attempt to rest indoors. In the cool of the dormitory, however, I scarcely slept a wink.

Later we rose again to cook our evening meal in the self-catering kitchen, then turned in for an early night, slept little, clambered out of our bunk at midnight and trudged off up the Talèfre Glacier – this time in the direction of the Aiguille Verte and by no means alone. As we progressed, we were concerned to find that the soft snow on the lower slopes of the glacier became no firmer higher up. We simply didn't reach the freezing level. This didn't bode too well for the ascent of the Whymper Couloir, a snow-ice gully notorious for stonefall when not well frozen.

At the *bergschrund* we could hear water running down the couloir underneath the snow. Two Swiss guides were also there with their clients and one was muttering about the dangers of descent later in the day. That was guaranteed to lower my morale. Sometimes I wish I couldn't understand any foreign languages. Les managed to cross the *bergschrund*, but I kept sliding back in the soft snow and that was when we decided to abandon the route, not wishing to risk our necks any further. Everybody else appeared to give up too and, after waiting for a little while, we followed the other parties back down the glacier to the hut. Soon we were packing our rucksacks and leaving for the Mer de Glace and Chamonix. We took one final look up at the Aiguille Verte and, to our disgust, glimpsed four dots in the Whymper Couloir. Two parties were climbing the mountain after all!

Twelve years later, however, I recalled that occasion, and knew then that we had taken the right decision. Probably those climbers in 1978 escaped unscathed from their mountain but their successors in 1990 were not so fortunate. The experience of hearing helicopters flying in to pick up the bodies of several climbers who had been hit by rockfall in the Whymper Couloir was sickening and confirmed that one can never be too careful. If in doubt about the conditions, there is no shame in turning back.

After this brief sojourn in the French Alps, our thoughts turned to the Weisshorn, one of those spectacular peaks in the Swiss Valais that we had picked out in the dawn from the top of Les Courtes. The Weisshorn stands high and proud at the northern end of the chain of peaks separating the Val d'Anniviers from the Mattertal. The relatively low Bishorn, which we had climbed in 1976, lies at the far end of the North Ridge of the Weisshorn. This time, it was not the North Ridge that tempted us, Les wisely assuming that we were not yet experienced enough as a two-person team to climb this with no other companions, but the Normal Route up the East Ridge. The Normal Route itself is serious enough and requires good conditions, unless one is prepared to risk a severe penalty.

When we arrived at the campsite in Randa, the man in charge dashed our hopes by telling us that the Weisshorn was completely out of condition. Further investigation supported this theory when we learned that the descent route to the Weisshorn Hut was covered with unstable fresh snow. Nine years later, I was impressed by Robin and Hazel Costello of the F&RCC, who safely climbed this route together in 1997 after recent snow-fall. Perhaps the conditions were less menacing when they were there, but in 1978 we did not go up, so never assessed the situation at first hand.

Instead, we stayed in the valley, awaiting the arrival of Pete and Patrick, two young men we had met in Chamonix and to whom we had suggested a joint venture up one of the easiest routes on the 4206m Alphubel. They were novices and Les had proposed this mountain as one of the most accessible Fourthousanders for beginners. By driving up to Ottovan, we reduced the walk to the Täsch Hut to less than one hour. This was luxury indeed. Moreover, the hut was not crowded that night and, apart from a little snoring which aggravated Les, we had a passable night's rest. After our midnight starts from the French huts, it was a joy to be able to lie in until 3.00 am.

In the course of the following year, I was to climb the Alphubel three times by three different routes, and for different reasons. Each occasion was a very special event. Our ascent that summer was unique in that we were accompanying two young men whom we had encouraged to go there to savour the joys of the 4000m peaks for the first time. This made me feel quite the experienced old hand. I was, in any case, in fine form by then, having climbed to 3856m on the Courtes and spent a few nights at high altitude the previous week.

The moon was full and the glacier so easy that we could walk along without recourse either to torchlight or a rope. Les and I reached the Alphubeljoch well ahead of the two boys, one of whom was considerably slower than the other, but it gave me the unique experience of time to spare whilst I sat admiring the dawn. It was at its best that morning. I couldn't help thinking how lucky these boys were to have their first Fourthousander in such perfect conditions.

When Pete and Patrick arrived, we roped up in two pairs for the ascent of the South-East Ridge and Les and I moved off in front. Every so often, Les would shout encouragingly to the others. There were no difficulties at all. It was simply an easy snow crest, in a splendid situation but with no notable exposure. About half-way up the ridge we came to the 4000m mark, at least that's what the altimeter registered, so Les yelled again to the others who were by now lagging further behind. I had secretly hoped that Les would let me rest a little longer in the circumstances but no, he had to show these young men what we were made of! The final slope looked steep, so I gritted my teeth and carried on. The reward soon came.

The summit plateau is extensive enough for a dance and in such fine weather it was like paradise. There was plenty of room for the various parties already there to enjoy their surroundings in comfort. The top of the Alphubel is a magnificent viewpoint, encircled as it is by a plethora of other Fourthousanders, the closest of which, the elegant Täschhorn, rises almost 300m higher, a bare 2km to the north. Warm and comfortable, I sat there admiring my surroundings, feeling completely at peace and at one with the world. This had been one of the most pleasant Alpine experiences, a straightforward ascent in perfect conditions, with the added psychological bonus of acknowledging how far I had progressed beyond the novice stage that the two boys clearly recalled for me. It was eight years since I had been in their position. I felt privileged to be involved in helping them to discover the pleasures of alpinism, even if they were finding the going not quite as easy as they had hoped.

Half an hour after we had reached the summit, our companions arrived and it was not long before Les was urging them to start on the descent. Those poor boys! I did feel rather mean at hurrying them, but it was becoming apparent to me that Les was already forming another plan for the two of us and we could not afford to delay too long.

Having assured ourselves that Pete and Patrick were safely down past any serious difficulties, Les and I pressed on ahead, cleared up our belongings at the hut, paid our debts and left for the valley. By the time our acquaintances arrived at the campsite, we were ready to leave. Just as we were driving out to the main road, the window down as we waved them goodbye, one of the lads rushed across and thrust something cool into my hands amidst a chorus of thanks – a bottle of wine. We drank their health a few days later and wished them many more Alpine climbs.

By the time we did that, however, we had driven all the way round from the Zermatt Valley, over the Simplon Pass, to Alagna at the head of the Sesia Valley in Northern Italy, just on the south side of the Liskamm and Monte Rosa. We had arrived at the one and only campsite, a ghastly place teeming with noisy children and their equally voluble parents, the ground so hard it was difficult to drive the tent pegs in. We were exhausted, having accomplished so much in one long mountain day, followed by a tedious drive all the way down Lake Como in the heat and long traffic jams. To crown it all, out of the blue, my period had just started. This was an inconvenience that I had to tolerate, but as menstruation became more unpredictable and unpleasant over the years, it was somewhat incompatible with serious alpinism. Despite all that, there was absolutely nothing to encourage us to linger the following morning in Alagna – which was just as well as it turned out. By going up that same day to the Gnifetti Hut, we barely had time to climb the East Ridge of the Liskamm before the weather broke with a vengeance.

We had hoped not only to climb the Liskamm, but also to traverse its entire ridge from east to west, so we were keen to make an early start the following morning. The Gnifetti Hut, however, presented us with a dilemma. Everywhere in this highly organised, splendidly modern, quasi-hotel style mountain hut there were notices, one of which gave the alternative rising-times for breakfast: either 1.00 am or 4.30 am! The latter sounded far too late for our purposes, so we opted for the early start.

We duly rose at 1.00 am and were absolutely amazed to see only two other people breakfasting – Englishmen. We were more or less thrown out of the door at 1.45 am into a somewhat cloudy night and presumably nobody cared what happened to us after that. We set off very slowly up the glacier, letting the two men go in front. I actually found the pace rather frustrating, as I was feeling quite fit. Perhaps it was just as well that we did go so slowly though, as we still arrived at the Lisjoch long before dawn. By now it was very difficult to see where the route went, as there was a lot of cloud swirling about. We decided to wait until daylight before setting off up the ridge. The two English lads had full bivouac kit with them, as they were intending to spend the next night out under the stars anyway.

They then wanted to carry on over Castor and Pollux and the Breithorn. However, Les and I only had our scanty emergency gear and I have now decided that in future I shall carry a large polythene bag. Lying on one rucksack with four feet squeezed into the other rucksack is not to be recommended. After an hour or so we were cold and decided to set off on our own.

At first it was most unpleasant as the snow was very soft, making upward progress difficult. I kept sinking backwards. After we had crossed the bergschrund, however, the snow became firmer and we reached the ridge fairly quickly. There was still no sign of our two compatriots, although it was light by now. On either side of the ridge the lower ground was shrouded by thick cloud and high above us thin wisps appeared to be heralding bad weather. The sun rose weakly …

At the summit we dithered about, ate some chocolate, looked at the views, worried about the clouds. Was a storm coming? Dare we go on?

I led tentatively off down the ridge in the direction of the West Summit but the snow was soft even at above 4000m and, as the clouds were moving in more quickly than before, we decided to abandon the traverse. All the same, I felt really cheated as we started back down in bright sunshine towards the Lisjoch. Despite the swirling clouds high above, the sky remained blue but there was an eerie light in the distance. Even further away, there appeared to be a slight roll of thunder. As we descended the glacier, passing goodness knows how many people on the way up, we were engulfed by dense, wet cloud and that was the last we saw of the mountains that day.

We returned to the campsite, packed up and left the Pennine Alps for the Dauphiné. After some more unsettled weather had disrupted our climbing plans in the Ailefroide area, we moved to the Alpes Maritimes. There, in the vicinity of the Verdon Gorge, a rock climber's paradise, torrential thunderstorms washed quantities of mud and rocks over the roads. Mean-while, back in the mountains we had just left, this same violent weather, which we had seen beginning to build up, caught out numerous climbing parties and a number of fatalities were reported. Our decisions to abandon the traverse of the Liskamm, and subsequently the ascent of Mont Pelvoux, were certainly justified. Any hint of an oncoming storm should always be taken seriously. Bad luck can befall an alpinist at any time, but danger signals can be heeded and the mountaineer's life may depend upon the judgments he or she makes.

PART THREE

Ski-Mountaineering

Skis were initially devised as a means of travelling over
terrain covered by snow and otherwise impassable.
— Peter Wilberforce Smith[1]

Panorama from Mont Blanc du Tacul to the Aiguille de Bionnassay

1 *A Little Walk on Skis* by Peter and Beryl Wilberforce Smith

1

Learning to Ski
in the Wild

One winter weekend in 1963, when living temporarily in Bordeaux, I joined a student trip to the Pyrenees. There I had my very first taste of standing on skis and, without any instruction whatsoever, attempting to slide downhill on the nursery slopes without falling over. We had great fun for a few hours but the idea of spending a whole week going up and down the pistes with crowds of other skiers didn't appeal to me very much. It seemed a crazy way of getting a broken leg. However, at the back of my mind, ever since early childhood, the idea of using skis to travel about mountains and forests had always attracted me. So when Les and I first decided to learn to ski six years later, I was delighted to discover that we shared the desire to ski-tour in the mountains, rather than spend all our time in crowded resorts.

Neither of us thought of learning to do Nordic skiing. In those days, we were barely aware of its existence. From the start, it was the downhill version that we tried to learn. We went to Glenmore Lodge, near Aviemore, and had our first lesson in some of the best snow conditions I have ever seen there. Unfortunately, our ski instructor, the well-known climber John Cunningham, was injured at the time and unable to continue teaching us after the first day. So our group was amalgamated with another and there were so many students that the instructor couldn't possibly have helped us all. Being one of the more timid beginners, and having little sense of balance on the ultra-long skis I'd been given, I didn't make much progress that first time. For several more years we continued to return to Glenmore Lodge at New Year and sometimes at Easter. We very much enjoyed being at the Lodge, one of the best Outdoor Centres in Britain, as we could chat about mountaineering with the instructors, some of whom were amongst the best climbers of the time in Scotland. However, it wasn't the greatest place to learn to ski in the limited periods we had available: in contrast to our initial visit, there was sometimes scarcely any snow at all and the pistes on Cairngorm were icy and riddled with rocks; the few ski lifts were slow, so we spent far too much time queuing and getting back up to the top of the runs; it was very cold indeed, especially at New Year, and from time to time there was a fierce, bitter wind. These factors militated against efficient learning, which in those days was a slow process anyway. First, you learned to snowplough; then you were taught the basic stem turn; after that came the stem christie; and, finally, the parallel.

Our hired boots gave little support, being made from soft, bendy leather and fastened with laces, and the wooden skis we used were very long indeed. Step-in bindings for downhill skiing were only just coming on to the market, so, at first, we had old-fashioned cable bindings. Your feet were relatively unstable and much less easy to release on impact than with the more modern bindings. The boots barely covered the ankle, too, so all in all there was a high risk of lower-limb injury.

A year or two later, we decided to buy skis. Because we had visions of using them to go touring across the hills in the Lake District and North Wales, we bought skis that were designed more for that than the piste. In fact, we rarely ever had such an opportunity. I am barely 5 feet 6 inches tall but I was advised to buy my first pair of skis at a length of 195cm; Les, who is six inches taller, bought a pair measuring 210cm. We also purchased leather ski-mountaineering boots which, apart from a few metal clips and a little notch at the back to fit into a ski binding, otherwise resembled the climbing boots of the period. Thus, we found ourselves at a disadvantage in ski school when we eventually started going on ski holidays abroad. By then, people were already beginning to use slightly shorter skis and these were much easier to turn on than ours. So it was a very long time, nearly a decade, before we felt confident enough to undertake ski-tours in the Alps.

In 1972, on our first resort-based ski holiday abroad, Les quickly attained a reasonable standard on the piste, but it was not until I acquired my second pair of skis, Rossignol Choucas, considerably shorter and wider than my previous pair of Fischers, that I began to master the art of turning in most situations. We were still extremely inexperienced off-piste: in those days relatively few holiday skiers ventured off-piste in resorts and we rarely did so ourselves.

Our ski-touring début was in 1976, just an overnight trip to a mountain hut near Val d'Isère, and a day on the Grande Aiguille Rousse with a French mountain guide and two other clients. This experience gave us enough confidence to arrange our own, unguided ski-tour at Easter 1977 with a small group of friends, including Paul Luton, whom we knew from the Lincoln Mountaineering Club. Paul had already had a little ski-touring experience with the Austrian Alpine Club and had climbed in all weathers in the Lake District, including in winter conditions. He accompanied us on several subsequent ski-mountaineering expeditions in the Alps. Our 1977 tour in the

Bernese Oberland was frustrated by poor weather but it was a grand experience and we all learned a great deal. Also accompanying us were Steve and Shirley Poulton from the Gloucestershire Mountaineering Club. We had known both these experienced mountaineers for several years, Shirley having been one of the very first people to take me on a rock climb, but back in 1977 neither of them knew any more about ski-mountaineering than we did. We were thus all well matched but were very aware of the need for caution.

Because of the snowy weather, we spent a considerable amount of time plodding about in whiteouts on the remote Oberland glaciers, as well as sitting at the Konkordia and Hollandia Huts, waiting for conditions to improve. I was grateful for having learned the snowplough and stem turns, as they were so useful in the conditions we had. In deep powder snow, however, I was at a great disadvantage because, at that stage, I hadn't really mastered the parallel turn. I looked with envy at the continental tourers who had probably skied since they were children. Their evenly curving trail in the snow was something to which we all still aspired.

Walking uphill on ski was much easier. On a touring course at Glenmore Lodge, I had been initiated into the technique of moving with nylon 'skins' attached to the sole of my skis. These are long strips of artificial fur, with the short hairs all laid in the same direction. When you go uphill, the skins allow you to glide forwards on your skis and prevent you from slipping backwards. Only when the slope changes abruptly to downhill, are you in danger of being propelled forwards with a sudden jerk if you don't remember to alter your stance appropriately. A fall is the usual result, and best avoided, especially if you are carrying a large rucksack.

The year after our début in the Oberland, the weather was even worse and we achieved nothing at all, despite having planned with another group of friends to tackle the High Level Route from Chamonix to Zermatt and Saas Fee. Our arrival in late March in the small Swiss town of Martigny in the Rhône Valley coincided with a large dump of fresh snow. We had intended to leave our cars there and take the train the French border to Argentière in the Chamonix Valley, but our plans were thwarted. There was no question of setting off on the High Level Route, so that had to wait for another opportunity. Les and I were most frustrated at being unable to make any progress in our ambition to become ski-tourers. It was now nine years since we had begun to learn to ski and, so far, our attempts to tour in the high mountains had suffered numerous setbacks.

At last our luck changed and, from 1979 onwards, we spent many Easter holidays skiing through the Alps.

THE HIGH LEVEL ROUTE

In 1979, we were lucky enough to make the acquaintance of Jeremy White-head through the Alpine Club, and he agreed to come along with us on our tour. Although we had no designated leader as such, Jeremy already had considerable experience of ski-mountaineering and his assistance was invaluable throughout the ten days we were up in the mountains. We were very fortunate that he had a brief gap in the busy sabbatical year he had taken from his teaching career and was happy to make up our foursome. Afterwards, he stayed on in the Alps to lead a tour for one of the Ski Clubs.

The four of us, Paul Luton, Jeremy, Les and I, set out in April from the Chamonix Valley for the Argentière Hut – the same base from which Les and I had climbed Les Courtes the summer before. As we made our way through the cable car station, bound once again for the Grands Montets, a Swiss guide commented to his party upon the idiocy of taking such immense rucksacks on the High Level Route. He said that we would get no enjoyment from either the ascents or the descents. He himself had a very compact sack and some of his clients seemed to have almost nothing at all, yet there we were, weighed down under large rucksacks piled up head-high, with ice axes and crampons strapped on the outside.

As for our ski-mountaineering attire, although my three companions had acquired the first generation of plastic ski-touring boots, I was still shod in leather. Furthermore, some of our equipment was home-made. The College welding shop had assisted Les in making our *harscheisen*, metal blades that make the ascent of steep, hard-packed snow so much safer and easier, the skiing equivalent of crampons. However, our *harscheisen* were clumsy to use, the design not being as practical as the commercially produced versions that we bought later. Whether the slope was sufficiently steep to require *harscheisen* or not, we always attached skins to our skis when we set off on an uphill stretch. At that time Paul, Les and I only had the old-fashioned type, fixed to the skis by means of straps and thus inclined to slide a little, allowing snow to pack into the gap between ski and skin.

The following year we acquired modern skins, made of the same material but with a layer of adhesive added to the back which permits the skin to remain in perfect contact with the ski until it is deliberately pulled away. Small wonder that we laboured under certain disadvantages that the novice ski-mountaineer today does not encounter!

The ski-tour began right there at the exit from the Grands Montets cable car station, high above the many pistes of the Chamonix Valley and in full view of the piste skiers. Conscious of my large rucksack proclaiming my apparent intention to set off on a serious expedition, I was somewhat nervous about skiing in front of an audience but determined to do my best. According to my journal:

I began with great aplomb. Then, down I went on my very first turn, with everyone looking!

This was before we had even left the 'official' off-piste run. Then:

I took the first steep slope very cautiously, but soon began to enjoy the fairly easy terrain. Then we had to leave this pleasant ground, slip under the tape at the edge of the run and start on the real thing – totally unpatrolled snow slopes, leading down to a glacier frequented only by climbers and ski-mountaineers! I managed quite well at first and Jeremy gave me the odd nod of encouragement, but lower down, the gradient increased, and I started to have trouble. In the end I decided to swallow my pride and do a few kick turns, but once I do these, I find it difficult to start skiing again.

Indeed, in those days there was no question whatsoever of me attempting to parallel ski with a huge rucksack on my back and my skis out of sight under a layer of soft snow.

An hour or so later, we arrived at the Argentière Hut for the night, along with hordes of other tourers, and, just before daybreak, set out on the first stage of the High Level Route. For the next few days we and many other people traipsed up and down over glaciers and passes under blue skies, with the sun burning down. The snow varied from hard-packed névé to slush, with plenty of variations in between. Occasionally, as on the very first day, we had to remove our skis and carry them where it would have been too dangerous to keep them on our feet. For me, it was a sustained and strenuous tour, requiring great stamina, more than would have been needed if I had not been so lacking in off-piste ski technique. The situations varied from sheer hell to sheer ecstasy and I have never for one moment regretted being there. This was for me the ultimate mountain experience: living up high amongst snow-covered mountains, travelling under our own steam from one part of the Alps to another. My journal describes part of the third day after leaving the Argentière Hut. We were in a remote place named '*le grand désert*':

What an apt name for this lonely, beautiful, white waste! As we slid silently across it, each in his own private world, my own thoughts turned to the people at home, wishing they could share my pleasure. Pleasure is an insufficient word, because for me this was an idyllic hour, an hour of delight at the moonscape surrounding me in the early morning light, a few clouds swirling around, the Rosablanche still dark on the horizon, virgin snow, occasional evenly sculpted hollows reminding you that danger lurked beneath the tempting surface. Here there was no need to strain the body, no cause to curse my lack of skiing technique, just glide forwards, onwards, gently upwards, as if towards heaven.

Of course, the idyll was soon broken by the next awkward, icy ascent and then the trials of an unskilled descent, but we duly arrived at our destination. Two days later we crossed the Col de Valpelline after one of the most gruelling mornings of the tour. It was a glorious sunny day but, when we reached the col, there was some low cloud and for a few minutes the view was totally obscured. Then the mist lifted and there before our eyes the great white peaks were revealed one after another: first, the Dent Blanche, then the peaks on the other side of Zermatt, the whole Mischabel chain and, at last, the Matterhorn and, quite nearby, the Dent d'Hérens, 'with its beautiful scimitar-shaped crest'.[1] This mountain was indeed spectacular, yet I was saddened and humbled by thoughts of my Alpine Club proposer, Freda Kemsley, and her husband, John, who had perished up there the previous summer.

That afternoon we arrived in Zermatt. We spent the night at the Bahnhof Hotel, where for many years in the earlier and middle decades of the 20th century the Biner family had actively encouraged a flow of British climbers. These were climbers whose aspiration was to make an ascent of, above all, the Matterhorn, as well as the other great Fourthousanders in the cirque above the Mattertal. By staying at the Biners' Bahnhof, we were following in the footsteps of some great women climbers, including various well-known members of the Ladies' Alpine Club, and many unknown British climbers too.

---

1 *Zermatt Saga* by Cicely Williams

Pete Fleming, our future alpine climbing partner, had spent several summers based there, and the famous ex-chief guide of Zermatt, Bernard Biner himself, had given him the benefit of much-appreciated advice. Cicely Williams, of the Ladies' Alpine Club, dedicated her history of women alpinists, *Women on the Rope*, to the memory of Bernard Biner, 'for over thirty years her guide, philosopher and friend'. She said that:

He was a real mountain lover, as well as a great mountaineer and he recognised an enthusiasm for mountains even if the enthusiast was young and insignificant.[2]

I am sure he would have recognised in us a similar enthusiasm and would have advised us wisely. Sadly, he died in 1965, so Les and I never knew him.

From Zermatt, we continued up to the Monte Rosa Hut and, the next day, climbed Castor, a snow peak situated between its twin Fourthousander, Pollux, and the Liskamm, which we had climbed in 1978. Castor was to be my first Fourthousander approached on ski and what a fine approach it was! Many other parties overtook me that sunny Easter Monday as I plodded wearily uphill but I still took great delight in making my way through the intricate ice fall at the bottom of the Zwillings Glacier. The gleaming ice walls reminded me of our ascent of the Bionnassay. My only concern on this occasion, however, was whether I would have the ability to keep on the narrow track when skiing back down through this labyrinth of yawning holes. At the top of the glacier, the col straddles the frontier between Switzerland and Italy, and we dumped our skis to make the final ascent on crampons up the narrow snow ridge to the summit of Castor. There I basked in the sunshine, somewhat reluctant to leave that fine viewpoint for the unknown perils of the steep ski descent. I had not yet reached the stage where a steep gradient seemed merely an exciting challenge – unlike the skier who, in front of our eyes, descended directly from the summit down what looked like an almost vertical slope.

We returned to the col, and put our skis back on. Despite visions of taking a bad fall on the intimidating slopes of the upper part of the glacier, I managed to turn unscathed. Soon we were up to our knees in the most delightful deep powder where, to my utter astonishment, I found that my skis slid round from one direction to the other with only the slightest effort from me. I became quite pleased with my progress, despite one inevitable plunge headfirst into the white stuff, and by the time I came to the bottom of that first steep slope, I felt far surer of myself than I had ever expected to be.

2 ibid.

Then the hard work began, as the consistency of the snow changed. It was heavier now and I no longer found it easy to turn. Jeremy, noticing my plight, took pity on me and gave me a brief lesson on how to cope. As I followed closely behind him, my skiing improved and I managed to turn in the heavy snow without falling too often. Eventually we came to the ice fall where, fortunately, the snow became firmer. The track, however, was narrow, requiring considerable control, but down we continued, back through the labyrinth, down and round and down, then up and down again, past blocks of ice and perilous cracks, until we came to a standstill to admire the magnificence of the scenery and await Jeremy, who had stayed behind to take some photographs.

I was thoroughly enjoying myself, and rather pleased that I had managed to ski this far without too much difficulty, but my ability was shortly to be put to the test. In the lower part of the ice fall, there was one awkward place where we had to shoot steeply down into a dip, where an extremely narrow snow bridge crossed a fearsome crevasse. On the far side, the track continued very sharply up a little snow wall, then disappeared round a corner. It was absolutely essential not to fall into the crevasse. Down I hurtled, over the bridge, up the narrow track, and then, forgetting to lean firmly forward, slid backwards, landing on my bottom in the dip again, fortunately missing the deep hole in the ice. Paul, behind me, had the good sense not to follow until he could see that the passage was clear.

The rest of the descent was easy and we were soon enjoying our reward at the hut. There was indeed plenty to celebrate: Paul had done his very first Fourthousander, Les and I had ascended our first Fourthousander on ski, and it was Jeremy's birthday. That was the moment when we learned that Jeremy had made his load even heavier than usual the previous day by carrying a large nut tart up to the hut from a baker's in Zermatt. Copious slices were cut and we all drank to his good health and many more birthdays to come. Jeremy probably spent most of his birthdays ski-touring, and maybe this is the recipe for a long, healthy life. He was reported as having celebrated his 80th in much the same way in April 2011, on the 4341m summit of the Ludwigshöhe in the Monte Rosa Range.[3]

After a day sitting out poor weather at the hut, we moved on towards Saas Fee. This time, we must have been the first party to leave the hut in this direction. Once again, I felt as if I were moving through a moonscape. The terrain between the Monte Rosa Hut and the first pass of the day was gently undulating and everything was covered in fresh snow. I felt as if we

3 Fell & Rock Climbing Club Chronicle Number 140, July 2011

were the only people in the world, a magic world of twinkling and glittering whiteness. It was easy enough for me to think like that, for I was not at the front of the party arduously beating down a trail. Even skiing downhill from the col, the snow was so soft that my companions at the front could do no more than shuffle forwards. As fourth in line, I was the only one lucky enough to have a compacted surface on which to slide. We then had the steep and lengthy ascent to the Adler Pass, situated between two Four-thousanders: the Rimpfischhorn, which I had not yet climbed, and the Strahlhorn, which we had ascended in 1973. From there, I struggled wearily all the way to the Britannia Hut, sometimes in a horrifyingly fast, icy rut, sometimes out of it in deep, slow snow, with tumbles and bad temper when my technique failed.

Our objective the next day was another Fourthousander, the Alphubel (my second ascent thereof, but this time on ski) before descending to Saas Fee. It was the last day of our tour. Our rucksacks were really light weight for a change and I set out from the Britannia Hut full of optimism for a splendid day. I was particularly looking forward to a second chance to enjoy the glorious views from the top of the mountain and then to what I hoped would be a magnificent ski run down.

I started badly, with a stupid fall off the traverse track from the hut to the Felskinn cable car station. A slight downhill slide took me by surprise and, with my ski bindings slackened off in the uphill position, over I went, nearly stabbing myself in the eye on the toe of one of my skis. I was sore and irritable as I picked myself up and hurried after my companions. From the Felskinn station, we took a steep, icy line for several hundred yards and I was soon sliding around all over the place, grumbling loudly. Things improved for a while as we reached the slopes of the Alphubel, where many other parties were heading in the same direction, having ascended from a different base. The climb steepened; I grew wearier and wearier, overtaken by one party after another. The long tour had evidently taken its toll on my energy. Once or twice, I stopped for a brief rest and Les kindly waited with me. At long last, the slope eased off and the sun streamed down into the sheltered snow bowl I had reached. Then I came to the final, steep, icy slope below the ridge and was so totally preoccupied with the business of making sure that my *harscheisen* gripped the narrow track, that I gave no thought to the horrors of having to ski back down over icy bumps and through crusty snow.

As I was staggering slowly upwards, I was about to pass a couple of continentals who were having a rest, when one of them thrust a water bottle towards me and invited me to drink. There was no question of refusing, I was parched anyway, and I gulped the liquid down. Cold, sweet tea! I grinned back my thanks and pushed on, wondering what Les would do if he was also offered a sip of the same stuff – he detests tea at the best of times. I didn't look back.

I had really been looking forward to arriving at the ridge, so it was disappointing to be met by a gale-force 'arctic' wind, so cold that a halt was unthinkable. As we hastened up the last slopes to the summit, the cold became more and more intense. This was no place to linger and I made an unsuccessful attempt to stand still and bare my face to the wind in order to admire again that glorious view I had seen one splendid, sunny day the previous summer. Bitterly disappointed, I turned about and prepared for the descent. With numb fingers I adjusted my bindings and skied off down as fast as I could.

The whole descent seemed atrocious. The top was steep and intimidating; then the snow became very deep and my poor technique let me down. A beautiful long straight followed and I was just beginning to feel more comfortable, when Jeremy yelled at me at the top of his voice. I couldn't hear what he said but his demeanour suggested that I should stop. I did so and realised immediately that he had saved me from a most unpleasant experience: there in front of me was an immense crevasse. After that escape, I went completely to pieces. I could scarcely ski at all. Watching a crowd of expert skiers wedeling down with apparent ease did nothing to boost my confidence. Weary and demoralised, I continued. I survived – but what a contrast to my previous ascent of the Alphubel!

That afternoon, after collecting our spare kit from the Britannia Hut, we glided easily down the long pistes back to civilisation. Relaxed and happy by then, I was overcome by the same sense of sheer exhilaration that I had encountered after my ascent of the Matterhorn nine years before.

We had done the High Level Route – all the way from Argentière to Saas Fee, right down into the village itself on ski. I was literally weeping tears of joy as I came to the final standstill.

Nor shall I ever forget the sensation of seeing the bright green grass and yellow spring flowers as we were driven down the valley from Saas Fee to Visp in the postbus. This was the first time I had experienced the contrast with the white world where we had just spent ten days. To say that I was briefly in a state of euphoria is no exaggeration.

3

THE ENGADINE ON SKI

The new decade began with downhill skiing in Switzerland at New Year and then, in April 1980, Les and I drove out there again with Paul Luton. The fourth member of our proposed ski-touring team, Richard Heery, had dropped out at short notice. It was not until some time later that Richard was at liberty to share his secret with us: his wife, Katherine, who had fallen into the crevasse on our ascent of the Strahlhorn back in 1973, was expecting their first child the following autumn.

Ski-touring is a fairly hazardous activity. Falling into a hidden crevasse whilst skiing unroped across untracked glaciers is just one of the objective dangers which threaten any ski-tourer, however experienced – and we were barely past the novice stage. There would have been a greater safety margin for us with a fourth person in the party, but our ski traverse from Chamonix to Saas Fee the preceding year had given us enough confidence to venture forth as a threesome. Knowing few ski-tourers at that time who might be persuaded to join us at the last minute, we decided to go ahead without filling Richard's place.

Andermatt was our initial destination but the weather was unkind. In dense, low cloud we skinned up to the Rotondo Hut in the hope that the sun would shine the following day. Not so. Having dried out our soggy clothes, made damp by the walk uphill, we awoke next morning to more cloud and far too much fresh snow for a safe ascent of any of the mountains beyond the hut. We returned to the valley to rethink our plans. The ski descent was most unpleasant, giving us practice in coping with breakable crust, where one ski remains on the surface whilst the other dives unpredictably at a different angle into the snow beneath. A tumble is inevitable. Although the snow conditions improved a little as we lost height, the visibility remained so poor that we had to strain our eyes in the grey light as we tried to follow each other.

Back in Andermatt, we telephoned for a weather forecast and learned that the Engadine might be a better bet for suitable ski-touring conditions, so we headed for Pontresina. The three of us had a great deal of fun during the following days and gained useful experience on the glaciers and summits around Piz Bernina, the only Fourthousander in the area. Even if Les and I hadn't already climbed that mountain in the summer of 1973, we would not have considered it a suitable objective on ski, so we concentrated on the surrounding peaks.

During our tour in the Engadine, we encountered all sorts of different snow conditions, skiing not only in sunshine, but also in thick mist. We even attempted to ski roped together across crevassed areas for the first time. That really was an interesting experience. It was particularly difficult for me as I was 'piggy in the middle', with Les pulling me from the front and Paul inadvertently catching me up when I was trying to turn. How we managed to survive without injuring each other is a mystery to me.

The highlight of our sojourn in the Bernina Alps was our ascent of the 3900m Piz Palü, a long block of a mountain with three summits joined by snow ridges. We set out from the Diavolezza Hotel, a fairly smart mountain refuge, and skinned up the Vadret Pers Glacier to the col below the eastern summit of Palü. There we dumped our skis at the foot of what appeared to be a daunting, blue ice cliff looming out of the mist. Until then, Paul had not done much Alpine climbing, so this was an interesting proposition for him. His experience in the British mountains in winter, however, would prove very useful.

With considerable trepidation, after fixing crampons on to our ski boots and attaching ourselves to each other with our worryingly thin 7mm rope, Paul and I followed Les over the very awkward *bergschrund*. Then we chopped our way with ice axes up the steep, narrow, icy ridge above the initial vertical step or 'cliff', as I had imagined it to be. When the slope eased off, the ascent became marginally more enjoyable but we could see absolutely nothing in the mist and every few minutes bitter gusts of wind slapped us in the face, nearly throwing us off balance. The ridge drops sharply away on both sides and so there was a considerable sense of relief when we reached the top. All we had to do now, I thought, was to climb back down again. I believe that Paul thought the same – but we were reckoning without the enthusiasm of our leader.

'Look, the sun's starting to break through,' Les announced, pointing at a tiny glimmer in the cloud. 'We could get to the Central Summit.'

After some hesitation, we agreed and Les led us on along another ridge just as daunting as the one before. This time, there were places where we had to move *à cheval*, one leg sinking deeply into the soft snow of the south side and the other cramponing into the solid ice of the north side. It was a unique experience in all my years of mountaineering. Despite my misgivings about what I considered to be foolhardiness, I was delighted to reach the true summit of Piz Palü. Nobody else had followed us up the ridge, but that was hardly surprising, given the weather conditions.

In all, we climbed seven peaks that April and enjoyed many miles of splendid skiing, surviving various minor mishaps on the way. We were entirely off-piste and mainly on crevassed terrain, learning more and more about mountain-craft every day. This was a breakthrough, not only for our skiing but also for our understanding of survival in poor weather and difficult snow conditions at high altitude. No 4000m peaks were climbed but the experience boosted my confidence yet again and whetted my appetite for further challenges.

The pattern of spring ski-touring followed by summer alpinism was now firmly established in our lives and continued almost unbroken for Les, if not for me, over the next two decades.

4

THROUGH THE BERNESE OBERLAND

An impending change of decade in an individual's age often seems to lead to an increased determination to maximise personal training in order to minimise the inevitable decline in physical strength. In eighteen months' time I would turn forty. This fact was already at the back of my mind during the winter of 1981 and, even more urgently, so was our plan to ski-tour in April with two very fit members of the Pinnacle Club, the all-female climbing association. Apprehensiveness stirred me into action. For thirteen weeks without a break, I either swam or jogged every single weekday during the college term and at weekends we were frequently active in the hills, despite very poor weather. It was a mild, wet winter with no snow or ice climbing.

Jay Turner and her friend, Sheila Cormack, joined Paul Luton, Les and me for a grand tour of the Bernese Oberland in April. I had known Jay for a few years, as she had briefly been a member of the Gloucestershire club before moving to London, where she was pursuing her career as a town planner. Younger than me and built more strongly, she was very fit, and we had walked and climbed together on numerous occasions. Jay had skied since she was eleven years old and had done some ski-mountaineering in the Alps. I was aware that she was capable of carrying far heavier loads than I could. Her friend, Sheila, also strongly built, extremely fit and a very good skier, was a mathematician at Edinburgh University. In 1980, she had organised a successful Pinnacle Club Himalayan climbing expedition to make first ascents in the Lahaul area of North India. Jay and six other members of the club had taken part.[1]

For ten consecutive days, in glorious weather, Jay and Sheila accompanied Paul, Les and me on ski at high altitude, from hut to hut, all the way from Andermatt in central Switzerland to the Lauterbrunnen Valley in the Bernese Oberland. Our itinerary took us to the source of the Rhône at

---

1 *Pinnacle Club, A History of Women Climbing* by Shirley Angell

the Furka Pass, then through the glaciated terrain from the Grimsel Pass, weaving our way past 4000m peaks to the Lötschental, and finally up to the Petersgrat and down towards Lauterbrunnen. We covered about 120km on ski. *En route* we climbed several mountains but, of these, only the Hinter Fiescherhorn, at 4025m, is high enough to qualify as a 4000m 'top', although not as a separate peak on Collomb's List.

From Andermatt we drove along the valley to Realp, where we left the car and shouldered our skis and heavy rucksacks to start the climb up to the Albert Heim Hut. My own rucksack weighed approximately 16kg and, in addition to that, I was carrying an ice axe. As well as personal clothing, cameras and other items, our loads also contained the usual ski-mountain-eering paraphernalia, including crampons, *harscheisen*, avalanche shovels and emergency bivouac gear, plus a share of eleven days' breakfasts and lunches and four lightweight evening meals. Many of the items we carried were considerably heavier in 1981 than the equivalent gadgets today. Amongst them were the bulky, old-fashioned transceivers we had hired from the Alpine Ski Club, electronic devices used to locate avalanche victims. Two people were also each carrying a thin, emergency rope. We were well laden.

It was a hot day and I struggled to reach the hut. After the first forty minutes, we were able to walk uphill on ski but, as the terrain steepened, I gradually fell a long way behind my companions. At one point, I had a slight tumble and the forwards movement of my rucksack thrust my head down into the crusty snow. I had to stop for a few minutes to patch up my scratched ear. That little incident should have warned me about the weight of the rucksack throwing me on to my face in a fall but it wasn't until the next day, on the final *schuss* after returning from our climb up the Galen-stock, that I fully appreciated the problem. That time, I broke my sunglasses, gouged my nose and acquired a black eye. In future years, rucksack manu-facturers would provide chest straps as standard items, thus helping to prevent the sack from bearing down on the wearer's head in such a situation.

The following day we skinned and skied across towards the Furka Pass where, in summer, tourists flock to look at the Rhône Glacier. Many years previously, I too had stood there, looking at my first glacier, disappointed to see the ugly, grey ice it presented in August. This time, however, we were alone in the snowy, wintry silence of the high mountains and we trekked across the beautiful expanse of virgin snow. Hard work and good navigation brought us a day and a half later to the Oberaarjoch. On a broiling hot day, the approach to the col via the Oberaar Glacier was particularly arduous. That was where Sheila taught me to put snow on my head under my sunhat to keep myself cool.

Over the previous two days, we had scarcely seen another soul and it was a joy to savour such solitude. This changed when we arrived at the Oberaar Hut where, despite the absence of the guardian, several ski-touring parties were in residence. It was a convivial evening, spent among like-minded companions. Some Germans encouraged us to climb the Gross Wannenhorn the following day, telling us what a wonderful run they had had that morning in perfect snow conditions. We took their advice and it was one of the loveliest mountain climbs on ski that I ever experienced. We were able to dump most of our heavy loads on the glacier, before wending our way up the mountain through an interesting crevassed ice field with overhanging séracs. It was bliss to be travelling lightweight for a change. At 3905m, the summit is a splendid viewpoint for the great Oberland Fourthousanders, the Finsteraarhorn being the closest. This was on our list for the ski-tour, but the guardian at the hut that night informed us that the conditions on the approach to the Hugisattel were very icy, so we abandoned the idea.

We did, however, celebrate Les's birthday on Easter Sunday by climbing two peaks at the head of the Fiescher Glacier: Ochs, with its huge, overhanging cornices, and the somewhat higher Hinterfiescherhorn. After another night with the Easter crowds at the isolated Finsteraarhorn Hut, we travelled on over the glacier to the Grünhornlücke and down to the Konkordia Hut, where Les and I had spent half a dozen nights during the 1970s. There we decided to have a rest day, as the Easter Monday weather was cloudy at glacier level, but we later realised that we had made an error of judgment. If we had spent the day travelling in the misty conditions to the Obermönchjoch Hut, we would have been in position on the Tuesday to climb the Jungfrau. We simply didn't dream that the conditions would be suitable but Tuesday dawned as fine as any day we'd had.

It was, therefore, in a greatly frustrated state of mind that I set out that day to cross the Konkordiaplatz in the direction of the Hollandia Hut. The devil got into me as I swooshed along as fast as I could go. Les had to chase after me to slow me down, saying that I would wear myself out before we reached the mountains we'd decided to climb on the way. But it was the Jungfrau I wanted to climb, not the Lauihorn and the Kranzberg that were our current objectives. This was at least the third time we'd planned to climb the Jungfrau, the first big, white mountain I had ever seen, several years before I became a climber. It was the peak I had always nurtured a desire to climb. Moreover, the Jungfrau is one of the great Fourthousanders of the Alps, completing the well-known scenic trio of peaks seen from Mürren, a ski resort above the Lauterbrunnen Valley: the Jungfrau, Mönch, and Eiger, at 3970m their slightly lower neighbour.

So there I was, thwarted again, but fortunately Alpine mountains don't have to reach 4000m to provide superlative experiences. Such an experience came our way that day, despite my frustration. We had an interesting time climbing our two peaks but it was the run back down on ski to the glacier that exceeded all expectation. I enthused in my journal:

We had a magnificent ski down from the Lauitor to the Aletschfirn – so different from 1977! [We had climbed to the Lauitor on our first ski-tour.] *This time the snow was in perfect condition – some light powder, mainly spring snow – and we have made such progress in our skiing technique since then. Ecstasy, but so short a pleasure …*

The plod up to the Hollandia Hut was hard grind by comparison. There we found the same guardian as on our last visit. Despite his surliness and disinclination to heat the sitting area for us, he was quite helpful when we asked him for advice about the route we wanted to take up to the Petersgrat from the Lötschental. He even made a phone call to see if the Lauchneralp lifts would be working.

In the meantime, we had one more peak to climb. The Ebnefluh, like the Gross Wannenhorn, is just short of the 4000m mark. At 3962m, it is easily accessible on ski from the Hollandia Hut and, the following day, it provided us with another superb descent. Indeed, it was one of those rare occasions when you can stop and look back to admire the beautiful curves you have made. An unexpected thrill, to be sure! If only skiing was always like that. A little further on, however, the snow became harder and so rutted that I was rudely reminded that I still had a great deal to learn. Then followed a disappointingly unpleasant descent from the Lötschenlücke to the village of Blatten. For many years, Les and I had dreamed of skiing down the Langgletscher, which we first ascended on foot with our friends in the summer of 1973. Unfortunately, the slopes were still icy in the late morning and were a nightmare of ruts and holes made by many skiers over the preceding days.

That night was spent in a very old lodging house up on the mountainside above the Lötschental. Our hosts were an ancient couple, who spoke in such a broad dialect that even those of us who knew some German found it impossible to understand them. Once again, it was bitterly cold inside the house and, although there was some water available, the facilities were so basic that we had to resort to a bucket in an outhouse in order to give ourselves the luxury of the first wash in a week. It was a primitive affair indeed.

Just one more day remained, and we were lucky with the weather to the end. Although we had now left the big peaks behind, the final day was no easy ride. We set off as early as possible from this minor ski resort on the first ski tow of the day. It was a T-bar and our enormous rucksacks didn't make it a very easy experience, but it was a quick way to gain height. After crossing the Petersgrat, there was one last, magical ski descent before we came to difficult ground covered in avalanche debris – a rather exhausting finish to this wonderful ski-tour through the Oberland.

Today, Les, Paul and I still agree that this was the best of all the tours we undertook together over the years. We had climbed eight peaks in eleven days and acclimatised up to 4000m. The exertion undoubtedly stood me in good stead for the coming summer, when Les and I climbed another sixteen peaks, including some of the highest Swiss Fourthousanders of them all.

5

REACHING AUSTRIA

Over the following decade, I took part in another seven ski-tours before my final one in the Vanoise in 1995. Injury prevented me from joining Les and our friends a couple of times in the late Eighties and then again, I missed another four tours between 1991 and 1994. This was very frustrating indeed, as I had come to view touring as an essential part of my life. Without it, I was grief-stricken. Each year when the group set off, my world felt black. Eventually I learned to cope with this and threw my remaining energy into other pursuits. So life changed.

However, in the years when I was fit and uninjured, and not recuperating from yet another orthopaedic operation, I accompanied Les on the annual ski-mountaineering trip. I was fortunate to be in the party on each occasion that a new section of the trans-Switzerland tour took place. Les and I had both been greatly motivated hearing about the traverse Peter and Beryl Wilberforce Smith had planned a route across the Alps on ski from the Mediterranean to Austria. They did the first leg in 1970 and continued to make their way systematically through France and Switzerland over the following five years. Then Peter died suddenly and Beryl decided that she must complete the journey as far as Kaprun in Austria. In 1978, at the age of 65, she did so. The book Peter had already started, *A Little Walk on Skis*, was finished by Beryl and published in 1987.

Unlike the Wilberforce Smiths, Les and I didn't attempt to cross the French, Swiss and Austrian Alps in one continuous line. Instead, we hoped that our annual fortnight's ski-mountaineering would give us the opportunity to cover as much as possible of a similar route, and Les would plan each year's trip according to the date of Easter and the consequent snow conditions expected in each area of the Alps. This not only depended upon that date, but also on the different snowfall pattern of each winter. By the time the Wilberforce Smiths' book was published, we had already skied across most of Switzerland, as well as a few parts of the French Alps. I never imagined that I would have the opportunity to complete the whole itinerary from the Maritime Alps near Nice to the Gross Glockner, on the eastern side of the Austrian Alps. Nevertheless, I was delighted when I suddenly realised, on the top of the Silvrettahorn in 1989, that I had reached the Austrian border of Switzerland exactly ten years after setting out on the High Level Route from the French village of Argentière near the south-western Swiss border. Between times, we had pieced together an almost continuous traverse of the whole of Switzerland. In just a very few places, we had been obliged to take a brief detour by public transport or car but, otherwise, we had crossed the entire country on ski.

Over the years we ski-toured with a number of different friends and I am grateful to them all for their companionship – and to some, on particularly difficult occasions, for their moral support. It was never easy to work full-tilt at college, with no half-term break, from early January to the end of March, sometimes even the middle of April, and then set off on the last Friday evening of term to start our tour as soon as we possibly could. Winter mountaineering weekends in the UK helped me keep reasonably fit and in tune with tough conditions in difficult terrain, and a morning swim a couple of times a week before the start of the college day became one of my most successful ploys to improve my stamina. Sometimes, however, the inevitable winter coughs and colds would set me back. It was very difficult to avoid viral infections when working indoors with so many other people. My journal notes just such a case in 1982:

By the eleventh week of term I had burnt myself out mentally and had fallen prey to a vicious cold which forced me to bed for the three days immediately preceding our departure for the Alps [as I hardly ever took time off work, it must have been really bad]. *I was extremely apprehensive about my ability to hold my own with this year's super-athletic team, but in retrospect I suspect that those few days of rest did more for me than all the training I had intended to do.*

That year we were accompanied by Paul Luton, Allan Brindley, from Kendal, and Ian and Sue Stirrups, two young friends who had joined the GMC three years before. This was a particularly successful group of tourers:

With the exception of Les, who seemed to be strong at all times, we all had our strengths and weaknesses, and this was probably why we got on so well together. There was no competitiveness, and there was a considerable amount of mutual encouragement. I hardly ever got demoralised and consequently never lost my temper with myself or anyone else – although I was by far the slowest on long easy ascents, where all my runner friends would go storming off ahead, my longer experience and superior technique allowed me to keep up and even occasionally overtake on the steep sections. On the downhill sections, I found that Sue and Ian skied at much the same speed as me, so I was usually in company on those sections too. Al is a real piste-basher, and I found it wiser to let him get ahead of me on descent, as the speed he skied at tended to frighten me ...

Although Allan was an excellent skier, he had only a little experience of ski-touring, and Ian and Sue had none at all. By comparison, Paul, Les and I had completed two successful weeks of ski-mountaneering at high altitude in each of the three preceding years. I had reason to feel competent.

Our tour began in Saas Grund and on the first day we traversed the Gruben Glacier beyond the Fletschhorn on our way towards the Simplon Pass:

The snow was very variable with a bit of crust here and there, and our novice friends found it quite hard. I, on the contrary, rather enjoyed the descent and didn't make too many mistakes. Then there was the bonus of a short wait from time to time as the others caught up! Les began to get rather impatient as he realised how long we were taking and he kept muttering about how far we had to go. So I threw my skins back on my skis again, stuffing as much food inside me as I could, and leapt back into action. The sun was beating down fairly relentlessly, and Sue asked me if it was always as hot as this. 'Hotter sometimes,' I chuckled, and plodded on, determined not to weaken until I'd reached the next col. I was having a really good day ... whilst they were all having a hard time.

I did feel rather pleased with myself just then – a rare event for me.

Four years later, in 1986, we skied the Swiss section from Andermatt to Cresta, a village near the south-western edge of the canton of Graubünden. Both Paul and Allan were with us once again, as well as Jay Turner and Brian Cox, a builder from Kendal. Brian, an enthusiastic skier, fell-runner, climber and ex-judo champion, joined us for the first time. He would accompany Les many times over the next two decades. Everyone in the group was a proficient skier, which was fortunate as our route involved some interesting terrain, including a long, steep, narrow gully where we resorted to sideslipping for several hundred metres on our approach to the Terri Hut. We had probably made a rare navigational error there. This was also the tour when we had one of the most perfect runs of all:

From the col beyond Piz Vial we were amazed to find the longest run in untracked powder snow that we had ever experienced. We had about 300m of vertical descent, right into the valley bottom, before the snow became heavy.

As we looked back up the slopes we had skied, we were delighted to see six elegant trails punctuated only rarely by the sign of a fall.

These memories were all I had to sustain me during the following two years, when a shoulder injury put a temporary halt to my ski-mountaineering ambitions. Then, in 1989, I was fit enough to go on tour again. With Jay Turner and Peter Kaye, an F&RCC member from Leeds, whom Jay had met through the Eagle Ski Club, we set out from Cresta, the village where I had completed my last ski-tour three years before. A short spell of poor visibility prevented us from traversing the mountains to Bivio, so we drove round there and began our journey from the Julier Pass to Zernez in the Engadine. I was past my peak as far as fitness for ski-touring was concerned and struggled throughout the two weeks to keep up with my companions. It must have been irritating for them to have to wait for me so often. Nevertheless, I am very glad they did, as our itinerary enabled me to complete the Swiss traverse.

This tour through the wild areas of the canton of Graubünden was one of the most varied we ever did and all my mountaineering skills were needed. Between the Julier Pass and Zernez, we climbed seven mountains, including Piz Kesch, a peak that an elderly acquaintance, Walter Kirstein, had recommended to us ten years previously. As we made our way from hut to hut through this remote country, we experienced a mixture of perfect heaven and sheer hell. On our way from the Kesch Hut to the Grialetsch Hut, as we passed through the flatter part of the Vallorgia, my journal recalls the way I felt at that moment:

Here, the scenery was idyllic, and the sensation of being somewhere special far away in a beautiful remoteness predominated both Jay's thoughts and mine. Then the slope steepened again …

The following day offered a complete contrast in my mood as I descended from Piz Sarsura on my way to Zernez:

The immediate descent from the summit looked steep and fraught with problems for any but the experts, so I watched the others before attempting it. Les and Jay gave me no cause for alarm, but Peter came a cropper, so I set out gingerly, taking a wide traverse, much to Les's irritation. He shouted at me to take a much steeper line. I reached him without incident, but then, several hundred metres lower down the glacier, the crust became impossible … I tried time after time to turn in the horrible stuff, but although I succeeded in one direction, my attempts to turn the opposite way seemed quite futile … For miles and miles we skied thus, the terrain changing all the time, the snow varying between crust and heavy and impossible … so it went on. At one point I found myself off course high on the hillside above the others with yards and yards of crust between us. I think we were all suffering – even Les began to fall over.

A day or two later we made our way by public transport back to the Julier Pass, where we returned to our car and Les drove us to Klosters to complete the tour. We stopped there only briefly to do a little shopping, and then set off for the Silvretta Hut. Struggling along some way behind the rest of the group, it was a long, hot five hours for me before I finally arrived. I had bought myself what I thought was a tasty chunk of cheese in Klosters and was looking forward to having a bite of it when I caught the others up at one of the brief resting points, but was dismayed to find, on opening my rucksack, that a vile smell overwhelmed me:

So it was at this point that I decided to get rid of the expensive little treat I had been so much looking forward to: out went the Appenzeller, it simply had to go. Without even tasting it, I left it for the birds. Perhaps they would have less sensitive 'noses' than me. Even when I was hungry later, I never missed it.

Although most of the approach to the Silvrettahorn the next day was fairly easy, parts of the slope at the head of the glacier were steep and very icy, so much so that it was only just passable with *harscheisen*. From just above the col, we had to abandon the skis and progress on foot up the ridge to the summit:

Here it suddenly dawned upon me that we had reached the Austrian border, indeed that over a period of ten years, we had virtually crossed the whole of Switzerland on ski! That knowledge gave me a long-lasting sense of satisfaction as well as gratitude to those who'd made it possible. Not just Les and all our other companions, but also the surgeon who had finally mended my shoulder sufficiently for me to get back on the mountains again.

After a while, we returned to our skis and sped off on a slightly descending traverse towards the foot of the Fuorcla del Cunfin. At the col, we once again left our skis in order to ascend to the Signalhorn on foot. This mountain also sits astride the Swiss-Austrian border, and our climb turned out to be most enjoyable, culminating in one of those narrow snow arêtes that always excite me so much. It was just wide enough to prevent fear, but just narrow enough for a sense of exhilaration: a fine summit on which to end our tour across the Swiss Alps.

Unfortunately, I had a major setback in 1995 and, as I was no longer able to carry a heavy rucksack, I was forced to abandon hut-to-hut tours. Although I continued to take advantage of opportunities to ski in resorts whenever they arose, I missed the sensation of adventure and the mixture of solitude and camaraderie that accompanies ski-touring. I particularly loved the challenge of journeying through wild places for several days at a time without descending to permanent habitation. It was the 21st century before Les and I learned to use cross-country skis akin to the Nordic skis used for travel in the Scandinavian winter. They have allowed us to ski through the forests of my childhood imagination and this new activity has to some degree compensated for the loss of high mountain tours.

PART FOUR

So Many
Alpine Summits

Our strong years are the years in which to learn the
complete craft of greater mountaineering.
– GEOFFREY WINTHROP YOUNG[1]

The Dom and the Täschhorn

1 *Mountain Craft* by Geoffrey Winthrop Young, 1910, from R. L. G. Irving's anthology, *The Mountain Way*

1

CONFIDENCE

Throughout the second half of the 1970s, we had continued our mountaineering activities all the year round without interruption. My confidence in all aspects of my life was growing enormously. Alpine summer holidays were by now an established part of our annual plans. There were so many places to go and so many mountains to climb in the Western Alps alone, without looking further afield. Although a few of our acquaintances did venture to other parts of the world, global travel was not as commonplace then as it has since become and our college holidays did not coincide with the monsoon-free seasons of many parts of the Himalaya. We would have had to take an unpaid sabbatical in order to climb in such regions and we were not prepared to do that.

In any case, Les really wanted to climb rather than trek or travel and, having had my appetite for Alpine climbing whetted, I wanted to accompany him wherever possible. I too wanted to reach the summits rather than just look at them from below. We enjoyed climbing together; it was an integral part of our married life. Three months away from Les in the autumn of 1972 had convinced me of that. I had put my desire to improve my German above everything else for a term, exchanging my post in Gloucester with a German college teacher in Nordrhein-Westfalen. Three months in the flat, northern part of Germany, with no opportunities to climb hills, let alone mountains, plus the absence of my husband of only three years, were more than enough to convince me of my priorities. By Christmas I could scarcely wait to get back to our chosen lifestyle.

There was another factor we needed to take into account. Although I was becoming increasingly unwilling to abandon an activity which it had taken me nearly thirty years to discover, my body clock was ticking away and doubts about the course my life was not taking were undermining my peace of mind. Children! Should we, or should we not, start a family? All around, our peers were taking the plunge. It was a question that we needed to resolve, unless nature simply resolved it for us – but nature did not come to the rescue. The choice, apparently, was still ours and during the mid-1970s we made our decision. The tension in my mind eased and we did not look back. Our lives swept on in a torrent of activity, leaving no pause for regret that our marriage would not result in that fundamental activity: the creation of new life.

The realisation that I wanted to continue spending so much of my time in the mountains undoubtedly influenced my professional life too. I was very happy teaching French and German. It was nearly a decade since I had left university and at last I was doing a job which really suited me and gave me considerable satisfaction. At the same time, there were enormous frustrations. I still lacked the key role I coveted, I was bursting with enthusiasm and initiative, and yet I seemed to be trampled upon at every turn. Throughout the 1970s I longed for a way out of the situation, but my options were extremely limited unless I was prepared to sacrifice some of the most important parts of my life.

Initially, Les and I had thought we would move further north to be nearer the British mountains. Les started to look for suitable lecturing posts in Lancashire and Yorkshire but soon became disillusioned by the dismal institutions he visited and gave up the idea of moving to a less attractive job. So I concentrated my own efforts on looking for a teaching post higher up the career ladder in Gloucestershire. Though I considered moving into the secondary sector, it wasn't really where my interests lay. I was, above all, interested in teaching people the skills to use their foreign languages in the business world and I thoroughly enjoyed working in the Further Education sector I had trained for. Careerwise, our main problem was that opportunities for lecturers in Chemistry and Modern Languages were few and far between, especially within reasonable travelling distance of the home we had just set up. Neither of us wanted to spend more time in transit than we needed to, as we already travelled a great deal at weekends. As it was, there was little enough time to see each other during the week since we both taught some evening classes and our free times rarely coincided.

Within the college where we worked at that time, career development for linguists was particularly poor, and little better for women in any subject area. The college was very much a male-dominated environment and many of the men were of the old school. They made it quite plain that they believed women only worked for pin money and that sooner or later a young married woman would leave to start a family. I was only in my early thirties and the overwhelming delight that I experienced in my mountaineering activities and in my life with Les compensated enormously for the difficulties and shortcomings of my professional situation. It also deterred me from taking any course of action to further my career. I remained in a very junior position for a very long time.

Year after year went by and our tally of alpine routes increased, in particular, the number of Fourthousanders. I was becoming increasingly competent. My rock climbing career had faltered very early on, one beautiful spring evening on the local crag at Cleeve Hill above Cheltenham, when I was boldly soloing up what was considered to be the easiest route. The crag is barely 10m high but it is steep limestone, with a fairly wide, gritty platform at its foot. At least, it was quite wide in those days – it is now very much eroded. Just as I was about to climb over the top edge of the crag, I slipped and hurtled backwards through the air. I must have touched down on one foot and then rolled over. Whilst I lay there, I felt the seconds tick away as I wondered whether I was dead or alive. Les and our other companion rushed over to see how I was and I realised that I was not in the next world after all. I was definitely on earth and had sustained a sprained ankle, nothing worse. Fortune had smiled upon me but the event undoubtedly clouded my perception of my ability to lead rock climbs, let alone climb solo, for many years to come.

From then on, I climbed almost exclusively as a second, not taking the lead until 1974, when Sue Wornham and I climbed together on a very easy route in Birkness Combe above Buttermere. Later that summer, in the last week of our Alpine holiday, we plucked up courage to go up the Normal Route on the Aiguille du Tour above the Chamonix Valley, whilst Colin and Les climbed a more serious route on a nearby peak. However, the weather disrupted this plan and it was some time before any similar opportunities presented themselves. In the meantime, I was only too happy to continue in my role as second on the many rock climbs and Alpine routes we undertook in the mid- to late-1970s. My confidence as a second had grown enormously, although, throughout this period, all my rock climbing was done in leather walking boots with Vibram soles. I didn't own a pair of specialist rock climbing shoes until the 1980s, thinking that I didn't climb hard enough routes to justify the expense. Now, in the 21st century, when technical footwear is *de rigueur*, this attitude would probably be considered quite astonishing.

At home, we continued to visit the English, Welsh and Scottish mountains all the year round, and when winter conditions were favourable, we would climb the classic snow gullies on the major peaks wherever we happened to be. These were mainly in Snowdonia and the Lake District, as our opportunities to visit Scotland in the winter were limited and we were rarely in the right place at the right time.

The Isle of Skye was another matter. Every year, without fail, in the early 1970s we went there at the end of May for a week. The Cuillin Ridge gave me invaluable experience of climbing and scrambling in vertiginous places. Les traversed the whole ridge on numerous occasions but, for me, it was a much more serious undertaking and we devised a strategy to ensure that I could complete the traverse of the Main Ridge within a 24-hour period. Even at my fittest, this ridge was one of the most arduous routes I have ever contemplated undertaking. It is a magnificent expanse of rock, with eleven peaks over 3000 feet above sea level. At one end of the range, the mountains rise almost directly from the seashore. In 1974, I spent one of the most memorable days of my life completing the traverse from Glen Brittle up to Garbh Bhein and thence along the whole ridge to Sgurr nan Gillean and down to Glen Sligachan. In order to meet the 24-hour deadline, we set off at 2.00 pm one day, accompanied by Geoff Causey and Richard Heery, and bivouacked overnight on the ridge near the Col na Banadich, then continued along the ridge and over the Bhasteir Tooth to Sgurr nan Gillean, reaching the pub in Glen Sligachan by 2.00 pm the following day.

Geoff and Richard were both very fit and competent. Subsequently, Geoff accompanied Les on the Greater Traverse of the Skye Ridge, including two outlying Munros, Clach Glas and Blaven, and it was Richard who was with Les on the Greater Greater Traverse, that took them back up and over Sgurr Dubh Mòr, to the starting place in Glen Brittle. The two traverses took them 16 and 36 hours respectively, with a bivouac on the latter. The Black Cuillin, undoubtedly the most exciting range of mountains in the UK, served us all in good stead as training for the coming Alpine season each year.

As a rule, we would only go rock climbing between April and September, and in the winter months, with indoor climbing walls in Gloucestershire still in their infancy, we would get no practice at all. I continued to climb mainly with Les, but occasionally I would tie on with other people, chiefly male since there was rather a dearth of female climbing partners in my circle of acquaintances. Most of my women friends climbed only for a few years before departing from the scene, as motherhood became their priority. My rock climbing standard in those years peaked at about Hard Severe, and in the Alps I would do the odd pitch of grade III.

Our Alpine climbs were usually mixed routes, with snow crests and easy rock ridges where we could scramble along in alpine style without belaying. Occasionally there were other routes too, such as the North-North-West Face of the Aiguille de Bionnassay in 1975, which involved scaling icy faces and climbing through terrain with fairly serious objective dangers.

Each year the scope and standard of my Alpine climbing subtly increased. Despite the terror I experienced in the electric storm on the Aiguille Purtscheller in 1976, and the doubts given me by the daunting snow-covered rock on the South Ridge of the Lagginhorn in 1977, my confidence grew through most of the decade. It reached a high point after the 1978 season, when we had climbed without the support of our usual companions. 1979 would prove to be the year when I finally believed in my own abilities.

2

BREAKTHROUGH:
A YEAR TO REMEMBER

In 1928, the redoubtable husband and wife team, Ivor Richards and Dorothy Pilley, had what they called their 'great year' in the Alps, when they made the first ascent of the North Ridge[1] of the Dent Blanche, amongst various other splendid climbs. For me, half a century later, 1979 was undoubtedly the 'great year' of my climbing career, culminating in my surprise election to the Presidency of the Gloucestershire Mountaineering Club and, a little after that, receipt of the hitherto unknown award of the 'Ladies' Roll of Honour' at the Lincoln Mountaineering Club Annual Dinner.

This presentation was really just intended as a moment of entertainment. However, before our ski-mountaineering companion, Paul Luton, presented me with this trophy, he made an extraordinary speech. My every foible was minuted in hilarious detail, and some were exaggerated beyond all reason, but I was touched by the apparent esteem of my friend who, beneath this catalogue of weaknesses, wanted to honour my achievements that year. It was the lighter side of mountaineering, commemorating our more serious labours. That spring, in the company of Paul, Les and Jeremy Whitehead, I had skied over the glaciers and mountain passes from Chamonix to Saas Fee on the well-known High Level Route. In so doing, I realised, I had now done at least fifty Alpine 'routes', as we had taken in four peaks along the way, including two Fourthousanders.

Which was my fiftieth route? It is impossible to decide whether it was the ascent of the Pigne d'Arolla, or Castor – a new Fourthousander for me – or the Alphubel, this time from the Saas Fee side. What, after all, is an Alpine route? Should I include our abortive attempt the year before on the Tré-la-tête, a minor outlier of Mont Blanc, when we had to abandon the route because of a broken crampon after several hours of traipsing up the glacier in the darkness? The ascent to the Lauitor, a high col in the Bernese Oberland, on our otherwise unsuccessful first ski-tour in 1977?

---

1 Now renamed North-North-West Ridge

Does the High Level Route itself, which takes a whole week, qualify as only one route? All things considered, I don't really believe that there is any hard and fast rule, any more than we can be absolutely certain which Alpine tops actually classify as 4000m summits or their subsidiaries. As far as I was concerned, I had spent at least fifty days of my life engaged in some form of Alpine climbing, not including all the walks to the huts or, for that matter, days spent on ski travelling over glaciers and passes between huts, but without actually ascending any peaks.

As for my unexpected elevation to the Presidency of the GMC, nobody could have been more surprised than me. (I had only intended to stand as Secretary, a post to which I did accede a few years later.) We were at the Annual General Meeting in November, when suddenly the current President made the unexpected announcement that he wished to resign with immediate effect. The shocked silence was quickly followed by a hubbub. Who was to take over? After a few minutes, one of the committee members spoke:

'Would Barbara agree to stand for the job?'

I gazed wide-eyed at the gathering of fellow club members. Would I? Could I even contemplate such an honour? I had never even been a committee member. If I did stand, who was going to be the Secretary? These thoughts churned around in my head.

A snap decision was called for and, after few minutes' reflection, I agreed to accept the nomination.

Although I was not actually the GMC's first female President, the diminutive Sandie Potts, a talented rock climber, having held the post a few years before, the local press learned of my election and made quite a fuss about it, simply because I was a woman. Even at the end of the 1970s, it was still considered unusual for a woman to be elected to the top position in a mainly male-dominated organisation. By the time I had been interviewed more than once on the subject, I began to feel that maybe I was not, after all, an unsuitable choice. I never regretted it. It was, I believed, an honour and an opportunity to give something back to the club that had given me so much. Perhaps, by taking on this role, I was also contributing in a very minor way to the ongoing struggle for women's equality. Certainly I set out to undertake my duties as well as I could.

With hindsight, I recognise that the Presidency gave me a much-needed opportunity to grow in self-confidence, to accept that I had achieved far more than I had realised and was capable of going further. One or two people who had known me only as a timid beginner on rock climbs in the UK, who had never climbed with me in the Alps and who were not aware of my gradually increasing ability to cope with climbs graded Severe, wearing boots with Vibram soles, did, however, express surprise that I was considered enough of a mountaineer to be elected President.

The 1980 Alpine Journal published an article of mine entitled 'Perpetual Second', in which I attempted to justify my secondary role in an activity I would now describe as 'unofficially-guided guideless climbing'. Even as I wrote the piece, I was beginning to hanker after something more than just following my leader. I knew by then that I was a confident and competent second in Alpine situations, capable of coping with certain types of emergency, though by no means all. Could every climbing leader in fact do that? In the late 1970s, I had proved, at least to myself, that on Alpine peaks I could climb and gain the respect of leaders other than my regular partner, Les. I did, however, and still do to some extent, share the opinion of the Australian climber, Louise Shepherd, whose views were probably concerned with rock climbing rather than alpinism:

By 'climber', I mean one who leads. The perpetual seconders-cum-portable-belayers that one sees, especially in Europe, I do not count as climbers.[2]

On British rock climbs with Les, I invariably climbed second. It never seemed to occur to either of us that I should take the lead. Indeed, I enjoyed climbing with him, as he rarely hesitated, rarely kept me waiting long on a stance whilst he looked for the way up, and I always had complete confidence in his choice of route. Where he led, I followed, becoming more and more capable as the years passed.

It was, however, more on the strengths of my recent Alpine climbing career than my abilities as a rock climber, that I felt by the end of 1979 that I had become a 'real mountaineer' at last. That summer season was one of the most splendid Alpine experiences I have ever had. The weather and snow conditions were good, the company was excellent and we achieved almost everything we set out to do, including the ascent of several Fourthousanders we had never climbed before. What more could one want? The Easter ski-tour, followed closely by a week in Scotland at the end of May, had laid a good foundation for the summer season. Not only had we walked miles in Scotland, slogging up and down some of the big Munros around Glen Nevis, but, even more usefully, Les and I had undertaken some classic rock climbs which boosted my confidence considerably. Splendid, delicate slab climbing on the 170m Severe Ardverikie Wall near

2 *Women Climbing* by Birkett and Peascod

Loch Laggan, the ascent of the 600m Tower Ridge on Ben Nevis, still complete with snow patches, and finally an interesting climb up the steep, exposed Agag's Groove on the Rannoch Wall of Buachaille Etive Mor in Glencoe, albeit as a second, never in the lead position, contributed to my Alpine training in no small measure.

Our first week back in the Alps in the summer was once again spent in the south-eastern corner of Switzerland, in the Engadine. The weather was perfect and we not only did a couple of training routes on Piz Morteratsch and the Bellavista, but also teamed up with our elderly acquaintance from the Alpine Club, the determined Walter Kirstein, aged 83, and his somewhat younger friend, Stuart Ferguson. With these two, we spent a whole day traversing Las Sours, a delightful rock ridge with an unrivalled view of the Bernina Alps. It was a unique experience for us, and a very pleasant one, followed by an excellent evening, dining with Walter and his wife, Bertha, at the luxurious Kronenhof Hotel in Pontresina. As Walter said at the time, one of the aspects he liked so much about mountaineering was the endless contrasts. That evening, after leaving the hotel, Les and I crawled back into our tent at the campsite near Morteratsch – a contrast indeed!

By the following week, when we joined our younger friends straight out from England, we were both fit and acclimatised. The weather in the Bernese Oberland was less settled than it had been in the Engadine. We met up with our alpine partners on a roasting hot and stormy evening in Meiringen: Geoff Causey and John Oaks, plus two of their acquaintances, Dave Hicks and Allan Brindley. Neither Dave nor Allan had climbed an alpine Four-thousander. How fortunate they were to be in the following two weeks.

It was our old friend, Richard Heery, who had introduced Dave to Geoff. Richard had moved to Doncaster, where he got to know Dave, a Maths teacher, at the school where he worked. In their spare time the two of them climbed together at Stanage, in the Peak District. Dave, despite his diminutive stature, was strong. Allan, who lived in Kendal, had first met Geoff on a winter's day on Helvellyn. Always an enthusiast, whatever activity he took up, Allan was keen to climb in the Alps. Though more of a skier than a climber, he was soon to combine both activities, joining us on ski-mountaineering trips year after year until knee problems finally put an end to that pursuit. He had a successful professional life, becoming headmaster at a school for children with a physical disability.

Our first objective, when we met up, was the Konkordia Hut where Les and I had already spent a number of nights both in summer and in spring. On this occasion, we set out from Fiesch in the Rhône Valley, taking the cable car to Kühboden and contouring the Eggishorn to reach the Marjelensee, where the route winds its way up on to the Aletsch Glacier. Next day, in somewhat indifferent, cloudy weather, we moved on over the Grünhorn- lücke to the Finsteraarhorn Hut. Then, despite poor weather in the night, the guardian woke us before it was light and, amidst mutterings about whether or not we needed to wear cagoules, we set off at about 4.00 am in the direction of the Hugisattel and the Finsteraarhorn. It was just spitting with rain. My journal gives a fairly detailed account of our progress:

Les steamed away uphill faster than anyone else intended to go and I headed the rest of the party rather too slowly up the unpleasant moraine at the back of the hut. Allan kept complaining that he was bumping into the ice screw that was dangling from the back of my sack. It was with great relief that we reached the top of the rocks, where Les was waiting below the steep ice slopes forming the edge of the upper part of the glacier. Here we roped up and put on our crampons and Les and I were soon away in front.

I was going quite well, and improved as the morning wore on and it became apparent that the other four were all struggling for lack of acclimatisation. By the time we reached the steep slopes below the Hugisattel, Les was tired of making the trail in the fresh snow and, refusing my offers to help, he suggested that one of the other pairs took over in the lead. Geoff leapt forward and we plodded slowly on until he had had enough. Then Allan took over and away we went at full speed until he began to realise his mistake. By then we were all begging him to slow down!

From the Hugisattel, a high col on the North-West Ridge of the Finster- aarhorn, the route becomes much more interesting. It is a fairly sharp rock ridge where many of the difficulties can be easily turned on the western side. It took us about an hour to reach the summit and I enjoyed every minute of it. The rocks were covered in some places by old snow and in others by the previous day's fresh fall, but it was straightforward to climb. I really felt on form. Les and I were the first to the summit, with the others close behind, and we sat for quite some time eating, taking photographs of each other and hoping for a view. The clouds were moving about and every now and then there was a glimpse of some blue sky or a snowy slope, but we would have had to wait at least another hour to see the other peaks. Not being prepared to do this, we set off back down the mountain without the privilege of viewing the whole Alpine panorama laid out at the foot of the highest peak of the Bernese Oberland.

Back at the Hugisattel, new distractions awaited us. There we met two German girls whose boyfriends had left them sitting by the rocks whilst they climbed on to the summit. The boys had spoken to Geoff and Allan, asking if they would accompany the girls back down to the hut. Much merriment ensued as our four menfolk were only too delighted to act as escorts to such charming young women. The consequences, however, were unforeseen: our party became involved in helping to keep the girls calm for several worrying hours.

We returned safely to the Finsteraarhorn Hut in time for a midday lunch but the German boys did not arrive back until 7.00 or 8.00 pm, by which time the two girls were in a serious state of anxiety. It seemed that the boys had gone to the summit and returned safely to the Hugisattel but their friends, who had climbed by a different route, had been very slow and no-one had thought to descend quickly in advance to warn the girls of the delay.

The next morning was perfect. It had frozen overnight and the sky was clear. Our objective was to traverse the Gross Fiescherhorn, then stay a couple of nights at a hut from which we could ascend the Mönch and Jungfrau before descending to the valley again. We had been intending to make for the Bergli Hut, about 200m below the Unders Mönchjoch on its north side, but the previous evening we had been chatting to a Swiss guide from Grindelwald. He suggested that we go to the new, privately owned Obermönchjoch Hut, and that is what we did. This saved us a slight detour.

The guide and his party were in fact going over the Gross Fiescherhorn too, and they set off more promptly than us in the morning. We could see them ahead of us on the glacier and as time went by they disappeared into the distance; they were moving really well. There was a beautiful dawn, but we only saw a little of it, as we were heading north-westwards and we didn't stop very often. I didn't feel quite as fit as the day before and when we reached the bottom of the ice fall, I was glad of a short rest whilst we put on our crampons.

We climbed the ice fall as quickly as we could, because there was a certain amount of objective danger from overhanging ice in the glacier itself and from stones falling from the cliff on the left side of the glacier. One small stone did in fact ping right past Les. In the middle of the ice fall there was just one rather entertaining step, where we had to move sideways in crablike fashion across the lip of a crevasse to reach the narrowest point where we could pull over it. We were roped together in two parties of three that day, John Oaks with us, and that made this particular manoeuvre very secure for me, the one in the middle.

Above the ice fall the pace eased off and we made our way towards the head of the Fiescher Glacier. There we paused and whilst we were having a bite to eat, we assessed the difficulties of the mountain in front of us, which we thought we were going to climb. It looked quite sharp, with large cornices on the far side, and there was no sign of the guided party. We set off again, and then, all of a sudden, Les stopped and shouted – we were going the wrong way! We were heading for Ochs; the Fiescherhorn was in the opposite direction! Although the guidebook stated that parties could easily lose their way here in mist, we had no such excuse as we stood there under bright sunshine and a clear blue sky.

We turned about and continued upwards to the saddle between the Gross- and Hinterfiescherhorn. From there, we had to ascend the 'easy' rocks (I quote from the guidebook). However, that was where I began to feel a little nervous. The previous day I had stumbled and taken a slight fall on my descent from the summit of the Finsteraarhorn. Probably this had unsettled me and I really didn't enjoy climbing the short ridge to the summit, an experience more awkward than it might have been as I was still wearing crampons. Indeed, at one point, John had to hold my foot in place as I squirmed around reaching for a high handhold on an exposed slab.

All that was forgotten when we stood on the summit of the Fiescherhorn. The view was superb: snow-capped mountains, knife-edge ridges, lengthy glaciers and, above all, the Finsteraarhorn, 'monarch of the Bernese Oberland', with the airy crest that we had ascended the day before. A chilly wind deterred us from spending very long on the top of our spectacularly situated Fourthousander and, as soon as our friends had arrived, John set off on the descent, with Les encouraging me from behind. At first we had to descend on narrow, exposed strips of snow on a fairly steep ridge. Then the gradient eased but, instead of continuing straight down over a rock step, we had to climb a rope's length down the 50° snow slope at the top of the Fiescherwand, the north wall of the Fiescherhorn. The top few feet were icy and then there were bucket steps made by previous parties. Despite the relative safety of these, we descended with extreme caution, facing inwards to the slope, and I was always belayed by one or other of my partners. A slip here could send you hurtling several hundred metres to your doom.

Once we were back on the ridge, the descent became much easier, and we were able to walk the rest of the way, even on the steepest sections. When we reached the glacier, we just kept going. Geoff, Dave and Allan followed us more slowly and, as soon as we had ascertained that they were safe, we carried on without waiting, as it was quite cold. Far away on the other side of the glacier, the Ewigschneefeld, we could see the hut perched just above the Obers Mönchjoch. This hut can be reached quite easily from the top station of the Jungfrau railway on the other side of the col, but from our direction there was still a long snow basin to cross and the sun was beating down relentlessly. Fortunately, the chill breeze had stopped the snow from melting and it was not too difficult to make progress. If the snow had been soft, we would have taken much longer. In fact:

I was going very well now, almost like a racehorse sensing the stable at the end of the run in past the post and it was Les, not I, who insisted on stopping for a couple of rests on the last slope up to the col.

The Obermönchjoch Hut was still very new at that time and seemed as smart as a palace, in contrast to the much older Finsteraarhorn Hut where we had spent the previous two nights. However, our new abode had one disturbing characteristic. We spent the next two nights there and, through-out both, suffered from strong gales. The hut sits on steel girders, which attach it to the lower slopes of the Mönch, just above the col, and as soon as the wind blew with any force, the whole hut seemed to heave violently like a ship on a tempestuous ocean. As I lay in my bunk by the outer wall of the hut, I felt as if I were receiving the full force of the storm. My imagination worked overtime. It was not conducive to peaceful sleep.

At least we didn't have to rise before daylight to climb the Mönch. A mere one and half hours was sufficient for us to reach the summit, so a 7.00 am start meant that we were basking in the sun at the top by half-past eight. The night storms had abated. There below us lay the South Ridge of the Eiger. It seems unfair that such a well-known peak reaches only 3970m, but for 4000m peak-baggers it is perhaps just as well: the Eiger guards its own summit jealously by offering a choice of approaches from the challen-ging to the downright dangerous. Even the Normal Route up its western flank is subject to stonefall.

Back at the hut we rested for the remainder of the day, then the weather deteriorated again and it began to snow. The white stuff fell all night and next morning we looked out into dense mist. There was no question now of climbing the Jungfrau, so we simply set out for the Rhône Valley – no mean undertaking in a whiteout. Les led us without incident through the maze of crevasses on the Aletsch Glacier and once below the Konkordiaplatz we were able to unrope and walk down the bare ice, leaping over crevasse after crevasse for mile upon mile on our way back to the valley. The weather improved as the day went on, and a glance behind revealed the mountains we had climbed and those we had not. In the vicinity of the Aletsch Glacier there were only two Fourthousanders I had never ascended: the Jungfrau and the Aletschhorn. These were two peaks we both wanted to climb and, for me especially, it was the Jungfrau that held a magnetic attraction.

After our Bernese Oberland tour, we all moved to Randa and from there went up to the Dom Hut. I still remember fondly my first walk up the steep slopes to that hut in 1976: the views behind us of the Weisshorn, the scent of pinewoods, the open pastures above and the goats peering over the rocks as we climbed the cliffs way up the mountain. I shall never forget how fit I felt on that occasion. We still have a photograph of my arrival at the hut, a striped cotton scarf shielding my head from the midday sun, a grin of satisfaction on my still youthful face as I strode happily towards the terrace. I have stood there several times since, transfixed by the glory of the Matterhorn.

In 1979, this second ascent to the Dom Hut seemed more arduous than I remembered, but it was very pleasant to be greeted once again by the friendly guardian. We were intending primarily to climb the Kin Face on the Täschhorn. None of us had voiced any thoughts of doing more than that, but the conditions of both snow and rock were excellent and so, after our ascent of that peak, we changed our plans, tempted by the sight of the ridge connecting the Täschhorn to the Dom. That was indeed my great year. I had health and fitness, perfect weather and conditions, and a partner who believed in my ability to move on to more serious mountaineering. During the main part of the summer season, I also had four other climbing companions who not only helped me in their various ways with the ascents and descents, but also contributed enormously to the sheer enjoyment of the whole experience. We had such fun and shared so much magic.

Later that year I felt so pleased with my achievements that I wanted to share my thoughts with others. So it was that, encouraged by Walter Kirstein, I wrote my article 'Perpetual Second' for the Alpine Journal. It describes our day on the Täschhorn-Dom traverse so clearly that I here quote parts of it, along with extracts from my journal. The following passage from the article explains how the day began:

As we set out in the night for the Kin Face [of the Täschhorn], I was rather grumpy. My enthusiasm for nocturnal starts had disappeared when I discovered that this time half the party had already set off without me up the moraine. Evidently I had been too inefficient at getting myself organised. So I spent the first hour and a half in very low spirits, wondering why I ever go climbing in the Alps at all! How much easier it must be to spend one's summer holidays just lazing on a Mediterranean beach.

Evidently I'd forgotten my feelings about the summer beach scene when we'd visited the Mediterranean coast at the end of our 1977 Alpine season.

That morning I was not at my best, either in mind or in body. Perhaps I should have taken a longer rest after our intensive tour in the Bernese Oberland. On the first part of the route to the Täschhorn we walked unroped for what seemed like ages up a long, stony band of moraine in the direction of the Dom.

Eventually we broke off to the right over the glacier, and on the other side the going became much steeper. There, I found that my physical condition was as poor as my mental condition. It was a real struggle to get up to the bergschrund below the Festi-Kinlücke.

After a little detour to find a point where we could cross this awkward *bergschrund*, we reached the ridge above, then had to descend a frighteningly loose scree slope to reach the Kin Glacier. I quaked at the thought of reversing this unpleasant step and abseiling back down the steep slope on the other side. It would also require a leap backwards over the yawning gap of the *bergschrund* in order to regain the Festi Glacier and the trail back to the hut. At that stage we were still intending to return by the same route.

As we started to climb the 830m Kin Face of the Täschhorn, despite feeling weary, I began to enjoy myself. That morning Les and I were in a rope of three with John and the snow was in excellent condition. Such can be the seemingly instantaneous transformation of one's mood! The scenery was superb: as we moved steadily towards some perilous-looking séracs three-quarters of the way up the face, I glanced as often as I could at the Fourthousanders on the western side of the Zermatt Valley: the Weisshorn, Zinalrothorn and Obergabelhorn. I also gazed upwards in awe at the ridge between the summits of the Täschhorn and the Dom. A question was forming in my mind. It was becoming obvious that the ridge would be in very straightforward condition, and I was well aware that for years Les had wanted to make the classic traverse from one peak to the other. Eventually we reached the ice barrier. In the AJ, I wrote:

At this point we cut across leftwards … to gain the steep, but less dangerous slope above. Some verglased rocks brought us on to the last few metres of the Teufelsgrat … Here the adrenalin suddenly seemed to start pumping round in my body.

Whatever must young Mrs. Mummery, bride of the formidable mountaineer Alfred, have thought in 1887 when she found herself not only making the first ascent of this dramatic ridge, with all its inherent dangers, but also having to endure the bitter cold of an ice-storm and the eeriness of approaching thunder as her husband and their guide led upwards into the unknown? She was made of stern stuff: she remained cheerful in the face of all their difficulties and even gave psychological support to the second guide who sustained a fall and became demoralised.[3] Almost a century later, I stepped out on to the uppermost section of the very same ridge. The AJ continued:

The situation reminded me rather of Le Rasoir on the Zinalrothorn – small gaps to be crossed on razor edges perched high above a staggering void. With my heart in my mouth I reached the summit, where a few moments' relaxation in the sun soon brought me back to my thoughts of only thirty minutes previously, as yet unvoiced: that this was an opportunity not to be missed, with the Täschhorn-Dom traverse literally at our feet in almost perfect condition. But I couldn't help wondering if I was up to it in my present frame of mind. So far this season fitness had been no problem, I had been climbing as I had never climbed before, but on this particular morning I had been going far from well. On the other hand, if I insisted on going down, Les would probably have been obliged to accompany me … I couldn't bear to let him down and, in any case, I myself … found the lure of that aesthetic knife-edge gleaming in the sun almost irresistible. The decision was made: we would go on.

Determined not to let the side down, determined not in any way to spoil the enjoyment of my two highly competent partners, I gritted my teeth and climbed as expertly and confidently as I had ever done. The intense sense of satisfaction and delight that this gave me was reward indeed. This much, at least, I surely share with Mrs. Mummery and the other 'petticoat pioneers' of the 19th century, as well as countless other intrepid women, such as Dorothy Pilley Richards, Dorothy Thompson and their peers in the Ladies' Alpine Club in the years before the Second World War. Yet there were marked differences. Their ropes were hemp, ours nylon; their boots had nails, ours Vibram soles. Then, too, although just a few were beginning to climb guideless and on ladies-only ropes, they mostly climbed with professional guides, whereas I always climbed with experienced amateurs and, in the Alps, was only ever on a mixed rope. And, in their day, the routes were less well known and less well documented. These women were naturally very talented climbers and some, if not all, had started walking and scrambling in the British mountains in their early years.

---

3 *Women on the Rope* by Cicely Williams

I, on the other hand – who only started mountaineering in my mid-twenties after an unathletic childhood – had spent years learning to steel my nerves and acquiring techniques which did not come naturally. Nevertheless, I am certain that the exhilaration, that sensation of utter joy, as I climbed these great classic routes of the Alps was very much the same as theirs.

We left the summit of the Täschhorn and headed for the Dom. The route starts by descending a long, very narrow, exposed rock crest, with a drop on either side of at least six or seven hundred metres:

John went in front and gave me kind, curt directions wherever the rocks were the slightest bit awkward. I followed him without hesitation, except at one point where short people had to grab a sling, and swing out over space in an effort to reach the comparative comfort of the next handhold, which was more than my arm's length away.

In my own journal I continued the story:

I excelled myself, no doubt much to the surprise of the others … Les secured me from behind, as we moved together … never hassling me. The situation here was so serious. The whole ridge from the summit of the Täschhorn to the col is extremely exposed. Saas Fee lies directly below you on the one side, thousands of feet down almost vertical slopes, and on the other side, equally vertiginously, lies the Zermatt Valley. There was a slight sprinkling of fresh snow on some of the rocks, so we had to be careful, but on the whole the ridge was in good condition. I began to grasp the hitherto rarely-used technique of hand-traversing fairly quickly as there was slab after slab to descend in this manner, precariously perched above the two valleys.

Well ahead of the other rope of three, after about two hours, we reached the col between the two mountains:

Two hours of acute mental tension, broken here and there by an equally acute sensation of delight. It was a lovely morning: perfect weather; no need to fear oncoming storms.

At the col we took a break and refuelled ourselves. When our three friends arrived, we roped up in three pairs and Les and I set off whilst the others took a break. As I was always likely to be the slowest when climbing uphill, we knew that they would soon catch us up.

Again my journal recalls my experience:

I was really looking forward to climbing up the ridge in front of us, as it was mainly in the sun and clear of snow. It looked most inviting. Within minutes I was to change my mind. The very first turret we had to ascend was completely loose – just one wobbly stone on top of another, like a rickety drystone wall – and so it went on. Into the bargain there was a team of four incompetent climbers in front of us, hell-bent on blowing our brains out with the rocks they kept showering down behind them. It was an age before Les succeeded in passing them and only then could I begin to relax.

By then, the other members of our own party had caught us up:

When we reached the final tower, I was beginning to flag a bit and Dave and John were climbing more or less level with me. In places I was beginning to find it quite a struggle to heave myself up the awkward moves. There was a helicopter flying around too, apparently filming, though we didn't know that at the time, and I found it slightly off-putting. At least the rock on this upper section was a little more solid. Just a few more rope-lengths and I could scarcely believe it – there we were a few feet below the summit cross! Dave and John went ahead so that Les could take a photo of them and then there we all were, squatting on rucksacks and coils of rope, celebrating our success on the top of Switzerland!

Delighted as I had been in 1976, when we first ascended the Dom with John Oaks and Andy Hodges, the feeling of achievement on this second arrival at the summit was overwhelming. Not only had I succeeded in supporting Les in his long-held ambition to do this spectacular traverse, but I had also completed it myself with considerable competence, stamina and enjoyment. I had overcome my few remaining doubts and fears about climbing in exposed places and I knew I had broken through to a higher level in my mountaineering career. I remember little about the long descent from the summit, the trudge from the Festijoch down the final glacier and the stony track along the moraine to the Dom Hut. It must have been quite gruelling after such a long climb but I was in a state of euphoria and cared little about the inevitable weariness.

About fourteen hours after our early start, we finally arrived at the hut, where the guardian greeted us with great cheer and praise for our achievement. We had lived up to his idea of 'British alpinists'. He supplied us with non-stop tea-water and an immense bowl of soup. After a nightcap of red wine, we slept soundly and next day gently returned down the steep path to the valley. Uncomfortable as the descent was for those of us whose knees were giving signs of wear and tear, our souls were still basking in a sensation of glory.

Fulfilled though we all were, the 1979 season was not yet quite over and we just had time for one more route. Whilst Les and John took the train up the valley to Zermatt to tackle an ice route on the Liskamm, Geoff, Dave, Allan and I drove above the village of Täsch to take the short, easy walk to the hut of the same name, where we were to spend the night. For the first time that holiday, I was to climb with someone other than Les and this contributed to a feeling of satisfaction at having become a climber in my own right. Even though Geoff was just as much my leader as Les ever was, just as expert a climber, and I was still a mere second, I felt much more responsible for my actions than usual, and acutely aware that I represented women climbers. For that reason alone, I was determined not to 'let the side down'. In the AJ I described this new experience too:

The four of us climbed the Rotgrat on the Alphubel on another perfect day. This was my third ascent of the Alphubel within 12 months! Yet each time I climbed a different route and each time the pleasures were very different. Everything about this climb was superb. We left the hut in the dark and dawn was just breaking as we were starting to climb the Wissgrat, which leads up to the rock knoll where you join the Rotgrat proper. It was cold and crystal clear, the mountains were bathed in the most beautiful pink glow, the rock we were climbing on was clean and dry and for the first few hundred feet there were alpine flowers peeping out of every tiny crevice.

Geoff must have seen many times how well Les always looked after me on a climb, especially a rock climb where I might be a little hesitant, but I hoped that he would now realise, after so recently seeing my assured performance on the Dom-Täschhorn traverse, that I had become quite competent. However, he was keen not to take any chances and I was grateful for that, so we roped up at a fairly low point on the rock ridge. Meanwhile, Allan and Dave carried on soloing for a while.

So we lagged a little behind the other two men, but we caught them up when we reached the top of the snow-shoulder, where the rock step seemed to present some navigational difficulties. Here we lost quite some time trying to find the gangway system mentioned in the guidebook, a line that was very obvious when we did eventually find it, just a few feet directly above the snow-shoulder.

Geoff now exchanged his cumbersome Dachstein mitts for a pair of gloves, and not just his usual old relics either. Out came a packet of brand new thermal gloves from Damart – nothing but the best that day! It was certainly the right choice. The traverse was on thin holds and the rock extremely cold to touch.

When we moved out rightwards on to the more exposed part of the ridge we were in the full blast of an icy cold wind and the more we delayed in our route-finding the more numb our fingers became. By the time it was my turn to follow Geoff up a delicate little slab overhanging the big gully on the right, my fingers were quite dead and I couldn't feel a thing.

Somewhere above this point, after we had warmed up a little, we came to a ledge completely covered with a layer of broken quartz. These little chunks of rock gleamed a brilliant white in the morning sun. It was quite stunning. We carried on without any more halts up to the rocky crest and within 100m of the top of the Rotgrat. There we opted to take the snow slope on the left-hand side to reach the summit ridge. At the start of the route, Geoff had seemed very protective towards me, perhaps concerned that he was taking Les's leadership role for the day. Now the atmosphere had changed and Geoff offered me the lead on the icy pitch. I was delighted to take responsibility for a change. It was exhilarating. Allan and Dave were now some way behind us.

The following entry in my journal completes the tale:

Geoff and I had somehow stolen the lead again, and we were able to enjoy the superb silence of the summit for a few minutes completely alone. On my two previous visits there had been several other parties standing or sitting around on this large snow plateau. My joy at being able to relax there in solitude was a bonus I hadn't expected. I scanned the slopes of the North Face of the nearby Liskamm for signs of John and Les on their route. In fact, it wasn't possible to see them, and even if they had known where we were at that moment, it is unlikely they would have been able to see us either.

The Alphubel really is located in one of the most magnificent spots of the Alps. It is lower than its neighbours, which tower around it in every direction, and therefore the view it offers is even more rewarding than when looking down from one of the higher peaks. I have never forgotten my disappointment at the view from the top of the Matterhorn, when the surrounding peaks all seemed dwarfed.

The first time I climbed the Alphubel, it was a sunny summer's day and I was able to sit gazing at the panorama laid out around me under a clear blue sky. The next time, we were not so fortunate, as a bitterly cold wind deterred us from admiring the view. On this third occasion, however, I was absolutely elated. Not only was the panorama so spectacular, but also I experienced a warm glow of satisfaction at having climbed a more challenging route than on the first two ascents, as well as the pleasing consciousness of having taken far more responsibility for my actions than hitherto, when I climbed on autopilot with my husband. My satisfaction was only slightly tempered by the contradictory sense of loss that I wasn't sharing such a delightful moment with Les, as well as Geoff, Allan and Dave.

For ten seasons I had climbed in the role of perpetual second. During most of that time, this fact barely registered with me but now I realised how much I enjoyed being at the sharp end of the rope. Certainly I felt confident that I could cope with situations that, a few years previously, would have given me an attack of nerves. I understood my limits so much better now, too, and knowing I couldn't lead everything I wanted to do, I saw no shame in continuing to second any route that I was capable of climbing. Leaders need a second, even if they don't share the lead, and I was confident that I could fulfil that role to the satisfaction of most of my potential Alpine partners. The year 1979 had convinced me that I had become a competent alpinist in my own right.

3

HYPERACTIVITY

Becoming President of our local mountaineering club had given me an opportunity at last to break out from my hitherto secondary role in most aspects of my life. I discovered that I thoroughly enjoyed taking the lead. For three years, I chaired the committee and the Annual General Meetings. It was a particularly busy period for the club, as the roof of our hut urgently needed replacing and we had to raise funding. We were also organising a grand reunion for the 25th cnniversary of the foundation of the club. All this kept me very active in a new way and, to a certain extent, compensated for the lack of opportunities for advancement in my professional life.

At the beginning of the 1980s, I was still working at the same old-fashioned technical college, where sexist attitudes towards promotion continued to prevail. Now in my late thirties, I felt more and more stuck in a rut. However, there was one advantage. Until now, my work had not been particularly challenging, so, after ten years, I was able to carry out most of my teaching commitments on autopilot. This gave me plenty of spare time to concentrate on mountaineering, but the downside was that I was beginning to hanker after work with greater intellectual depth. My solution was to enrol for a part-time Master's degree course in 1981 and so, in addition to my full-time college work, for two years I travelled once a week to evening lectures in Birmingham and spent a vast amount of time on all the associated academic activities. Exhausting, it may have been, but it was extremely fulfilling and, despite the enormous extra workload, I still managed to fit in a considerable amount of mountaineering.

It was also at this time that I became more conscious of being not just a mountain climber but a female mountain climber. It seemed to me that I needed to rock climb with other women in order to gain some independence from the male leadership that I had accepted without reservation up to this point. It was not that I resented my situation vis-à-vis my husband and our men friends. Indeed, I enjoyed climbing with them all and was happy to push myself on routes that I would never have dreamed of leading. What I needed to do, however, was to prove to myself that I was competent within my comfort zone. For that, I had to start leading the easiest rock routes.

At that stage, I knew very few female lead climbers and had never understood until now just why an all-female organisation such as the Pinnacle Club existed. It was founded in the 1920s, 'when women wished to concentrate on their rock-climbing skills and lead expeditions', as Shirley Angell says in the introduction to her history of the Club.[1] It was not a case of women disliking men or never climbing with men. It was simply that women wanted to climb on their own terms and, in 1980, I was beginning to have a similar attitude.

What I did not understand at the time was that I wasn't really a rock climber at all. I was a mountain climber. The two terms are not synonymous. I did know, however, that in order to be a totally independent, competent mountain climber, not just a mountain walker, I needed to improve my rock-climbing skills to the requisite level for the mountain routes I was likely to climb.

Over the next few years I took the opportunity whenever it arose to climb with partners other than Les – and sometimes to share the lead on easy rock routes. Les was pursuing his own climbing ambitions on harder routes with other partners but I had no desire to complicate my already hectic life with trips away from home with yet another organisation, such as the Pinnacle Club. So, despite encouragement from a few women friends, I made no effort to diversify in that way.

We continued to travel to mountain areas on a couple of weekends each month and, between times, we would rock climb in the Wye Valley and other places not too far from home. New friends encouraged me to try off-road running, but I soon found that this caused sciatic twinges, so I never took it up seriously. Thanks to the opening of an excellent new pool near the college, I also started swimming regularly so, all in all, I was not only active at every conceivable opportunity but was greatly improving my fitness and stamina. Frequent hill walking was still the essential basis of my training for mountaineering.

It never occurred to me, whilst taking all this exercise, working full-time and running a home, that I might be overreaching myself. After all, our college jobs still gave us extremely long summer holidays. The official break of eight weeks was entirely ours to spend as we wished. It was not until the 1990s that the terms of our employment changed and college vacations for the staff were radically reduced. There was never any need for either Les

---

1 *Pinnacle Club, A History of Women Climbing* by Shirley Angell

or me to do lesson preparation or any other work during the summer. Each year, Les would have more or less the same timetable during college terms and needed to make few changes to his well-rehearsed teaching routine. This suited him very well.

My situation the previous decade had been more complicated. Although some of my work was foreseeable, approximately half my timetable consisted of teaching French and German to adults, not only in the daytime, but also in the evenings. The college day ran from 9.00 am to 9.30 pm, and I never had any exact idea of what new classes I would have until the enrolment phase was over in September. At that point, I would have to dive straight in, using all my energy and abilities to devise a programme of work to suit the customers who had signed up. This was stressful but not difficult, as the academic level was well within my competence. Now, in the 1980s, reorganisation was taking place on a grand scale. My teaching duties continued to be very straightforward but, at last, my work schedule was becoming more predictable from year to year and most of the evening classes disappeared from my timetable. In that respect, life became much less complex. Even during the period when I was studying for my Master's degree, I managed to fit in a great deal of walking and climbing at weekends.

Throughout the decade, we continued to go to Scotland for our halfterm holiday at the end of May every year. We were now concentrating on doing the Munros, the mountains over 3000 feet (914.4m), and, whenever the weather permitted, climbing classic rock routes. All through the 1980s, this week of sustained mountain activity played a vital role in keeping us fit for the summer visit to the Alps, when we would climb as many peaks as circumstances permitted, occasionally stopping for a day's rest. Over the summers of 1980, 1981 and 1982, I made a great many Alpine ascents, including scaling sixteen new Fourthousanders. Some of these were amongst the highest in the Alps and via routes that required considerable skill and stamina. I was on top form, energised and contented with my lifestyle.

4

THE BEGINNING
OF A NEW ERA

A sustained period of poor weather endured throughout the summer term of 1980, both in England and the Alps. There was a great deal of precipitation and very little sunshine. Thus, the Alps were still covered in a thick layer of spring snow when, in early July, we returned to Switzerland for the third time that year. Grindelwald was not the ideal destination in these conditions: the Bernese Oberland peaks were too high to be in condition until the snow had melted off the rock routes and consolidated on the glacier approaches.

Les and I had several new companions for the summer season. Ian and Sue Stirrups and Pete and Margaret Fleming were with us for three weeks. John Howe, a member of the Lincoln Mountaineering Club, was also one of the party. He was a proficient rock climber but had little experience on Alpine snow routes. We had walked and climbed with him on LMC meets in the Lake District.

We had first met Ian and Sue on a meet at the George Starkey Hut in Patterdale in February 1979. At that time, they were living in Croydon but, to our great surprise, one evening in the early part of that summer we met them again, at the foot of our local crag. That was the beginning of a long friendship. Ian, an actuary in his late twenties, had recently taken a new job in Gloucester. They were both quite experienced rock climbers. Sue, several years younger, had started climbing at Harrison's Rocks, a sandstone crag in East Sussex, in her late teens. They had already done some Alpine climbing and were very fit, enjoying running as well as climbing. In fact, Sue had been a successful competitive cross-country runner for many years. She encouraged me to try running, as a means of keeping fit, and for a few years I did a little jogging, mainly on the hill behind our house. They also encouraged me to rock climb wherever we went together at weekends, whether in the mountains or on the Wye Valley crags not far from home. Ian, in particular, pushed me to lead easy pitches on easy routes. Thus they both helped me to improve my fitness and my confidence.

Pete and Margaret Fleming were from Barrow-in-Furness. We had got to know Pete on a meet he was leading for the Alpine Club and ABMSAC in March 1979 in Wasdale. During that winter weekend, Pete and Les walked together and discovered that they had a great deal in common as far as Alpine mountaineering was concerned. That summer, Pete spent his spare time in the Himalaya, so it was not until the next year that we had our first opportunity to climb with him in the Alps.

On leaving school in the early 1950s, Pete had discovered the hills of the Lake District and that soon led to his first Alpine season. In 1956, he was in Zermatt and, like Les, wasted no time in getting to the top of the big peaks. His first Fourthousander was the Matterhorn. However, as a marine engineer, away in the Merchant Navy for several years, his opportunities to climb in the Alps were somewhat curtailed until he returned to live and work in Barrow. By the time we first met him, he had had many seasons in the Alps. Pete was also a long-term member of the F&RCC; he had become an accomplished rock climber and had a reputation for walking extremely fast on the hills.

Margaret also enjoyed the mountains and was happy to walk, but didn't climb. In the years that followed our first meeting, she accompanied us on our trips abroad, supported us in many ways and became a trusted friend whose company I greatly valued, particularly when we were alone together at campsites, awaiting the return of our husbands from climbs they undertook without me. I never ceased to be amazed at Margaret's patience and tolerance of our frequent absences, when all three of us were up in the mountains without her. It is unlikely that I would have been as understanding in such a situation.

From Grindelwald, that July in 1980, the Wetterhorn and Mittelhorn served as training routes, enabling acclimatisation, but were hard going in soft snow. It had been our intention to climb several of the 4000m peaks in the vicinity, but the conditions were against us. The Lauteraarhorn was an early objective: Pete, Les and I set out from the Strahlegg Hut to climb it but it soon became clear that deep snow would prevent us from reaching our target. We settled for the considerably lower and nearer Strahlegghorn instead.

Our party split for a while after that. Whilst Ian, Sue and John stayed in the Bernese Oberland to climb another peak there, Pete, Margaret, Les and I left Grindelwald and drove to Chamonix, where Les and Pete had several objectives. Pete was intent on finishing his list of Fourthousanders and had inspired Les to consider doing the same, especially when he realised that he and Les each had almost as few peaks left to collect as each other. So, from then onwards, although they both continued to climb any mountain or route that appealed to them, some of their plans became specifically focused on the Fourthousanders they had not yet climbed. They made a formidable team: swift and highly competent. I was very privileged to have two such companions and especially fortunate that they wanted to take me along on routes that were within my competence. When they decided to climb harder routes, however, there was no question of me accompanying them, and indeed I had no wish to overreach myself. What I was already doing seemed daring enough. So I was only too happy to have some extra rest days in the valley with Margaret. We had some really pleasant times together, sometimes walking, sometimes simply relaxing, whilst our husbands were away 'up the hill'. In this way I was able to gather strength to return to the higher peaks a few days later.

It was from Chamonix that I tackled my next Fourthousander. The Aiguille Verte had excited my imagination in the early 1970s when I walked with Sue Wornham on the big hills on the other side of the Arve Valley, looking across at the Dru. It is a great pillar of rock but seems almost to melt into the face of the snow-capped Verte behind. Magical mountains, they seemed to me. Two years had passed since Les and I had first walked up the Talèfre Glacier to the foot of the Whymper Couloir on the Aiguille Verte, then turned back because the night was too warm and the snow too soft. Now, with Pete, we set out again for the same route. At a quarter to one on a very dark night, we left the Couvercle Hut. Only one or two other parties had risen at the same time and, of them, only one pair climbed the same route as us. We trekked in silence up the glacier on the approach to the mountain, taking some time to find the best place to cross the *bergschrund* at the bottom of the couloir. This time the snow was firm enough to start the climb. The first problem was immediately evident: we were faced with some six metres of vertical climbing above a gaping hole, with only a thin snow bridge connecting the upper lip to the lower edge. In the dark, however, I was not too intimidated by the delicacy of the situation; it was not until later that morning, when we descended, that I could really see the void below.

Once over the *bergschrund*, we continued steeply up a snow gully until it became easier to move on to the rocks on the left. There we climbed an awkward crack – at least it seemed so in the dark – leading us to a mixed snow and rock rib. When we reached the main couloir, I felt as if the climb would never end. The couloir just continued on and on upwards at an ever-steepening angle, attaining about 55° towards the top. The snow was hard and for much of the way we were on the front points of our crampons, with the result that our calf muscles ached more and more. We were in the

Whymper Couloir for about three hours and for most of that time it was dark and seemed as if the night would last forever. It was nearly 6.00 am when daylight came.

At last we stepped out on to the col at the top and could see a party coming up on the other side from the Couturier Couloir. That may be a more serious route than the Whymper Couloir, but it is all a question of what the limit of endurance and skill is for each individual climber. At 7.00 am we reached the summit and I was almost weeping with relief, our route having sapped so much of my physical and nervous energy. It would have been an appropriate reward to take a long rest there in warm sunshine, savouring the delight of achieving this long-held ambition to reach the top of one of the most aesthetically attractive peaks in the Mont Blanc Massif – but it was not to be. It was bitterly cold and we only stopped long enough to take a few photographs and have a quick bite to eat before turning back to our couloir again, this time just behind the other two climbers who had followed us up our route. None of us could afford to delay our descent because once the sun starts to warm up the snow, the Whymper Couloir is very prone to stonefall.

Every so often, in all forms of mountaineering, it is the case that there is only a very brief time at the top of a route to relish the sensation of joy. John Oaks once reminded me not to become too elated until we had returned safely from the climb. At the time, we were at the top of the 'Forty Foot Corner', the crux pitch halfway up Great Slab, the fine VS route on Clogwyn D'ur Arddu. I have never forgotten this sensible advice. On the summit of the Aiguille Verte, Pete, Les and I respected the 'Forces of Nature' and decided not to delay our retreat any longer than necessary. The time to savour the reward of our successful ascent of the hostile couloir would come later, when we were safely back at the hut.

As a rope of three, facing inwards most of the time on this descent, we had to make haste rather slowly. It was tedious and nerve-racking. Despite the fact that there were only two of them, the other party was progressing no faster than we were and the noise they were making discomforted me. After a while we managed to pass them and we kept pressing on down to beat the clock. Stones were beginning to fall. By the time we reached the steep gully above the *bergschrund*, I felt as if I could hear my calf muscles screeching in agony. I kept thinking to myself, 'How much longer do I have to endure this pain?' By then, my mood was such that I had no wish to climb any more mountains at all that summer. At last we were on the glacier, unroped and at ease. Les shot away to the hut, leaving Pete and me to slither along at our leisure in the soft snow. It was twelve hours since we had set out that morning and we still had to carry all our gear back down the Mer de Glace to Montenvers, where we would take the railway down to Chamonix and to Margaret, waiting for us at the campsite.

I would have appreciated a rest in the valley, but the Stirrupses and John Howe had arrived after their detour in the Western Bernese Alps. They were now acclimatised and keen to get up high as soon as possible in the Mont Blanc Massif. I was persuaded to join the three of them in the traverse of the Rochefort Arête, a classic snow ridge that connects the Dent du Géant with the Aiguille de Rochefort on the frontier ridge between France and Italy. Both of these points are 4000m peaks but, at that time, this fact still had no great significance for me. Thus, I didn't give any thought to the Dôme de Rochefort, which also qualifies for the List and lies a little further to the east along the same ridge. Leaving Les with Pete and Margaret at the campsite in Chamonix, we four drove through the Mont Blanc tunnel and took the cable car up from La Palud towards the Col du Géant.

From the top téléphérique station at 3375m, weighed down by more gear than usual, including a litre of milk and a bottle of red wine, I puffed my way up a long, steep staircase to the Torino Hut. In 1980, this refuge was in a state of considerable disrepair. When we checked into our dormitory, which reminded me of a youth hostel with its ugly, iron bunk beds, I didn't realise that the roof above me would leak when it rained. The afternoon was sunny and fine, so no such thought crossed my mind. We spent some time outdoors and were pottering about on the glacier, looking to see where the route led up towards the Géant, when Ian discovered we had left the guidebook at the campsite. Later, I was able to borrow a French route card from a friendly fellow climber and copied down the description. Unfortunately, the French instructions gave more information than the English synopsis and I discovered that there would be a 30m abseil. That got the wind up me straightaway, as Les had lent John and me his short rope. Would it be long enough?

Whilst we were on the glacier that afternoon, there had been a stiff breeze. By evening it was growing stronger and the sky closed in with strange cloud formations. By the time we rose in the darkness for an early breakfast, there were no stars to be seen and visibility on the glacier was poor. We hoped that dawn would bring a change. It did, but for the worse. Rain began to fall and the glacier completely disappeared from view. We went back to bed.

By 8.00 am it was lashing down with rain and we decided to lie in, drinking tea that we had brewed in the dormitory. What a luxury! But, very soon, water began to drip through the ceiling at the end of my bunk and within three hours the floor was awash. We were forced eventually to evacuate to another dormitory, when the guardian was finally disposed to let us move in. I have limited experience of hut guardians in Italy but, generally, I found them inclined to be fairly rigid in their approach to accommodating us.

We turned in that night, still unsure whether we would be able to climb the following morning, as thick cloud and rain had persisted all day. By 4.00 am the stars were out and it was a sparkling, clear night, so we set out an hour later and were rewarded by a fine, sunny day. How strange the weather can be.

Our route had the great merit of starting downhill for a quarter of an hour. John and I roped up and followed Ian and Sue. Ahead of us, a trail of several torchlights progressed towards the couloir below the Géant and we caught up with some of them before the route steepened. There were no problems at all but we moved quite slowly, taking care not to disturb loose rock. Near the top, I made a route-finding error, so John and I were temporarily out of touch with Ian and Sue; we soon caught them up again, however, as they were debating about a snow section. Here my makeshift 'route card' was called for and a decision made: just one tricky rock slab to be traversed, which looked more awkward than it really was, and beyond it a little gully with some ice and snow. We arrived at the Salle à Manger, a broad area of snow on the ridge at the foot of the South Face of the Géant. There we had a brief rest before moving on. None of us intended to climb the Géant that day and, indeed, I could not at that moment imagine that I ever would. The Dent du Géant is a steep rock 'tooth', rising 150m directly above the point we had just reached. It would be another nine years before I considered the possibility of climbing it myself.

We now moved away on the snow ridge in the direction of the Aiguille de Rochefort. Here I began to feel slightly frustrated as John and I were still in the rear. Sue was not yet as accustomed to airy snow ridges as I was and I found myself wishing to move faster. The ridge was, in fact, surprisingly wide, with a well-trodden track. The snow was firm. The inclement weather of the previous day appeared not to have made progress particularly difficult. It was only when we reached the 30m abseil point that we encountered anything to make me nervous.

Ian and Sue were still in front and climbed together down this steep snow-ice slope without belaying, so we followed suit. This was an unwise decision on my part, but we survived. A belay would have been much safer. An easy section followed, but then we had to descend another ice slope before traversing beneath bulging rocks and climbing back up to the ridge. On the final slope up to the Aiguille de Rochefort, icicles adorned the rock but the climbing was straightforward, with just one steep pitch. What concerned me, however, was the fact that this section was littered with many loose stones and I worried about the descent, which would be via the same slope. Meanwhile, the summit was glorious: a big snow platform enabled a dozen people to sit comfortably and admire the superb situation.

I looked eastwards along the frontier ridge and for a moment the Grandes Jorasses, beyond the Dôme de Rochefort, deceived me, this aspect being so very different from the views from south or north to which I was accustomed. Ian quickly put me right. I felt quite stupid. After all, I had been coming to this area now for several years. To the west, Mont Blanc and all the surrounding snow peaks and rock pinnacles rose in their glory before us. Then, turning northwards, I could admire at leisure the route we had done a few days before on the Aiguille Verte. This really was a moment to savour.

On the way down, I made sure that John would belay me on the one steep section. For all my confidence on snow, he was by far the stronger on rock. We complemented each other well and gave each other mutual support. I felt that this route was a breakthrough, because at last I was climbing with a partner who had no more experience than me. I had to make decisions, and this gave me a very pleasing feeling of responsibility. At the end of the summer, this was the route that I remembered with most satisfaction. It gave me a great sense of achievement and I shall always be grateful to John for having had the confidence to climb with me.

The misgivings I had experienced after climbing the Aiguille Verte had by now evaporated. The Rochefort traverse had restored my enthusiasm and I was eager to try another big route. The Grand Combin was our next objective. Situated just over the French border in Switzerland, it was within easy reach of Chamonix. Pete and Margaret had now come to the end of their holiday, so that left only five of us to motor over to the area just below the Grand St. Bernard pass.

The Combin is an enormous, bulky mountain, topped by a vast snow plateau broken up by four separate summits: the Combin de Valsorey, 4184m at the western end, the Combin de Grafinière, at 4314m the highest summit, the Aiguille du Croissant, 4243m, and then to the east, the Combin de la Tsesette, 4141m. From many points in the Alps, the Grand Combin can be identified without difficulty as it rises high above most of the surrounding terrain. All approaches are long and the traverse of the mountain, though not particularly difficult, is a serious undertaking, whether on ski in the winter or spring, or on foot in summertime.

We decided to take one of the easiest routes up the mountain and therefore walked up to the Valsorey Hut on the west side. At 3.15 the following morning we roped up in two parties: John Howe in a threesome with Les and me, and Ian and Sue as a rope of two. By daybreak we had all reached the Col de Meitin, from which point the West Ridge rises approximately 570m to the Combin de Valsorey. There are three rock steps, of which the first is 300m high, and I found that the climbing was mainly quite easy, though not particularly pleasant on the sections where hands were needed because it was a very cold morning and we were in the shade. Sue was suffering badly from her ankle, which she had broken earlier in the summer, and Ian was hampered by a headcold, so they weren't moving as quickly as we were. When we reached a flat area beyond the first rock step, we came into the sun and waited three-quarters of an hour for them. Then we pressed on up the next two rock steps, Les somewhat impatient when I struggled to heave myself up the awkward pitches. I moaned back irritably because I could see no point in hurrying. Then I remembered that we were not alone and that John could overhear our domestic bickering. Poor fellow! At last we reached the top of the Combin de Valsorey.

Rather than wait for Ian and Sue, we decided to continue to the Combin de Grafinière, thinking that they might abandon their attempt to go to the highest point if they were really struggling. There was no need to go that far in order to descend to the Panossière Hut, our next objective. In fact, we left our rucksacks and rope at the col between the two summits and soloed up the easy snow slopes to the Grafinière. When we were about half-way up this ultimate peak, I looked back and saw that Ian and Sue were in view and actually pushing on towards us.

A little later, whilst we were all enjoying the satisfaction of having reached the true summit of the Grand Combin, we made an error of judgment. Our experience on our ski-tour in the Bernese Oberland in 1977 should have warned us not to listen to the advice of local guides. Then we had been led astray on the descent from the Hollandia Hut. This time we allowed ourselves to be talked into joining a Swiss guide and his client on a descent route to the Panossière Hut.

There are various ways off the Grand Combin, the Corridor Route being the most traditional, but we knew it was dangerous as it passed beneath a long chain of unstable séracs. We had therefore anticipated using another route that a guide at the Valsorey Hut had shown us on the map. Now, however, a second guide was proposing that we should accompany him down the north-west flank and this is what we did. The guide was concerned not to descend that route alone with his client, who was very inexperienced, and he wanted to avoid returning by his ascent route, which he had decided was rather unsafe. That route was the one we ourselves had intended to descend.

Despite the fact that the top of the face was obscured in thick cloud, the guide persuaded Les to help by going down the steep slope on the north-west flank first, in order to secure a good belay somewhere in the gloom below. Then the guide lowered the rest of us down to Les, and finally came down himself, having acted as anchor to us all from above. This manoeuvre was repeated many times, as the slope was several hundred metres long, and most of us climbed down facing inwards for a considerable distance. On one stance, Sue and I looked at each other in horror as the client slipped, his cramponed feet hurtling towards our heads. Fortunately, the guide arrested his fall before he reached us. All in all, as I noted in my journal, it was a very time-consuming descent, three hours, in fact:

It got beyond a joke. I was worn out and my calf muscles were giving out again by the time we reached the glacier below.

From there it took another hour and a half to reach the Panossière Hut. It was already dinnertime and the guardian, who had been watching our descent through binoculars, voiced his disapproval of our choice of route. He provided us with food, drink and a bed for the night, nevertheless, and we were thanked for our efforts by the client, if not by the guide. The client lived in Montreux, by Lake Geneva, and from his home had a view of the Grand Combin in fine weather. That was why he was so motivated to climb the mountain, despite his inexperience. He was a friendly soul and invited Les and me to leave our skis at his home so that we could come out unencumbered in wintertime. We never took him up on his kind suggestion.

The following morning we left the hut and returned to our base at the campsite in Sembrancher. Down there, at the foot of the Grand St. Bernard pass, lazing in the sun on a wonderfully peaceful, almost empty campsite, the last thing I wanted to do just then was to go up any more mountains. The long, steep descent from the Combin had made my knees ache and my whole body felt racked with pain. This summer I seemed to lack energy. Ian, Sue and John, almost at the end of their holiday, were keen to do one more route before they went home, so they left us there. Les, meanwhile, perhaps knowing that I might be tempted despite my reluctance, had a new plan for me: we were to go to the Weisshorn.

Back in 1975, Les had gone up to the Tracuit Hut from Zinal with Colin Wornham and other friends in order to climb the North Ridge of the Weisshorn. I had also walked up to the hut on that occasion, but not with a view to accompanying them on the route, as I was still quite inexperienced and not as fit as the rest of the party. Although, in 1978, we had hoped to climb the Weisshorn by its Normal Route from the Mattertal, by 1980 Les considered me to be so much of an alpinist that he was prepared to undertake the traverse of the mountain with me as his only companion and was keen to try the route forthwith. Unlike me, he had had several disappointments during this holiday: the serious routes he and Pete had wanted to do together, both in Grindelwald and Chamonix, had all been out of condition. So I agreed to go along, despite my tiredness and my dread of the long steep walk up from Zinal. Afterwards, I was immensely pleased that I had made the effort.

The first time I'd walked up to the Tracuit Hut, I had found it hard going, as the refuge is situated at 3256m, approximately 1400m above the village. This time, however, I made my rucksack as light as possible and found the walk much less strenuous than I remembered. Unfortunately, the hut was just as crowded as on the previous occasion and a large party of overexcited schoolchildren was in residence. This meant that we had very little sleep in the evening, trying to rest before our 2.00 am start.

Taisez-vous, s'il vous plaît! ('Silence! Shut up!') We tried over and over again to quieten our dormitory companions but with no success at all. This was very frustrating indeed, as we knew that we had a long and demanding day ahead of us.

We rose at 1.00 am as planned and breakfasted along with just two other parties, both with a guide. To reach the Weisshorn from the Tracuit Hut, you must first traverse the Bishorn, which itself is classed as a Four-thousander. From the Bishorn to the summit of the Weisshorn, the route follows a very fine ridge of rock and snow, interrupted at one point by a distinctive gendarme that is instantly recognisable from many viewpoints in the Valais Alps. It is 2km from summit to summit.

By 2.00 am we were on our way up the Turtmann Glacier and, an hour or so later, to my consternation, my torch faded out. We had no spare battery. It was very dark and, although I had been going quite well hitherto, I now found I was staggering about off-balance on the snow. There was a stiff breeze too, which became stronger and colder as we climbed and I was cursing myself for not having worn my long johns under my breeches. At the top of the Bishorn we put on our crampons and moved off in the wake of the other parties down the snow ridge in the direction of the Weisshorn. By now it was daylight and walking on the snow was easy, but when we reached the first rocky section near the Weisshornjoch, we were subjected to frequent gusts of strong wind, which threw me off-balance again. Memories of Palü flashed through my mind. At times I was down on all fours, though the men, I noticed, were brave enough or, more likely, strong enough, to stand up to the force of the gale.

Various rock steps now had to be down-climbed and I found the crampons rather a hindrance. After a while I began to wonder if these rock steps would never end. From the guidebook description, I hadn't realised just how many there were. However, the rock was mainly solid and, if the wind had not been blowing so strongly, I would have found these sections quite enjoyable and our progress would have been considerably faster. Eventually we came to the 'chimney'. We were always within sight of the second of the other two parties and, as we approached the bottom of the cliff, the client was just moving away up the pitch. I noticed that he was no longer wearing crampons and told Les, who, after trying the first few feet, agreed that we might take them off too. This pitch is described as a '*dièdre*-chimney' and is a series of blocks and cracks. Although the climbing is technically easy, I found it strenuous, perhaps partly because of the altitude, but mainly because I was wearing so many clothes. Because of the cold wind, I was still clad in my bulky down jacket, which I would like to have removed, but once on the ridge again, I was glad I hadn't stopped to take it off.

After the chimney, there was still a quarter of an hour's climbing to do around the Grand Gendarme and a further rock section to descend before we reached the snow ridge. When we arrived, the other two climbers were just setting off, so we took their resting place to have a snack and put our crampons back on. I had been so looking forward to the snow, thinking it would be easy and relieve my mind of all tension, but I was wrong. The wind was as strong as ever, and several portions of the ridge are very exposed indeed. On one or two sections, I felt it was the narrowest snow crest I had ever been able to walk along without resorting to the *à cheval* position, as on Piz Palü. The tension never eased one iota, the most delicate part of the crest coming just as I approached the summit itself. One foot broke through the surface of the snow, as I inched forward and, for just a second, I thought I was going to slip.

All the way up the snow ridge, I had struggled with fatigue. This could have been the effect of altitude – the Weisshorn summit, at 4506m, is one of the highest in the Alps – but it may simply have been exhaustion. At last I arrived at the top. The route had taken eight hours. The first party had passed us in descent ten minutes below the summit, so they must have returned by the same route to the Tracuit Hut. After all, the guide was the guardian's son, so perhaps he was going back 'home'. The other two climbers were, however, still sitting on the summit when we arrived, which gave a boost to my morale – I had climbed almost as quickly as they had. Exhaustion and nervous tension gave way to elation: what a view! What a feeling! I was overwhelmed to think that I had climbed the North Ridge of the Weisshorn, a route that, five years previously, we had considered far too serious for me. It was wonderful to have shared that experience with Les alone, just the two of us. This was the first time we had climbed such a demanding route on one of the highest Fourthousanders with no other companions.

The descent to Randa in the Mattertal was a contrast. Unlike the airy North Ridge, the East Ridge, despite falling sharply away from the summit, starts with a wide snow slope that gave us no difficulty. It was, in fact, a joy to romp down until it reached the top of a rocky section which, thanks to my tiredness, I found increasingly awkward to descend. Then came a long rib of soft snow strewn with sections of loose boulders, interspersed with sections of scree. This was quite unpleasant and I was so exhausted by then that I no longer cared how much of it was accomplished on my backside. At the foot of the rib we unroped and soloed the last part of the glacier to the Weisshorn Hut, where we stopped just long enough to drink a cup of tea laced with as much sugar as I could find. I needed the energy to cope with the final hour and half down the steep descent to the valley. My knees ached and ached and ached.

They still ached a fortnight later when I was writing up my journal:

Am I really crazy enough to subject myself to all the agony again next year?

Of course I was. Mountaineering, and especially alpinism, was a vital part of my life. It fed my soul. It satisfied the urge I had to counteract the constraints of my everyday occupations. I needed these opportunities to escape into a more primitive environment where I could commune with nature and companions of a like mind.

5

ENCHAÎNEMENT:
TRAVERSING THE SKYLINE

In the summer of 1981, we deliberately set out to climb some more 4000m peaks but, although Pete Fleming and Les had embarked upon a mission to reach their target of 52 Fourthousanders, I was still climbing without any such goal. That year Pete didn't join us in the Alps, as he and Margaret were visiting China. So, it was with friends from the 1973 summer that Les and I returned to Sembrancher in the Valais Alps for the first week of our holiday. From there, six of us went to the Chanrion Hut. Les and I teamed up with Stuart Cooke to climb the Bec d'Epicoun, La Ruinette and Mont Gelé. Then the two of us departed for the Swiss Val Ferret, where, from the delightful little A'Neuve Hut, we made an ascent of both the Tour Noir and Le Grand Darrey. None of these peaks reach more than 3900m. This was climbing purely for its own sake. It was also excellent training and acclimatisation for the bigger routes we were about to tackle.

It was time now to move to the Zermatt Valley once again and we settled into the Atermenzen campsite near Randa to await the arrival of Ian and Sue Stirrups. This year Sue was back on top form, her ankle having long since healed, and she was keener than ever to climb some really interesting mountains. Because they needed to acclimatise, we all walked up to the Bordier Hut. Les encouraged this idea, as the hut was also a starting point for two Fourthousanders that he had not yet climbed: the Dürrenhorn, and the Hohberghorn, now renamed the Dirruhorn and Hohbärghorn. It is straightforward to join these two peaks together in one expedition, as they are situated next to each other at the end of a long chain of mountains. For a really grand *enchaînement*, you could start at the Alphubel and continue over the Täschhorn, Dom, Lenzspitze and Nadelhorn, finally reaching the Hohbärghorn and Dirruhorn. This fine ridge, the Mischabelgrat, at least 7km long from summit to summit, separates the Saastal from the Zermatt Valley or Mattertal. The complete traverse would take the alpinist along some of the sharpest crests of rock in the Alps, from one snow-topped 4000m peak to another, and would require considerable competence and stamina. One night could be spent at the bivouac hut on the Mischabeljoch between the Alphubel and Täschhorn, but any further bivouac would have to be in the open. When Martin Moran and Simon Jenkins attempted to do this long ridge in the opposite direction in 1993, as part of their continuous alpine traverse, they found it preferable to drop down off the crest to a makeshift bivouac site on the Hohbärg Glacier below the Lenzjoch. Their plan to continue beyond the Dom the following day was defeated by an unexpected storm, and they were forced to retreat for a night at the Dom Hut, much lower down the mountain, and thence to the valley.

Les and I had been to the Bordier Hut some years previously and had not been very impressed by the guardian, a churlish individual. His hut had burned down sometime later and we rather hoped that a new guardian would have replaced him, but this was not the case. Our reception this time was no more welcoming than on the first. This was a pity, as the guardian's attitude can make all the difference when you have just arrived after a very long, gruelling walk uphill. The approach to the Bordier Hut from Grächen is just that.

The next morning it was cloudy on the mountains but not bad enough to deter us from going out, so we accompanied Ian and Sue up to the flat open bowl of the upper Ried Glacier, where we parted company. They carried on towards the Ulrichshorn, whilst we headed for the gully leading up to the Hohbergjoch. Visibility at this altitude was poor and we found the way by using a compass and following old tracks in the snow. The gully was steep and we moved slowly up hard-packed old snow, keeping to a runnel until it ran out. Then we partly pitched it out on the open slope above but mainly were able to move together. At the top of the gully we had to climb over a very small cornice to reach the col. The mist was still as dense as ever but, for just a few moments, it looked as if the sun might break through. We left our rucksacks at the col and, without crampons, walked up to the Dürrenhorn. The rocks were very easy to climb but were covered with a few centimetres of fresh snow, so we had to be very careful.

When we arrived back at the col, I knew that Les wouldn't change his mind about visiting the summit of the Hohberghorn – it is, after all, a Four-thousander. However, the weather was not improving. It had been our intention to traverse the Hohberghorn and climb on as far as the Nadelhorn, from which we could descend to the Windjoch and make our way back down to the Bordier Hut. By now, we were not entirely convinced that we would continue beyond the first peak, but we hadn't yet completely abandoned the idea. Just as we were starting off from the col, we met a guide descending from the Hohberghorn with his client. He seemed quite shocked that we should be attempting the ascent, especially as we were still not wearing crampons, and did his best to deter us in his best English:

'It is dangerous! … Ice on the rocks … Very windy …'

We decided to ignore his advice. I trusted Les implicitly to make the best decision for the circumstances and knew that he would turn back if he felt it was too dangerous to continue. Previous experience with other people's guides had made us both wary and we preferred to keep our own counsel.

For a long way it was quite safe without crampons, though the rocks were more awkward than on the Dürrenhorn. When we came to the snow slope higher up, we put our crampons on and, as the wind was fairly brisk and clouds were still rolling all around us, we decided to leave the rucksacks there and return by the same route. The traverse to the Nadelhorn and Windjoch would have taken too long in these conditions – the guide's advice was not so wrong after all – and the rest of the route seemed much easier without the rucksacks. This was the first day of the holiday that I had been up to 4000m and the altitude was making me feel a little weary. The conditions hardly helped, either: it was more like a Scottish winter climb in the mist than a summer's day in the Alps. We had seen nothing at all apart from the terrain of our immediate surroundings: a monochrome picture of rock and snow. The only real pleasure came from the satisfaction of having made the best of a day of poor weather.

From the summit we returned the way we had come, picked up the ruck-sacks, descended to the col and pitched the whole of the slope down to the *bergschrund*. I sank exhausted on to the glacier below but there was no respite. Immediately we trudged off again, and it seemed a very long time until we reached the moraine path down to the hut. When we did arrive, we found that Ian and Sue had just left, the guide we met having told them that we would be out for many more hours as we were doing the Nadel-horn … Several hours later, the four of us met up again in Randa.

The Rimpfischhorn, via its North Ridge, was to be my next Four-thousander. This was one of the peaks that Les had climbed in his very first alpine season several years before we met. However, he wanted to climb it again, as he hadn't done the North Ridge and this classic route appealed greatly to him. By now, I was quite prepared to accompany him on this type of climb. A fine rock ridge with a series of gendarmes, the North Ridge is graded AD and must be a delight in perfect summer conditions. Unfort-unately, the conditions were far from ideal.

Although the four of us all went up to the Täsch Hut together for the night, Ian and Sue decided to climb the Alphubel, so Les and I were on our own again. Just as fresh snow had lain upon the rocks of the two Fourthousanders we had climbed two days before, so there was also a layer of fresh snow on the North Ridge of the Rimpfischhorn. This time, however, it was a beautiful sunny day. On the glacier approach, the snow had frozen sufficiently to support our weight in the early morning but when we came to the ridge leading up from the Allalinpass, Les began to find that he was sinking in and getting quite tired. This slowed us down a little, but I had no objection to taking a more leisurely pace.

We traversed the Grand Gendarme on the east side but this was none too easy because of fresh snow and loose rock and seemed to take ages. Although I was very hungry by then, there was no question of eating until we reached the ridge again. When we did get there, we were confronted by an icy cold wind and only stopped for a moment. It's hard work climbing in the Alps! Who would do eight hours' hard labour at home on just a few nuts and a Mars Bar? The ridge was now mainly rock, though snow-covered, and seemed endless. The airy situation reminded me of the North Ridge of the Weissmies, the South Ridge of the Lagginhorn, or even the Täschhorn-Dom traverse, but particularly the first two, as we had climbed them in similar conditions. We climbed the entire ridge, whether rock or snow, in crampons, and that made for slow progress. For a while we could see a party on the summit, but they had left long before we arrived.

The North Ridge of the Rimpfischhorn was quite tough for me and had a real sting in its tail: the last pitch below the summit was very awkward and strenuous. For all that, I was mentally in much better form than on the Lagginhorn South Ridge in 1977, where I had really struggled with the combination of exposure and poor conditions. Here on the Rimpfischhorn, I benefited from the successful traverse I had made in 1979 from the Täschhorn to the Dom. I knew that if I could cope with that, I could certainly cope with the difficulties on this ridge. It was simply a matter of pacing myself.

I was so looking forward to a rest at the top – but within five minutes we were on the move again. We had already taken far too long on the ridge and we didn't want to have to struggle through soft snow on the glacier. So down we went, until we came to a halt: there in front of us was the party we had seen on the summit, and another party coming up, all struggling, ropes entwined on a simple pitch of rock on the Normal Route. We had no intention of waiting till they had finished – we would have been there for ages – so, amidst a certain amount of abuse, we descended swiftly past them and shot down the snow gully at the side. Then, it was back on to the ridge and down to a col, where we rested briefly, before starting the long, weary plod back across the glaciers to the Täsch Hut, where Ian and Sue were on the lookout for us. Despite the lengthy time the route had taken us, it had been a grand day.

The climax of this summer season was about to come. I called 1979 'the great year', but 1981 is a strong contender for that nomination. Including our ski-tour in the spring, we visited 27 Alpine tops that year, of which 24 classified as separate mountain summits. Eleven are Fourthousanders on the Collomb list. In 1979, the year that signified a great breakthrough in self-confidence for me, both in climbing and ski-mountaineering, I had, in fact, only climbed twelve separate mountains, of which five were Four-thousanders that I hadn't done previously.

It was not only the number of peaks ascended that made these two years so special, however. It was also the companionship of our fellow climbers: 1979 was the last year when we were still climbing with trusted friends from our earlier years – Geoff Causey and John Oaks in particular. I owe them both so much in terms of psychological support, as well as the occasional anchorage as third person on the traverse of a steep slab, or a push-up from below on a steep rock step. Geoff, and then John, both took the life-changing step of marriage in 1981 and we didn't climb any more Alpine peaks with either of them again, although Geoff and his wife, Pauline, were in the party at the Chanrion Hut that summer. Both Geoff and John continued to be active mountaineers, however, but neither had any further direct influence on my own climbing career.

By 1981, we had moved on to a new era with our new acquaintances, who were already becoming very special companions too: Pete Fleming, who spurred us on to attempt to complete the Fourthousanders, and his patient, understanding wife, Margaret, who supported us all so well from our valley base; also Ian and Sue Stirrups, who had by now joined us for a number of very memorable ski-tours and two summer seasons. Our old friend, Paul Luton, was still with us in both these great years, as a participant in our spring ski-tours, though never during the summer Alpine climbing season. His presence was invaluable and he was much missed when he decided to abandon ski-touring after 1986.

6

STAYING UP HIGH

The last week of the 1981 summer holiday was the most exhilarating. Our first outing started with a cable car ride from Zermatt to Trockener Steg. From there, Ian and Sue, Les and I all walked across to the Gandegg Hut, where we spent the night after a glorious evening watching the sun setting over the great peaks of the Valais. The next morning we returned to Trockener Steg to await the start of the service up to Klein Matterhorn. At 7.30 am, this was a really late Alpine start for us. Walking along the Italian side of the Breithorn to the far end, we dumped all our excess gear at the Cesare e Giorgio Bivouac Hut, which we were relieved to find empty. We immediately commandeered all four bunks, making it quite obvious that we intended to spend the night there. What a hut! Shaped like a Nissen hut, it slept six, if two people lay on the floor under the bunks. There was only about eighteen inches of headroom between each narrow shelf and, in the centre of the hut, a space no more than two feet wide. The overall length was that of a normal bunk, and that was it. Strangely enough, I slept very well there, perhaps because there were no nocturnal disturbances as in other huts. This hut no longer exists, having been replaced by a larger, more modern version near the original site.

We were now ready to set out for Pollux, which is immediately to the east of the Breithorn. It didn't take us long to reach the foot of the West Face, where we had noticed a trail zigzagging up the steep slope towards the summit. I must have been really fit and acclimatised, as I found it very easy going uphill. In fact, my ego was boosted for a change, as Ian and Sue were moving more slowly. Usually I was the slowest in the party. We were rapidly catching up a really incompetent group of climbers further up the slope and this caused me some concern, since it would have been difficult to arrest a fall caused by a body hurtling down from above. Apart from human missiles, there was no fear of any other objects falling upon us: no cornice, no rocks. We waited for Ian and Sue when we reached the upper part of the West Flank and then all four of us walked up the easy snow arête to the summit. Here we basked in the sun at 4092m, taking many photos and enjoying our exalted situation: the Breithorn on one side, Castor, Liskamm and the Monte Rosa on the other. Castor and Pollux are named after the twins of ancient Greek mythology and it seemed a shame not to be climbing them together, but Les and I had already climbed Castor and our companions didn't feel sufficiently acclimatised, preferring to conserve their strength for the following day. It was, in any case, getting a little late now for a deliberate trek over the glacier: the sun was becoming quite fierce and the snow would be softening fast. Instead, we descended the West Flank and returned to our bivouac.

Later that day we were joined there by two more climbers, a Japanese and an Italian. They were both climbing solo and the following morning set out on their separate ways. It was unfortunate for them that we had arrived first at the hut, because they were obliged to sleep beneath us on the floor. To our astonishment, one of them managed to eat his breakfast under the bunk as well.

Since our bivouac hut was situated at about 3800m, we didn't have to get up too long before dawn and we only had a fairly short climb to reach the Roccia Nera, before starting the traverse of the Breithorn. The clear moonlight of the night very soon gave way to early morning sun as we cramponned along the airy snow arête from the Roccia Nera towards the Grand Gendarme. The cornices to our right hung perilously out over the precipice that drops down to the glaciers on the Swiss side, but the relatively low gradient of the snow slope on the Italian side gave us a pleasant sense of security. I lost this agreeable feeling as I teetered across the top of the Grand Gendarme, where soft fresh snow on the very narrow rock crest made me feel extremely insecure. I was in front and did my utmost not to show the others how I felt. I clambered carefully down the rocks and Les followed with ease, before belaying me down a tricky little ice gully below an overhanging slab. I then belayed him from below as he lowered himself down on the rope and the others did likewise.

Another easy snow arête followed and we reached the East Summit, at 4139m. After the first easy snow slope, the descent was quite awkward. We came to a series of rocky slabs with pegs in place for belays and it was a steep but easy climb down to the bottom. However, this was the kind of obstacle that always made me slow and Sue, although the better rock climber, found it no easier than I did.

The next difficulty was the ascent of the three large rock steps to the Central Summit, 4159m. Here, the climbing was delightful; the rock was warm in the sun, the holds were plentiful and the situation incomparable.

Most of the rock was good solid stuff, with only a few loose sections here and there. Les and I made more rapid progress than our companions and I felt I was simply strolling along. Such was the psychological boost I gained from being at the front for a change. By the time we had completed the rock steps, I was in the seventh heaven of delight and we had the bonus of a half-hour wait, munching all the food we were carrying, before attacking the final snow slope to the Central Summit.

This snow slope was a trifle icy but went well in crampons and soon we were all contemplating the view of the West Summit ahead of us. At 4164m, it would be the highest point of our day. The difficulties were all over now and it was just a question of keeping going. The final summit was not nearly as enjoyable as it might have been, though, as the perpetual shouting and singing of enthusiastic tourists who had walked up from the cable cars now shattered the beautiful silence we had experienced all morning. One of those same cable cars whisked us back down to Zermatt, where, to round off the trip in style, we had to run the gauntlet of a festival procession coming, group after group, with bands playing, up the street towards us. It seemed a very long way to the railway station at the far end of the village.

After a rest day in Randa, we took the train from Zermatt up the Gorner-grat railway to Rotenboden, just as we had done in 1979 on the High Level Route. The Matterhorn dominates the view all the way up the railway. From Rotenboden we descended via the easy summer path to the Gorner Glacier, which we crossed with ease amidst the many tourists walking up to the Monte Rosa Hut for a drink and a snack.

Tourism was precisely what made the hut so inhospitable as far as we were concerned: the guardian had no time at all for mountaineers. It was the usual story of not allocating your bed until late in the evening, giving you no possibility of resting earlier. Although the guardian sold ready-made tea, we still preferred to make our own hot drinks but the only 'hot' water supply made available to guests was a tepid trickle from large urns in the living room. Even if this water had initially been boiled, having undoubtedly come from the glaciated terrain around us, it was an insufficient temperature for us to make a palatable cup of tea. In smaller huts, the guardian would usually have a constant supply of boiling water on his stove. Here the objective was to make as much money as possible from the day-trippers.

The following morning we were up at 3.00 am. Swiss time was one hour forward that year, so this was the 2.00 am of 1980. There was a chilly breeze, which was perhaps just as well as Les, Ian and Sue set a cracking pace up the moraine. After an hour or so we arrived at the glacier, where we roped up and put on our crampons, our feet growing really cold. The going became harder as we pressed on steadily upwards, eventually leaving the main Dufourspitze track and all the other parties on it. Alone, we four headed for the Silbersattel, which lies between Nordend and the rest of the Monte Rosa. Four and a half hours after leaving the hut, we reached the col. I was exhausted and dying for some food but it was so unpleasant in the bitterly cold wind that it was quite out of the question to stop for more than a minute. To my immense relief, however, we left the rucksacks at the col and, with the weight off my back, new life surged into me and I almost enjoyed the walk up to Nordend. Here again, it was icy cold as we climbed one by one up the final rocky point. It was not a place to linger long.

We returned the same way and picked up those wretched sacks. Immediately I felt bowed down again. We were at an altitude of some 4500m and that was probably the cause of most of my discomfort. The snow slope ahead turned out to be very solid ice and we decided not to go straight up after all, but to traverse round to the left on to the crest of the ridge. After he had reached the rock, Les spent at least ten minutes trying to lasso a spike to belay himself on a very blank slab. We were beginning to think that we were stuck, and I am sure that none of us fancied reversing the ice slope. At last Les was successful and he hauled me up the difficult part. From then on, the ground was quite straightforward but it seemed a long way over the Grenzspitze to the Dufourspitze, at 4634m.

The Dufourspitze is the highest peak of the Monte Rosa. Five other points in the range also qualify as Fourthousanders on Collomb's List and, as Nordend is one of the six, we had now reached two. It was our intention to visit the other four as well: the Zumsteinspitze, the Signalkuppe, the Parrotspitze and Piramide Vincent.

Just before we reached the Dufourspitze, there was one most awkward section of down-climbing, followed by a delicate traverse of an exposed slab. When we were at last on the summit, it was warm enough to rest a long while. We were by no means alone there, other parties having arrived by a different route, but, despite my love of solitude on a summit, their presence did not detract from the splendid feeling of sitting once more enthroned upon one of Western Europe's very highest peaks.

After retracing our steps across the difficult section, we took the south-east ridge of the Grenzspitze down to the col below the Zumsteinspize. It was quite easy rock, so it was some time before Les realised that he had left his ice axe at the top of the Grenzspitze. We shouted back to our companions and were relieved to learn that they were bringing it down to us. Waiting for them in a breezy spot, we cooled down significantly and so, when they arrived, we moved off again at speed to warm ourselves up.

From the top of the Zumsteinspitze, we could see our destination: the Margherita Hut on the Signalkuppe. It was within easy reach now and I found myself moving faster and faster towards it. In fact, Les had to ask me to slow down on the last zigzag up to the hut.

At 4554m, the Margherita Hut is probably the highest house in Western Europe and, in 1981, it was very smart indeed, having recently been rebuilt. We were allotted a room for four, with a balcony from which you could have jumped straight down into the depths of Italy. Unfortunately, the cost was fairly high and, having no Italian lire, we were obliged to pay with Swiss francs at an extortionate exchange rate, so had to be fairly cautious in our purchasing. We decided to spend the little money we had on hot water with which we made various brews. As far as eating was concerned, we relied entirely on the cold provisions we had carried up from the valley. So it was salami for lunch and salami for dinner. I think that Sue ate salami for breakfast too. By morning, however, Ian was no longer eating at all. He had spent most of the night upright, feeling very queasy, whilst Les and I watched silently, also unable to sleep at the unusually high altitude. On the other hand, Sue slept soundly all night long. I was a little unnerved by the fact that you were almost expected to feel sick: on every wall there were little notices asking you to use the plastic bags provided … It reminded me of the bags supplied for the same purpose on an aeroplane.

The main blessing the next morning, apart from the late start, was that the route simply had to go downwards. I was, however, caught unawares by the icy steepness of it and was soon left behind, slowed down by my sense of caution. We were all walking solo: there seemed no need to rope up until later that day, when we started on the descent to the Monte Rosa Hut. The Parrotspitze, our first summit, was very easy indeed, apart from one section of about 15m of blue ice. Then we ambled over to the Ludwigshöhe, climbed up and down the Corno Nero, greeting the Madonna on the summit, and finally reached the Piramide Vincent. Of these tops, only the Parrotspitze and the Piramide Vincent count as separate mountains on the Collomb list.

It was a magnificent day up on top of the Monte Rosa Range, but down below us the Italian plain looked gloomy and there was little to see on that side. The great peaks around us were more to my liking and we were fortunate in having had each of that morning's summits to ourselves. A little later in the day, this would have no longer been the case: we could see hordes of people coming up from the Gnifetti Hut.

To reach the Grenz Glacier, we had to climb back up the snowfield and skirt round the north-west side of the Ludwigshöhe. We then roped up, as the terrain ahead of us was extremely crevassed. I was dreading the pounding of the descent and, even more, the heat of the glacier lower down but, to my relief, I barely suffered at all. There was just one very steep snow slope. Apart from that, we could keep moving comfortably and enjoy simply being there.

The day slipped slowly by: we unroped for the last part of the Grenz Glacier, coming once more on to the moraine of the morning; there we continued each at our own separate pace, until we met again at the Monte Rosa Hut. Ian was still feeling unwell but insisted that he would be all right. Les and I set off across the Gorner Glacier, Sue and Ian caught us up again on the far side, then we trudged off one by one: Les, then Sue, then me, then Ian, last of all, on the track to Rotenboden station on the Gornergrat railway. Whilst we waited for the train that would take us back down to Zermatt, we sat for a while in the sun admiring our peaks. This was the end of another Alpine season and the sense of achievement was considerable.

PART FIVE
MÉLANGE

My heart aches and a drowsy numbness pains

My sense …

– JOHN KEATS[1]

The Finsteraarhorn

1 'Ode to a Nightingale' by John Keats

1

FEAR

We scampered along the narrow mountain-top one cool, early morning at the end of May, the stony corries and peat bogs of the Isle of Skye spread out on either side, stretching away from the foot of the Black Cuillin Ridge far below. As I stepped down and round a corner below the crest, there was Les waiting for me on the far side of a chasm. Aghast, I stood on the brink of a deep cleft. Just one bold step was needed to bridge the gap, but beneath was a void waiting expectantly to suck down the unskilled long-jumper who didn't reach the other side with both feet. There was a ledge wide enough to land on but, above it, the adjacent crag leaned intimidatingly towards me.

'You can do it,' Les called to me from his comfortable stance beyond the notch. 'Of course you can.'

'Can I?' I muttered to myself. Standing there, with no rope to protect me, my stomach churned. 'Yes, I can. If Les knows I can, then I will.'

I had implicit faith in my husband's judgment of my abilities, even though my nervous system was trying its best at that moment to make me believe otherwise. I jumped.

Relief surged through every fibre of my body as I landed. Pausing only momentarily to catch my breath, I continued calmly on my way to our next objective, the Bhasteir Tooth, one of the only two sections of this airy ridge where we would use our rope.

In his book, *Unjustifiable Risk*, Simon Thompson claims that:

As people have grown richer, healthier and better educated … so ever increasing numbers have deliberately undertaken dangerous climbs in order to expose themselves to risks that are clearly unjustifiable by any normal moral or rational standard.[2]

---

2 *Unjustifiable Risk* by Simon Thompson

Whilst this may be true of some people, neither I, nor any of my close companions, as far as I know, have ever undertaken climbs simply for the sake of exposing ourselves to risk. We accepted that there was a risk and the knowledge of that risk may have added to the feeling of satisfaction we experienced after completing a climb safely. However, each time we embarked upon a climb, we did everything possible to control that risk and, if the risk became too great, we would turn back or escape from the situation. We didn't climb deliberately to put ourselves in danger, to get a thrill of fear. We climbed because we wanted to climb.

Fear is a necessary adjunct to a climber's equipment, as it emits warning signals, without which you might overstep the limits of safety. When you feel the first pangs of fear, it is time to remember that you have your own personal limitations. We all have our own threshold as far as vertigo is concerned. Your own fitness and ability will only allow you to climb to a certain level of difficulty, both physically and psychologically. Fear may also prevent you from straying into terrain that is inherently dangerous: a child learns not to put his fingers in the fire; a climber learns not to pull on loose rock, and not to linger beneath hanging séracs.

What happened when I was on the verge of being overcome by fear? How did I prevent myself from overstepping my personal limit? In the early days, when I had little experience, I learned to rely to a certain degree on Les's judgment. On the Zinalrothorn, for example, when I was confronted by my first high Alpine hand-traverse on the Rasoir, an exposed flake of rock hundreds of metres above the glacier, Les knew I could make the move, especially as he was protecting me with a rope passed behind the flake. I had already undertaken this kind of manoeuvre in the UK, though never with the experience of being able to look down between my knees and see the drop quite so terrifyingly far below. His belief in me gave me the confidence to curl my fingers round the sharp edge of the rock above and trust the soles of my boots to the smooth surface of the blade, even though there didn't seem to be any footholds.

By the time we came to traverse that other narrow ridge, from the Täschhorn to the Dom, in 1979, I had no fear of hand-traverses but I had never completely rid myself of a tendency to vertigo in exposed situations. However, I was determined to do the route, not only because Les and all our companions were keen to try, but also because the sheer fact of joining these two mountains together by this long crest seemed to me one of the most beautiful excursions I could ever make in the Alps. My decision was justified. The route gave me a profound sense of enjoyment. It was a privilege to be there, and my head acted accordingly. I found I could look down and see into the very depths of the glaciers below, just as Robert MacFarlane did from his elevated position on another route:

My eye followed the face down ... I could see glimmers of blue ice far down inside the body of the glacier. That was where we would end up if we fell.[3]

True, that was where I would die, if I fell, but falling was something I decided not to do. I knew I had the skill to make the traverse without mishap, so I made a conscious decision to believe in myself. That was my solution to any underlying fear that might threaten to spoil my day.

Fear of rockfall, perilously fragile séracs, hidden crevasses and, particularly in the skiing season, the fear of snow avalanche, is an integral part of Alpine mountaineering. You accept this, you never ignore it, but you do your best to avoid spending any more time than absolutely necessary in places where such events might occur. When you are forced to take a route through such terrain, you take appropriate precautions. You take note of the weather, the snow conditions and the size of your party. You try to avoid putting more than one person in danger at any one time. Despite all these attempts to minimise risk, there will probably be a few occasions when even the safest alpinist has to contend with immediate threat. A cracking sound above, or a shout from a climber higher up the route, would always send a chilling sensation down my spine but, at the same time, my autopilot would switch on and I would leap into whatever action seemed appropriate. In such circumstances, you do your utmost to avoid disaster. Without the stimulus of fear, you might not act. On the other hand, terror, that most intense form of fear, can strike you rigid, just as it does when you wake from a nightmare. You are simply paralysed, in mind and in body. That is how I felt when I was trying to shelter from the falling rocks as we descended from the Droites in 1990.

---

3 *Mountains of the Mind by Robert MacFarlane*

2

A Strange Season

After our very successful ski-tour at Easter 1982, working our way from Saas Grund via the Simplon Pass and Binn to Oberwald in the Upper Rhône Valley, the summer season was very strange indeed. Les and I left England in July, intending to do a couple of weeks climbing together before the arrival of Pete and Margaret Fleming. Then we would do a few 'training' routes to help Pete acclimatise and, finally, Les and Pete would have a further two weeks climbing harder routes whilst I opted out with Margaret. A few days before we started out, however, Andrew Hodges decided to join us, so we took his tent and spare rucksack in our car and he followed us by coach a week later.

The real bugbear throughout the holiday was the weather. Counting carefully, I noted that we only had six whole days of sunshine in the entire month. For at least four days it poured with rain, two weeks were disturbed by severe storms, and the rest of the time it was simply overcast and dull. It was, however, never particularly cold and the snow conditions were on the whole quite passable, chiefly because the few weeks before our arrival had been extremely hot and sunny.

Our first destination in Switzerland was the western end of the Bernese Oberland, where we just had time to climb the Gspaltenhorn before two days of continual rain. With a sodden tent, we set off for Lausanne, where we were due to meet Andrew at a friend's house. It was there that Les and I both picked up really bad head-colds, which manifested themselves a few days later. In the meantime, despite poor weather, we managed to fit in an ascent of Mont Vélan with Andrew. After that, he returned to Lausanne to go climbing with his friend, whilst we did one more route before meeting Pete and Margaret near Brig.

By now, Les was suffering severely from the head-cold but, despite that, the four of us took the cable car from Blatten to Bel Alp and walked up to the Oberaletsch Hut on a fairly sunny day. There were only a few parties there, some of whom climbed the Aletschhorn the next morning, but Pete wanted to start with a lower peak to acclimatise. So, in misty conditions, we set out at about 6.30 am to go to the Gross Fusshorn. It wasn't long before I stopped. I was feeling really dreadful – a sore throat was accompanied by difficulty in breathing – and, in any case, the Gross Fusshorn didn't appeal to me very much. I was worried that I would be in no fit state for the Aletschhorn the following day, so I retired to bed. I lay there until midday, coughing and spluttering. Les was in no fit state either but, if he hadn't gone out, Pete would have had to solo his training route.

On the second morning, we rose at 3.30 am. Nothing would have stopped me from joining the men: not only is the Aletschhorn one of the Four-thousanders, but it has always seemed a most alluring peak to me. We had passed below its northern flank several times whilst trekking between the Konkordia and Hollandia Huts on the Upper Aletsch Glacier, but this was the first time any of us had approached it from the south. We chose to take the easiest route up, via its South-West Rib.

What a long way it seemed from the hut to the point where we reached the snow. It took an hour or more to cross the moraine. When we started up the rock ridge, clambering over wobbly boulders, I was suddenly taken aback to notice the huge drop to the glacier to my right. A coating of fresh snow hampered our progress a little but at last we reached the snow ridge and roped up. Very soon I began to feel really nauseous. Was it the altitude or my cold? Fortunately, whatever it was, it passed. I was, no doubt, helped by the fact that Pete wanted to rest at frequent intervals, presumably because he was not yet acclimatised. Thus Les, still suffering from his own cold, was alone at the front, making steps for us all in the fresh snow. All traces of the previous day's ascent had been obliterated. I was a little concerned about the safety of our descent in the soft snow, with its underlying layer of hard névé, but my companions seemed confident that we would come to no harm.

The ascent seemed to drag on endlessly but the sun kept shining on us and eventually, in a little over guidebook time, we made it to the summit. We signed the visitors' book hidden in the metal cross and had plenty of time to sit and admire our splendid, solitary position. We were the only people on the route. Around us, all other peaks near and far, even Mont Blanc, were hidden below clouds but, amazingly, we remained in the sun all day. Although the Aletschhorn, at 4193m, is the second highest peak in the Bernese Oberland, it is considerably lower than many of the mountains of the Valais to the south and the great French peaks a little further west. Usually, then, you would expect to see at least the highest of those summits protruding through the cloud base. Today, however, our summit was the

Monte Rosa (L) with Liskamm, Castor, Pollux and the Breithorn.

Barbara in the Cesare e Giorgio Bivouac Hut on the Breithorn, 1981.
Overleaf: Ian and Sue Stirrups on the traverse of the Breithorn, 1981.

Les leading a rock pitch on the Breithorn, 1981.
Photo: Barbara Swindin.

Pete Fleming looking towards the Aletschhorn, 1982.

The Dent d'Hérens.

Barbara traversing under the icicles on the Dent d'Hérens, 1982.

Les Ecrins from the south.

The South Face of The Grandes Jorasses.
Opposite: The WNW Face of the Dent d'Hérens.

Barbara and Les on the summit of the Dôme de Rochefort, Les's final Fourthousander, 1985.
Photo: Pete Fleming.

The campsite at Silvaplana, near St. Moritz, in the snowstorm, August 1985. Photo: Pete Fleming.

Crevasses on the Fiescher Glacier after snowfall in the summer of 1986.

Pete Fleming with Les and Barbara on the summit of the Finsteraarhorn, Pete's final Fourthousander, 1986. Photo: anon.

The Arbengrat.
Opposite: The North Face of the Obergabelhorn with the ENE Ridge (L)
and the Arbengrat (far R).

The Swiss Alps from the summit of Monte Disgrazia, 1988.

The Aiguille du Géant with the Burgener slabs in the sun, and the Rochefort Arête. Photo: Pete Fleming.
Opposite: Looking back along the Corda Molla on our way up Monte Disgrazia. Photo: Pete Fleming.
Overleaf: Climbing the fixed ropes on the Burgener Slabs, the Aiguille du Géant, 1989. Photo: Pete Fleming.

*Mont Blanc and the Aiguille Blanche de Peuterey (far R),
with the Brouillard Glacier (L) and the Frêney Glacier (R).
Photo: Pete Fleming.*

The Jungfrau (centre) from the south-east.

Barbara signing the visitors' book on the summit of the Schreckhorn, 1990.

Les Drus, the Aiguille Verte, Les Droites (R of centre) and Les Courtes from the west.
Overleaf: The Schreckhorn (centre L) and Lauteraarhorn (centre R) from the west.

Fiona Turner, Bill Turner and Alan Jonas at the Gonella Hut, 1993.
Opposite: Climbing the East Ridge of the Aiguille de Bionnassay, 1993.
Overleaf: Looking across the Frêney Glacier to the Aiguille Blanche de Peuterey.

Les at the Eccles Bivouac Hut, 1993. Photo: Pete Fleming.

*Barbara with Walter Bonatti at the 150th Anniversary
celebrations of the Alpine Club, 2007.*

only one in the whole area to be touched by sunlight. When we stood up again, we noticed our shadows stretching out over the cloud layer below us: a Brocken spectre, just like the one Les and I had experienced with John Oaks and Andy Hodges many years before on the summit of Mont Blanc.

The descent was much easier than I had imagined it would be, but the rocks soon slowed me down and brought back the old familiar jarring sensation in my knees. Fortunately, I had a temporary respite from my cough and cold, and was able to appreciate an afterglow of pleasure at having had such a delightful day out, snatched from the clouds and storms. We were too tired to go down to the valley that afternoon, so we spent a third night at the Oberaletsch Hut. It was almost deserted now. No newcomers arrived, even though it was a Saturday. Presumably the weather deterred them. The next morning, accompanied by Margaret, who had patiently waited at the hut whilst we were out climbing, we walked down to Bel Alp and then drove to Randa, where Andy joined us again.

Losing no time, we four climbers set off on the Monday morning, Margaret too, for the Schönbiel Hut. The Matterhorn was still wreathed in clouds but, by the time we arrived at the hut, the Dent d'Hérens was unveiled in all its majesty. This was our next objective and one that I looked upon with mixed feelings. Once again, I found myself thinking about John and Freda Kemsley, who had perished up there in 1978. We had met Freda, originally a member of the Ladies' Alpine Club, and her husband in the early 1970s in the Lake District, at a meet of the Association of British Members of the Swiss Alpine Club. They were devoted alpinists and we found their enthusiasm inspiring. Freda must have seen in us a like-minded couple and encouraged me, in particular, to recognise that I was beginning to build up an interesting record of Alpine peaks, though, sadly, she was never to know how long that list would become.

Now we were to climb this special mountain, forever associated in my mind with her. When we told the hut guardian of our plan, however, he was very concerned indeed. He thought the big peaks were completely out of condition and there was so much fresh snow on the upper part of the glacier that we would be in danger of falling through a snow bridge into a crevasse, or, worse still, we might be overwhelmed by an avalanche as we approached the Tiefmatten Col. We explained that we did not intend to go to the latter, and finally convinced him that it would be worth our while going to have a look at the current situation.

My peace of mind was disturbed for the rest of the evening. I never asked Margaret how she felt. She was to stay at the hut alone to await our return from the mountain. She would not have the all-embracing excitement and hard physical work of the climb to distract her mind from the potential dangers.

At 2.00 am we rose and were on our way within the hour. There was a full moon, so we were able to make progress without having to rely too much on our torches. For the first three hours, the terrain was most unpleasant, with a continuous mixture of loose boulders, scree and dry glacier. We made our way along the Schönbiel Glacier until we came to our first obstacle. From the hut, we had been able to see two ice falls but it was only the second one which we had to climb. Here lay the difficulty. It was at the foot of this ice fall that Les and Andy could not agree on the line to take. Les (and the guidebook) said that we should climb on the left, but Andy preferred the right-hand option as that was where he had descended only the year before. He maintained that the guidebook was old and possibly out of date. Pete and I stood aside listening to the discussion, Pete determined that we would not separate into two teams, each going its own way. Finally, it was decided to take Les's option but, later in the day, when descending, we looked across at the other side and, despite being unable to see a safe way down, we could see footprints, indicating that a party might recently have gone that way.

The ice fall was, in fact, very intricate indeed but Les led up it without making any errors, and we all followed. In places it was fairly steep, and sometimes there were wide gaps to be crossed. The largest crevasse of all, higher up on the glacier, was where, on the way back down in the soft snow, I had to jump so far that I ended up flat on the ground in order to avoid falling backwards into the yawning hole. We had a brief halt when we reached the bottom of the West-North-West Face of the Dent d'Hérens. It was now daylight, with the promise of blue sky and sun as long as we required.

As we stood there, we deliberated whether to climb the face or go to the Tiefmatten Col after all. I was against the latter idea, because the guardian's dire warnings had made me nervous, and we started up the face. Immediately Les was sinking up to his knees in soft snow. By contrast, up to now, the glacier had been frozen hard. We struggled up the first few pitches in these conditions, still wondering whether to try the other route instead and concerned about the safety of the descent later on. For the time being, we were in the shade but that would not last more than a few hours. Les pressed on, then made a false move, and Andy overtook us by a better route, which we followed. By now we seemed to have committed ourselves to climbing the Dent d'Hérens by its West-North-West Face, though I don't recall any statement of agreement having actually taken place.

The snow was now consolidated and we found ourselves moving steadily upwards through some of the most beautiful terrain I ever experienced. The ice towers and séracs were impressive, yet I didn't feel threatened. When you are so involved in climbing in terrain like this, although you know that there is objective danger, you are by then so committed that you just continue with the job in hand. You appreciate the privilege of being immersed in an environment that so few people ever experience, whilst trusting that chance will allow you to remain safe. Even though you have already assessed the apparent safety of the situation – and I believe that my three companions were all eminently capable of doing this and had indeed done so – there is still, and always will be, a slight chance of Nature taking the upper hand.

So I continued on my way, totally absorbed in the magical white world. It was easy to kick steps into the firm snow, as it never became too solid. We didn't have to dig the front points of our crampons into an ice slope here, so, despite the steep gradient, it was not a repeat of the endurance test I had experienced on the Whymper Couloir. At one point we came to the base of a huge overhanging sérac from which icicles, a metre or so in length, hung down like an inverted forest. We traversed directly underneath them and exited up a steep ramp into the open space above. The angle eased off and, once we had crossed the *bergschrund*, there were no further difficulties. Andy and Pete kept moving at such a comfortable pace ahead that I had no difficulty keeping up.

From the point at which we reached the Normal Route from the Italian side, we had to gain another 300m in altitude. It was a case of 'head down and just keep going' until we came to the rocks below the final snow ridge. It was airy up there and I peered gingerly down the North Face. There, on the other side of the glacier, was the Schönbiel Hut and I wondered if the guardian could see us through his binoculars and if Margaret knew we had almost arrived. I climbed on carefully in this exposed position, two or three more rope lengths, to the summit. Andy and Pete had stopped lower down for a breather, so Les and I stood there alone for a few minutes, savouring the view and the sensation of achievement. The sky was a vivid blue and totally cloudless. The Matterhorn was right there, next to us, that splendid, so familiar outline. Les, took out his monocular and could see someone standing on the summit.

The four of us, reunited again, called out the names of all the peaks we could see in the Swiss Valais and the Mont Blanc Massif. We had half an hour's rest on the summit before returning the way we had come. It was important not to leave the descent of the West-North-West Face till too late, better to get down before the sun warmed it up too much. We descended quite easily and two hours later were wading down the softened glacier. Several hours after that, I stumbled across the last boulders, heaved my aching body up the cliff and flopped down on the hut terrace to swallow some much-deserved Apfelsaft. There I relaxed at last, gazing with deep satisfaction at the magnificent mountain we had just climbed. The Dent d'Hérens, ascended by its West-North-West Face, would remain forever etched upon my mind as the climax of the 1982 season and, indeed, one of the most impressive routes I ever climbed.

3

HIATUS

The year 1983 was destined to be a hiatus in my climbing career. At home, I was busy with the second year of my part-time Master's degree course and had to cut back on the number of weekends when I could travel to the mountains, though I continued to keep as fit as possible. We spent the Easter vacation in the Alps trying to ski-tour as usual, but the weather was against us and we returned home having done very little. In the meantime, my gynaecological problems were becoming very unpleasant. Dealing with unpredictable and excessively heavy menstruation on an increasingly frequent basis was not particularly easy out in the wilds on mountaineering expeditions. So I consulted my doctor:

'Have you considered a hysterectomy?' he brightly suggested.

I flinched. He had mentioned the idea before, and I had refused to consider it. Such a radical solution to my problems had until then seemed completely unjustifiable. However, after much soul-searching and trying some medication that made me feel extremely unwell, I decided to go ahead and get my problems resolved once and for all. I was over forty now, and had no intention of starting a family at such an age.

I spent the following few months in a state of considerable Angst. As soon as I had completed my academic duties that summer term, I took leave of absence from college and was admitted to hospital for the first internal operation of my life. After it, I spent the summer heat wave convalescing in the garden until I reached the point when my surgeon agreed that foreign travel was again possible.

So we went abroad with our now regular summer companions, the Flemings. Whilst Pete and Les set about tidying up their lists, Margaret and I relaxed at a lower altitude. Strangely, I was not frustrated and managed to reap a considerable amount of pleasure from wandering about and admiring the scenery, firstly in Chamonix and then in the Bernese Oberland. By the time we reached Grindelwald, I was well enough to walk all the way to the new Schreckhorn Hut, where the four of us spent the night.

Unfortunately, after his climb with Pete, Les tripped on the glacier, putting a crampon spike through his knee, and so mountaineering came to an abrupt end for that season. It is unlikely there was any connection with that incident but, back at home a few weeks later, Les himself was hospitalised and also submitted to the surgeon's knife. One of his spinal discs had prolapsed but he was fortunate to be in the hands of someone who practised the very latest and least invasive techniques of microsurgery.

4

STARTING AGAIN

By April 1984, we were both fit enough again to resume our normal lifestyle, albeit a little cautiously at first. With Paul Luton, we planned a gentle ski-tour in the French Vanoise. In fact, we did so well and the weather was so good that, after completing the intended route, we drove over to Italy to attempt the Gran Paradiso, a Fourthousander that none of us had climbed before and which could be done on ski. For Paul, this would be his second Fourthousander, having climbed Castor with us in 1979, and for me, it was my first in Italy. The only other Fourthousander on Italian soil is the Aiguille Blanche de Peuterey, on the south side of Mont Blanc, which Les and Pete had climbed in 1982. It would be another five years before I seriously considered attempting the Aiguille Blanche myself.

On a scorching hot day we drove to Aosta, where we appalled ourselves by spending what seemed like a fortune in Italian lire on a lunch of omelette followed by ice cream. We then drove up the long, narrow valley to Pont and spent the night at an inn. Suddenly the weather changed and the following morning we looked out to see low cloud completely masking the mountains. As time was running out, we decided to go up to the Vittorio e Emmanuele Hut with enough food and money for two days, in the hope that the weather would improve. We were allotted places on the vast *matratzenlager* under the roof where there was room for dozens of people to lie down. I dreaded the night to come but fortunately, probably because of the poor weather, only a few other people turned up to share our attic. The majority of guests had paid more than us and were accommodated in smaller rooms on the floors below. At dinnertime, the dining room was more or less full, but the hut wasn't crowded.

We were lucky; the next day was perfect again and we skinned steadily up the highest mountain in Italy. The only part of the climb of any note was the 'sting in the tail'. To reach the summit cairn we had to clamber delicately across a very sharp, rocky ridge with a huge drop to one side. The last two steps were the most daunting, and I experienced surges of vertigo as I teetered gingerly in my ungainly plastic ski boots over an exposed block. What confidence I had built up in previous years seemed to have ebbed away with the traumas of the previous summer. Finally, I arrived at the comforting safety of the Madonna on the summit, where Paul and I posed for Les to take a photograph.

As we skied back down the mountain, we realised that it would have been a more pleasant descent if we had waited until later in the morning, when the snow had thawed a little more in the sunshine. We were, however, in a hurry to drive to Chamonix and ski the Vallée Blanche before returning home.

The summer was dominated by Les's intention to complete his list of 4000m peaks but, although he only had two left to do and succeeded on one, the other resisted all his attempts that holiday. Once again we were joined by Pete and Margaret Fleming and headed for the Dauphiné at the end of July. Perfect weather gave us good climbing conditions and, with Pete, we climbed a number of routes, including the traverse of the Ecrins from south to north. Margaret, patient as ever, waited for us down in the valley.

Les and I had climbed the Barre des Ecrins from the northern side ten years before but Pete was keen to add this Fourthousander to his list too. This gave us the opportunity to undertake a more exciting expedition than our original one. The first south-to-north traverse of the Ecrins had been accomplished in 1888 by Katy Richardson with two French companions, J. B. Bich and le père Gaspard. Almost one hundred years later, we hoped that the English guidebook would help us find the route easily but the description of the ascent of the South Face of the Ecrins was poor and the tips that the hut guardian gave us were not particularly helpful. Finding the route difficult to follow, we picked an interesting line up increasingly steep rock of very good quality, which we enjoyed immensely, but which would have been very difficult to reverse. Pete, who was behind me at one point, voiced his misgivings about getting ourselves into such a situation, but Les, out of earshot, led on upwards, relentlessly towing us behind him, or so it seemed to me. It became quite strenuous and my nerves were on edge.

The route was by no means over when we reached the summit. Once more I had to steel my nerves, having forgotten the airy nature of the rocky *Barre* that we had to traverse to descend to the Col des Ecrins. Miss Richardson would have had no such fears. From the col, we had to reach our campsite far below at La Bérarde. First of all, this necessitated an unpleasant 150m descent on a series of chains, my hands becoming so sore that I could barely hold on by the time I reached the bottom of the last one. It had already taken eight or nine hours to reach this point and still there was a walk of two hours or so left to do. I did, however, describe this route in my journal as 'a magnificent day out'.

We left the Dauphiné for Italy and camped in the Val Veni on the south side of Mont Blanc. There Les was hoping to climb the Dôme de Rochefort, one of his two final Fourthousanders, but the weather spoilt each attempt he made. In the meantime, he and I made an ascent of the Grandes Jorasses. Les may originally have thought that this large mountain straddling the border between France and Italy would make an appropriate Fourthousander for him to complete the Collomb List. He and Pete would not have planned to climb the awe-inspiring Croz or Walker Spur routes up the North Face, but they might have considered climbing the mountain by its North-East (or Hirondelles) Ridge. That would have made a very fine culmination to Les's ambition.

In the long term, however, it was fortunate for me that the weather never presented the right window of opportunity for such a course of action. I wouldn't have accompanied the men on the Hirondellles Ridge, as it would have been too hard for me. Instead of that, Les settled for the idea of climbing the Grandes Jorasses by its Normal Route from the Val Ferret, taking me along as his second, whilst Pete and Margaret spent some time together at a lower altitude. Pete had already climbed the mountain in 1971.

It was a long, steep walk to the Grandes Jorasses Hut and it was a hot day. I took about four hours to get there. Next day, we had fine weather for the climb but there was a cold breeze and we were unable to sit comfortably on the summit crest to savour the splendid views and relax. In any case, Les was disinclined to spend any more time than necessary on the route, being concerned to descend to the valley to catch the last cable car up to the Torino Hut with Pete. They planned to have another attempt on the Dôme de Rochefort the following day.

Not only was this undercurrent of haste somewhat irritating for me, but I was also in need of more rest, having found the Rocher Whymper, the long rocky ridge that we had climbed, somewhat strenuous. Though I had recovered a great deal of stamina, I still lacked core strength, and some of the rock steps had tested me to the limit.

Whilst the descent from Pointe Walker was less strenuous than the morning's climb up to Pointe Whymper, it was tricky in places. I had a moment of panic on the lower glacier, when my feet shot from underneath me: the snow was melting fast on its firm base and balling up our crampons. We took them off to stop our boots from sliding, but it was just as slippery without them as our Vibram soles skidded instead. In this hazardous way we succeeded in reaching the last of the snow. Once we had descended the steep rock promontory below the hut, Les abandoned me, as agreed, and I continued alone, wandering down to the valley, where Margaret pressed a lovely cold beer into my hand on arrival. The men had already left for Entrèves and the Torino Hut.

That night the weather broke again and, once more, the men's plans were thwarted. We left the area, Les still having one last tick to write on his list, and moved to the Pennine Alps, where Pete had a mission to add the Hohberghorn and Dürrenhorn to his own list. By the time the men were ready to set off, I had recovered enough to tag along and we went up to the Dom Hut. Although I had already climbed both mountains, my previous ascent had been from the other side, so I was content to approach them by a different route. If everything went according to plan, we would spend a second night at the Dom Hut, and climb the Lenzspitze the day after that, before returning to the valley.

My journal explains how we fared on the first day after our arrival at the hut. Even as we approached the upper glacier on our way to the first two peaks, my thoughts weren't very positive, and they continued in much the same vein:

What a long way it is to the Festijoch [the col between the two glaciers on the west side of the Mischabel Ridge]*! And each time I go there, I loathe the traverse of the rocks. By the time we eventually reached the col between our two peaks, I was so exhausted that I let the other two go to the Dürrenhorn without me. I belayed myself to a rock and fell asleep. It took the men an hour and by then Pete was feeling shattered. We therefore climbed the Hohberghorn at snail's pace, which suited me, but Les was most frustrated. The descent from the Stecknadeljoch to the Hohberg Glacier was foul: loose scree with light snow cover. I held the men up now. I was so concerned I might send a boulder down on top of Les. On and on we struggled, over the next glacier all the way back to the hut. We had been out for about twelve hours. So we abandoned our thoughts of staying at the hut that night and climbing the Lenzspitze the following day. We were much too tired.*

We had barely had time to sit down on the terrace outside the hut, when we were forced to reconsider. A familiar voice hailed us from the path just below the hut. It was Margaret, who had decided to come up and join us for the night. The expression on her face bore witness to the great sense of relief she felt at reaching the hut after completing the gruelling 1500m ascent from the campsite on such a hot day. As he served her with a welcome cold beer, the guardian congratulated Margaret on her determination to reach her target with nobody to keep her company on the way. She was so much looking forward to a relaxing evening followed by a well-deserved night's rest at the hut. Her horror was palpable when she learned we were intending to go back down to the valley immediately. I quickly suggested that we modified our latest plan, and we stayed at the hut for a meal. After that we had all regained enough energy to make the steep descent to Randa in the cool of the evening. It took us two hours of steady walking to reach our tents.

Les and Pete then made yet another attempt to climb the Dôme de Rochefort but this time got no further than a campsite in Chamonix. Rain set in and brought all their hopes for that year to an unsatisfactory conclusion.

I, too, had had a fairly difficult time that season, despite the fact that I had climbed one very fine new Fourthousander. I had a problem and it was a psychological one. I was concerned that my pleasure in my Alpine activities was no longer as deep as it had been. Was this a recurrence of the feelings I had experienced after the demanding climbs in the summer of 1977? The fact that I had climbed seventeen new Fourthousanders during my last four Alpine seasons, and many other peaks besides, didn't seem to register as a satisfying achievement. Perhaps I really was trying to do too much? As well as juggling my mountaineering and professional life, my hormones were in turmoil and, burdening myself still further, I had proposed that we move house that year. My new garden was stimulating my creative instincts and consuming much of what little spare time I had.

5

TWO MEN COMPLETE THE FOURTHOUSANDERS

If I had known in 1984 what difficulties the following few years were going to bring and how much my mountaineering life was going to be disrupted, I might have counted my blessings at the time. I had imagined, when I opted for gynaecological surgery the year before, that after a temporary disruption I would be restored to perfect health, which I was, and to an athletic lifestyle no longer disrupted by female problems, which was also the case. I had, however, never appreciated how permanent could be the disruption caused by minor accidents and I blithely expected my body to accept without complaint or long-term damage the hammering I continually gave it on the mountains. After all, we knew quite a number of elderly alpinists by then, and some were still very active in the high mountains.

For a while, life continued in its usual pattern. At Easter we would tour the Alps on ski and in the summer we would return to climb a few peaks. We continued to climb mainly in the company of Pete Fleming who, along with Les, was still determined to complete the Collomb List of Fourthousanders. This was the main focus of our Alpine exploits in 1985 and 1986. The result was that I inadvertently added a few more Fourthousanders to my own growing tally, as well as repeating a few that I had previously climbed with Les. I didn't know that fate was waiting to put an unplanned, temporary halt to my activities, so it was fortunate for me that we focused on the remaining Fourthousanders that Les and Pete had to collect because, by doing so, we also reduced the number I would have left to climb in the years following the disruptions caused by injury.

At the start of the 1985 summer season, all three of us, Pete, Les and I, had the same prime objective to climb the Dôme de Rochefort, but first we needed to do a training route, so that we would be fully acclimatised. Starting once more from the Val Veni in Italy, we went up to the tiny Giovane Montagna Bivouac Hut, where we enjoyed a delightfully peaceful evening. At dawn the following morning, the sky glowed orange, enhancing the many familiar dark outlines on the horizon, with Mont Blanc towering immediately above us. We climbed the Petit Mont Blanc and the Aiguille de la Tré la Tête in excellent conditions. Then we were ready to go back to the Torino Hut for Les to make one more attempt to reach his *bête noire*, the Dôme de Rochefort. After the previous year's fiasco, I had vowed that on the next occasion I would accompany them as their lucky mascot.

Up at the Torino Hut, we were not so sure that all would be well. Storm clouds began to gather round the big peaks that evening and were still with us the next day. Luckily, the Rochefort Arête was almost entirely free of cloud and the snow conditions were first-rate, so we were able to move much more quickly than on my previous traverse of the ridge with John Howe and Ian and Sue Stirrups. This time, the icy step wasn't icy and the rocks on the slope below the Aiguille de Rochefort were dry. They weren't decorated in an array of icicles on this occasion, either. Thus we were able to make really good time to the Dôme. At last Les had reached his target: he had climbed all the Fourthousanders! We offered him our congratulations and we, too, were pleased to have reached another previously unclimbed summit. After all the efforts Pete and Les had made to get to this awk-wardly placed, unimpressive Fourthousander, which from Italy looks no more than a pimple on a long snow ridge, the sense of relief was tangible. A few years later, when I decided to complete the List too, I was very pleased that I had accompanied them and didn't need to return to the Dôme.

Pete now had just seven Fourthousanders left to climb, so he and Margaret drove to the Val Sesia, and went up to the Gnifetti Hut. From there, Pete soloed the Piramide Vincent and Parrotspitze. Meanwhile, Les and I installed ourselves in the Silvaplana campsite near St. Moritz, hoping to do a route somewhere in the Bernina Alps whilst waiting for Pete and Margaret to join us again. Poor weather deterred us from setting out for the moun-tains, but Pete was luckier, with blue skies and sunshine, although he had the inconvenience of gale-force winds on the Monte Rosa Range.

Despite the apparent lack of satisfaction that Alpine climbing had given me the previous summer, the passage of time seemed to have healed this brief dip in my enthusiasm. In the Alps, that summer of 1985, I regained a sense of peace once I was back at high altitude, surrounded by the peaks I loved so much. Thoughts of our life in England were banished by the overwhelming happiness I felt when immersed in this environment of rock and snow, whether the sun shone benignly from a cobalt blue sky or the clouds shrouded the mountains, giving them a sense of mystery. This was where I experienced a profound sense of belonging. My fitness had improved greatly since the previous year, too, and that boosted my morale. At home, we were comfortably installed in our new house and I was back on track with a training regime of swimming and cycling. In my forties now, it was becoming a matter of keeping my body in good form for the chief athletic activity in my life. That was definitely mountaineering.

Pete's next objective was Piz Bernina and we were both keen to help him achieve that goal, especially as it would enable us to return to the Biancograt, a route we had much enjoyed in 1973. A brief period of fine weather began when he and Margaret arrived in the Engadine and this enabled us to make the traverse of Piz Bernina once again. This time, however, although Pete was able to savour to the utmost the joys of the Biancograt, Les and I found it crowded compared with our previous visit, and the magic was spoiled. After the Bernina, we climbed Piz Palü again, this time by the North Pillar of its East Peak. Though not a Fourthousander, it held the same attraction for Pete as it did for us. Ticking mountains off lists may have given us a great deal of satisfaction but, for all three of us, mountaineering was, and always would be, about climbing mountains or specific routes for their own sake.

Back down in the campsite, the season came to an abrupt and most unusual end. We barely had time to change our clothes and have a cup of tea before the blazing sun disappeared behind a rapidly approaching weather front and we were engulfed in torrential rain. The temperature dropped swiftly and by morning our tents were surrounded by four inches of fresh snow. This was the middle of August ...

The following year was to be Pete's year. He fully intended to complete his list of Fourthousanders and we were both keen to be there with him. Our annual ski-tour that Easter was a success and throughout the summer term I walked and climbed as usual at weekends. Unfortunately, in mid-June, I had a trivial accident at work using a paper punch and felt something click in the back of my left shoulder. Not realising that I had torn a tendon, I went climbing on the local crag a few evenings later and it was only after a fairly active hour or so that I realised all was not well. I dutifully adhered to the period of six weeks' rest advised by my doctor, and physiotherapy gave some relief from discomfort, but the Alpine season was fast approaching. Apart from this apparently trivial injury, I was on fine form, rock climbing better than ever and thoroughly looking forward to going out to the Alps. All the doubts I had had in 1984 were now well behind me.

Exactly six weeks after my little accident, Les and I arrived in the Alps and were soon carrying heavy rucksacks up to huts. No doubt my shoulder was still unready for such a burden: most of the time I had no problem, but I began to realise that vibration on descent was causing irritation. Before Pete and Margaret arrived, Les and I enjoyed several short training routes in the Pennine Alps. Above the village of Fionnay, the approach to the Panossière

Hut took us through meadows where the flowers were noticeably abundant. From the hut, we had two days acclimatising on the surrounding mountains, including the Combin de Corbassière, where the final rock ridge to the summit, too, was bedecked with vivid Alpine flowers. Only once before, on the Besso above Zinal in 1970, had I experienced such a colourful route to a summit. Our ascent of the Corbassière was further rewarded by clear views of Mont Blanc in one direction and Monte Rosa in the other.

A few days later we accompanied Pete to the Moiry Hut to help him acclimatise and then we were all ready to make a start on the higher peaks. For his first new Fourthousander that year, Pete decided to climb the Bishorn from the Turtmann Hut. After that, we turned our thoughts to his three remaining peaks, all in the Bernese Oberland. It was there, on the highest of that range of mountains, that he intended to complete his list of Fourthousanders.

Placed as we were in the Rhône Valley, it was possible to gain access to the complex glacier system of the Oberland from the Eggishorn cable car system. Margaret waved goodbye to us in Fiesch, as we were whisked up over the hillside as far as Kühboden, and then we walked round to the Marjelensee. The trudge up the Aletsch Glacier seemed endless, just as it had done in 1977 when we embarked on our first ski-tour. This time, unluckily, I began to feel unwell and that evening at the Konkordia Hut I was sick. I stayed at the hut whilst Les accompanied Pete up the Gross Grünhorn the next day but, on the third day, I managed to summon up enough energy to reach the Obermönchjoch Hut via the Jungfraufirn. By the fourth day I was restored to normal, so, despite a sprinkling of fresh snow that had fallen during the night, we were all able to traverse the Gross Fiescherhorn on our way to the Finsteraarhorn Hut. At last, we were in a position for Pete to climb his final Fourthousander. We were now in the most remote part of the glacier system of the Bernese Oberland, in a place that is about as far as one can be from an inhabited valley base in Western Europe. The only easy way out in an emergency is by helicopter.

On the fifth day of our expedition we set out for the Finsteraarhorn, repeating the route Les and I had taken in 1979 to the Hugisattel, and then the North-West Ridge to reach the summit. Pete's moment of triumph had arrived! It must have been very satisfying to finish the Fourthousanders there: the Finsteraarhorn is remote, it is dramatic in shape and it is the highest peak in the whole area. Sharing that moment with Pete was a privilege. The fact that I had climbed most of those Oberland Fourthousanders before was of no consequence. If there had ever been an opportunity since then, I would happily have climbed them all again.

In his own account of climbing all the Fourthousanders, Pete admits to having felt a mixture of relief and sadness on this occasion. For him, it was 'the end of an era'[1] that had begun exactly thirty years before. He was suffering from a chest infection and, consequently, it had been a struggle to breathe on the way up. Moreover, there was no view: the clouds had rolled in whilst we were climbing the ridge from the Hugisattel.

On the other hand, I felt a great sense of elation. As far as I was concerned, it was almost as if I had completed the Fourthousanders myself. The occasion contrasted with the ascent of the Dôme de Rochefort, when Les had completed his list the year before. Then, after so many previous attempts to reach the summit of the Dôme, we all three shared a huge sensation of relief, but Pete had still not achieved his own ambition. As it had initially been his idea to complete the Collomb list, it seemed a little unfair that Les had inadvertently overtaken him in the number of peaks climbed and arrived first at the goal. Now, on the Finsteraarhorn, the record had been put straight. Would it be my turn next? No such thought occurred to me until three years later.

---

1 *One Man's Fourthousanders* by Peter Fleming

6

FATIGUE

The day we climbed the Weisshorn in 1980, we had been out on the mountain for at least twelve hours. Now, on an easy track at last, I was alone with my aching body. I was on the descent from the Weisshorn Hut to the railway station in Randa, and away from the adrenalin-fed action of climbing up and down narrow crests of rock and snow. Les had 'abandoned' me, to allow his body to relax at its own pace, always so much faster than mine. In Randa we intended to catch the Zermatt train on its way down the Mattertal to Visp, where we would change to a fast train along the Rhône Valley for one brief section, before catching the postbus back up into the mountains. Our tent awaited us on the campsite in Zinal.

We had left the Tracuit Hut at two o'clock in the morning and at 10.00 am we stood on the summit after the long climb up the North Ridge. It was now about 3.00 pm and we had rested for barely half an hour at the Weisshorn Hut on the way down. Both mind and body were trying their hardest to rebel. Thoughts jostled with each other for my attention: if only I could sit down again just for a moment… if only I could stop to enjoy the view of the mountains over there on the other side of the valley, the Dom, the Täschhorn, the Alphubel … Those great snow domes and rocky crests were all begging me to stop and gaze at them.

Then my knees intervened. Oh, the pain! How much more of this could I bear? My knees ached so much, I wondered if they would ever recover from the torture of pounding downhill on the hard stony path.

Reason stepped in: I must keep going. I mustn't stop. We might miss the last bus up to Zinal from Sierre. I really couldn't bear the thought of another night without getting back to the home comforts of our little tent.

Several hours later, back in Zinal, I crawled into my down sleeping bag and slept one of the most relaxing sleeps of my life. The following morning I awoke totally refreshed, the residual aches and pains of battered muscles and damaged joints temporarily dismissed. I glowed instead with intense delight at having traversed such a magical, yet so demanding, mountain.

My fourteen-hour day of sustained activity on the Weisshorn was nothing compared with the experience of Mrs. Le Blond when she first climbed the Matterhorn. She started by walking all the way from Visp to St. Niklaus, a distance of 16km, before continuing to Zermatt. At that time, there was no rail service up the Mattertal. The line from Visp wasn't completed until 1890, and the extension from St. Niklaus to Zermatt didn't open fully until 1891.

Having reached Zermatt, Mrs. Le Blond didn't linger. Instead of spending the first part of the night in a hotel, as she usually did before a climb, she and her party, 'tempted by glorious weather',[1] set out for the summit, hoping to return to Zermatt the next day by descending the Italian Ridge and crossing the Theodule Pass back into Switzerland. However, the rock on the descent was so icy that they made very slow progress, and were forced to spend the night sitting on a rocky ledge until daylight, when they would be able to see their way down the remaining part of the ridge. They were in poor shape by then, as they had run out of food and drink and had 'tongues swollen like sausages'.[2] It must have been not only exhausting, but also very cold and uncomfortable. Because of their distress, they had to continue down the Italian slopes beyond the foot of the Matterhorn as far as the village of Breuil in order to obtain food and drink, but they then turned around immediately and walked back up to the pass and down the glacier on the Swiss side to Zermatt. It had taken them 43 hours. It is astonishing how will-power can overcome fatigue on such an occasion.

One of Katy Richardson's best-known early feats of endurance was in 1882. At the age of 26, in one week at the end of July, she climbed no fewer than four completely separate Fourthousanders in the area around Zermatt: first the Zinalrothorn, then the Weisshorn, followed by the Monte Rosa and finally the Matterhorn. With the St Niklaus-Zermatt stretch of railway not yet open, a climber descending to the valley from the summit of the Weisshorn would either have had to walk or possibly take a lift with a mule pack for the 20km up the valley to Zermatt. From there, it was still more than another 12km as the crow flies to the summit of the Monte Rosa, with 3000m of ascent. (It wasn't until 1898 that people could use the Gornergrat rack railway to alleviate the effort of the uphill approach from the village to the Gorner Glacier.) It is likely that Miss Richardson and her party took a shortcut via Täschalp, entirely avoiding Zermatt, though it would still have been a lengthy and strenuous undertaking to get from the summit of the Weisshorn to the summit of the Monte Rosa in two days.

---

1 'Then and Now', article by Mrs. Le Blond, reproduced in LAC Final Yearbook, 1975
2 ibid

Six years after my endurance test on the Weisshorn, perhaps I should have been more aware of the dangers of fatigue. If nothing else, my year-long experience of recovering from abdominal surgery should have warned me. By 1986, I was in my mid-forties, but I didn't feel that old. Unfortunately, where physical ageing is concerned, the mind doesn't always seem to keep pace. I forgot how long it took for injuries to heal and I was frequently tempted to undertake new ventures when I had barely had time to relax after my latest exploits. Fatigue is an enemy: it causes you to make errors of judgment as well as putting undue strain on the body. Moreover, excessive fatigue is exhaustion or 'burnout'. I hadn't yet reached the latter but I was in danger of acting carelessly and accidentally hurting myself.

Another decade later, in 1995, my life suddenly changed. Eventually I realised that excessive fatigue had undoubtedly played its role in undermining my ability to continue working and playing at such an intensive level. Dorothy Pilley Richards referred to 'the disproportion between what one really believes one can do and what one has somehow done'.[3] Then she wrote:

What a good thing that one did not fully know how far one had to go.[4]

Indeed it was.

---

3 'Looking Backward', LAC Yearbook 1975, article by Dorothy Pilley Richards on the occasion of the merger of the LAC with the AC in 1974
4 ibid

7

ONE PEAK TOO MANY

Once Pete had completed his list of Fourthousanders, he and Margaret left us to spend the remaining days of their holiday in a less demanding environment, whilst Les and I returned yet again to the Zermatt Valley. The Obergabelhorn was one of the few big mountains in the area that I had never climbed and when Les suggested that we might round off the season with an ascent of its Normal Route, the East-North-East Ridge via the Wellenkuppe, I was tempted, despite my concern that a descent of the rocky Arbengrat, its West-South-West Ridge, might not do my shoulder injury much good.

Forgetting that I had been unwell only a few days previously, and not leaving our bodies very much time to recuperate from the strenuous tour of the Bernese Oberland, we set off up the steep path above the Trift Gorge to the Rothorn Hut. This refuge is situated at 3198m, some 1600m above Zermatt, and the walk up takes four or five hours. The sun was blazing down and several times I felt so dizzy that I had to stop. Once we had emerged from the top of the gorge, Les pressed on ahead to make sure of good sleeping spaces for us. By the half-way stage, I was on my own, making my way up the relentless moraine of the Trift Glacier. The heat suddenly changed to a cool breeze but this made me feel no better. By the time I arrived at the hut, I was in a very sorry state indeed, so exhausted that I could barely speak. It took me quite a while to recover.

Despite the arduous nature of the hut walk, I felt able enough less than twelve hours later to set off on our route. Thinking back, it is easy to see just how inappropriate this whole venture was for someone in my state of health. I was obviously exhausted and not entirely well; moreover, I had one shoulder in a fairly lamentable state and should have been resting it. However, some deep psychological factor was at work: I felt the need to climb this Fourthousander which I had never climbed before and which I had admired on my very first evening at a mountain hut in Switzerland. It was in 1970 and we were spending the first night of my Alpine career at the Mountet Hut, surrounded by a cirque of mountains with the North Face of the Obergabelhorn at its heart. Today, our route was going to take us along the two ridges that formed the silhouette of that 'perfect mountain'.

At the Rothorn Hut, there were more British climbers than I had seen all summer, but most headed for the Zinalrothorn the next day, so we were one of only a few parties setting out in the direction of the Obergabelhorn. We soon realised why. When Les had climbed the East-North-East Ridge in the late 1960s, it had been a fairly easy route, mainly on snow. Now, nearly twenty years later, we were to discover that conditions had changed.

The only obstacle of any note on the way to the Obergabelhorn via the Wellenkuppe is the Grand Gendarme, where fixed ropes supposedly ease the way. I have always found such ropes and cables unpleasant to handle and this occasion was no exception. After that, we continued without difficulty until about half-way up the East-North-East Ridge on our way to the summit. The snow ridge of Les's memory had now become a series of smooth rock pitches, with no alternative means of ascent. Climbers were appearing in increasing numbers above us, swinging down on ropes protected by belays at intermittent abseil points. There must have been a dozen or so people, all apparently having spent the night at the Arben Bivouac Hut on the other side of the mountain. It was certainly easier to descend than ascend this route. At one point a guide, who was waiting for us to pass him, offered Les a belay on a particularly smooth, exposed groove and, probably for the only time in his Alpine climbing career, Les accepted the offer. I followed on a very tight rope.

It was a relief to reach the summit, but the wind was very cold and there was hardly any space at all in which to shelter from it. The Matterhorn, quite close by, looked spectacular and I realised that this was the first time that morning since we had stood on top of the Wellenkuppe, that I had had time to appreciate the view. It was to be my last enjoyable moment for many hours.

I was never very adept at climbing long rock ridges, and particularly not in descent. Thus the Arbengrat, which many rock climbers would relish, proved rather trying. There were few parts where I was prepared to move roped together with no kind of protection and there were some places where I would not move at all without a really good belay, so Les had to exercise considerable patience. This must have been hard for him, as he found the climbing easy and was hoping to descend quickly enough to get back to the valley in good time. We were due to dine with Richard and Katherine Heery at their home near Geneva that same evening. A few years previously, Richard had taken a teaching post at an International School there and he and Katherine had decided not to return to live in the UK.

Eventually we left the ridge to wend our way down the grit-strewn South Face of the Obergabelhorn. A cautious descent brought us to the Arben Bivouac Hut, a very fine new building at that time. We rested there briefly but the need to press on was never far from Les's mind. The route then took us down a crevasse-ridden glacier, followed by what seemed like miles of moraine, and finally there came a point where I could no longer tolerate the pain. So I stopped and exchanged my heavy boots for lightweight trainers. Carrying the boots was preferable to the agony of sore feet.

When I eventually reached Les, who had been waiting for me further down, he simply hauled his rucksack back onto his shoulders and, without displaying the frustration he must have felt, said:

'Right, now let's get motoring.'

I exploded with rage. I simply could not go any faster. A few minutes later, we saw a signpost that indicated: 'Zermatt, 2½ hours.' I was appalled – but needs must and I was at the station two hours later. The walk had seemed interminable. The agony of feet and knees was temporarily replaced by the agony of carrying the rucksack, only to be replaced by the knees and feet again and, finally, just sheer exhaustion. I simply could not get the commands from my head to my body.

Down in Zermatt, the train was waiting and so was Les. He had tried to buy me a litre of milk to drink but a festival was in progress and all the shops were closed. Instead, he found me a can of fizzy drink, which I relished all the same. It was thirteen hours since we had left the Rothorn Hut.

Les had been right to hurry, though not just in order to get to Geneva that evening. By the time the train had delivered us to its first halt in Täsch and we had retrieved our car, rain was beginning to fall. This quickly turned to hail and the wind began to blow furiously. Driving along the Rhône Valley towards Geneva, we experienced a gale that littered the road with debris from fallen branches. What a contrast to the many hours of unbroken sunshine we had just experienced up on the mountain, and how lucky we were to have descended before the storm broke.

I was reminded again of Walter Kirstein. Mountaineering is indeed all about contrasts, though that is hardly the reason we would ever quote when asked why we climb. It is not just the variations in weather that come to mind when I consider my Alpine experiences. This particular day had been such a contrast to the one we had enjoyed so recently on the Finsteraarhorn with Pete. It was days such as that which made it all worthwhile. Conversely, although our ascent of the Obergabelhorn resulted in an addition to my tally of Fourthousanders, and I was glad to have climbed a mountain I had long known and admired, it was an experience that made me write the following lines in my journal a few weeks after returning home:

I had not enjoyed a single moment of the whole thirteen-hour day, except perhaps a fleeting sense of pleasure at the top of the Wellenkuppe. [So the moment at the summit of the Obergabelhorn, despite the view of the Matterhorn, had not actually registered as a pleasure.] *It had been gruelling, and now I was only too aware of the self-inflicted damage to my shoulder and possible repercussions. What is the point of it all if you don't get any pleasure?*

My concerns about my shoulder, too, had proved justified. Down-climbing seemed to have been the very worst exercise for my left arm and, at home, I had to start on a long round of doctors to get it repaired.

However, the Obergabelhorn was the only mountain I had not enjoyed that summer. What a pity that my experience of the traverse was so different from Dorothy Pilley's in 1923.[1] She was clearly a far more proficient and daring climber than me, and consequently found the Arbengrat consisted of 'magnificent rocks, nowhere very difficult, but continuously interesting'. They are – but sadly I was in no fit state to enjoy that descent route. Then, too, the Arben Glacier may have been covered in a great deal more snow, and thus much less arduous than it was in 1986. Above all, Dorothy Pilley and her guide had perfect snow conditions on the ascent of the East-North-East Ridge. They made 'leisurely, effortless and exciting progress' along the 'sweep after sweep of the clear white ridge … [that] … led up to the final rocks'. It was only on the ascent of the Grand Gendarme that she and I shared a similar experience: 'From its most repellent corner we found hanging an immense cable. The ascent of this was the least attractive and most fatiguing aspect of the day.' This indefatigable young woman (she was about thirty years old at the time, whereas I was now in my mid-forties) then rushed off to continue her climbing season with a grand traverse of Monte Rosa, Lyskamm and Castor. I, on the other hand, was only too grateful after my exhausting traverse of the Obergabelhorn that we were at the end of our holiday.

Did I really want to continue spending my summer vacations in this way, or was this just a 'blip'?

---

1 *Climbing Days* by Dorothy Pilley

8
SETBACK

A year later, in July 1987, I wrote a short note in my journal. I wondered if the sentiments I had expressed at the end of the previous summer were, in fact, a plea to stop, to finish with the grind. If so, that plea was answered. From the autumn of 1986 onwards, my shoulder injury gave me endless trouble. Although my work at college continued as usual, the rest of my life was on hold. I consulted doctors, tried physiotherapy, osteopathy, homeopathy, acupuncture, cortisone injections and minor surgery, all to no avail. I was quite unable to carry even a small rucksack. The idea of ski-touring at Easter had to be abandoned and the summer alpine season was ruled out too. This gave me no sense of relief whatsoever. After that day on the Obergabelhorn, one might imagine that it would have been a delight to sit back and let other people play. Instead, I wrote: 'The future is bleak, and my heart grieves.' Depression had set in. I was by no means ready to give up mountaineering: the apparent plea to stop held no substance.

Fortunately, I eventually found a surgeon, Paul Stableforth in Bristol, who correctly diagnosed my injury and was enthusiastic to help me return to the mountains. MRI scanners were few and far between in those days, but he was in a position to request a scan at Frenchay Hospital. I believe I was part of a research project. The scan confirmed the diagnosis and, in February 1988, I succumbed to the surgeon's knife again. My supraspinatus tendon was at last released from its entrapment and became free to help itself. I was advised that I could resume normal mountain activities and I duly did so. There was an immediate and considerable improvement after the operation, although mobility was impaired for quite a long time, and within a few months I was able to rock climb again. Cneifon Arête above the Ogwen Valley, First Pinnacle Rib on the West Face of Tryfan and Amphitheatre Buttress in the Carneddau, all in North Wales, were the first routes I climbed that year. A trip to the Lake District added Bowfell Buttress to my growing list. These were all routes I had climbed in the past, but it was such a pleasure to find that I could do them again, now that I had a new lease of life. These easy V Diff climbs were my only serious preparation for joining the Alpine Club meet at the end of July in the Zermatt Valley, and the Gloucestershire Mountaineering Club meet in the Bregaglia after that. Having done so little general mountain walking over the previous two years, I found that I was slow going uphill, and my knees were very painful in descent, but overall I was well pleased. Climbing in the high mountains that summer gave me an unexpectedly profound sense of joy.

Once again I had to curb my natural tendency to fear in exposed situations. I needed to retrain my mind to cope with narrow rock ridges and steep precipices. I also needed to gain confidence in the strength of my mended shoulder. Between such moments, however, my long-starved soul was overjoyed to be back amongst the snow and rock of the great peaks of the Alps. After acclimatising on the Pointe de Zinal, Les and I made easy ascents of two previously climbed Fourthousanders, the Allalinhorn and the Weissmies. Pete Fleming and other Alpine Club members were with us on the latter. After that, I relaxed for a few days whilst Les and Pete went climbing on their own.

Without my realising it at the time, Les was subtly steering me towards increasing the number of Fourthousanders I had climbed. At that stage there was still not a shred of expectation that I would attempt the Aiguille Blanche de Peuterey, which we all considered far more serious than any of the other mountains on the list, nor had I ever fancied climbing the Dent du Géant, because I found seriously exposed rock routes so unnerving. Thus I never imagined that I would complete Collomb's List. However, above all because it is a Fourthousander, Les and I decided to ascend the Lenzspitze and traverse the Nadelgrat to the Nadelhorn, which I had previously climbed. This is a classic Alpine route and Les had done the traverse many years before with a few friends.

It was a fine day when we set off from Saas Fee for the Mischabel Hut but there was a threat that the weather might become unsettled. Our attempt to sleep fairly early that evening was disturbed by the hut guardian setting off the traditional fireworks just outside our dormitory window. It was 1st August, Swiss National Day, and as we were long accustomed to this practice, we should have been expecting it.

Next morning we left the hut as early as possible, having breakfasted at 3.00 am. The sky was fairly clear but there were big cloud formations scudding rapidly past, signs of a very strong wind at high altitude and precursors of the storms to come. Evidence of my growing interest in completing all the Fourthousanders is to be found in my journal:

I felt fairly tense [on account of the signs of changing weather] but all the more determined to climb as fast as I could to get this steep, rocky peak in the bag. There only remained seven 4000m peaks to complete the list of fifty-two, and I didn't want to be obliged to return to the Lenzspitze, because I feared that my knees might soon prevent such steep descents. [I was referring to the descent from the Mischabel hut to Saas Fee after the climb, one of the steepest hut walks that I knew in the Alps.]

We moved as quickly as possible and made good progress up the East-North-East Ridge towards the Grand Gendarme, which I climbed somewhat nervously, very conscious of my rigid new boots. This was the first season I had climbed in plastic boots and, although I found them more comfortable than any previous pair of Alpine boots, I missed the flexibility of leather. I sincerely hoped we wouldn't have to reverse this part of the climb. My hopes were dashed a little later when I was descending an awkward chimney and Les called from his belay above. When I looked up, I saw that little flakes of snow were falling. The weather was coming from the other side of the mountain and Les could see a dense, dark cloud formation over the summits of the Täschhorn and the Dom, just to the left of the Lenzspitze. Ensconced in my chimney, I was unaware of this but the deterioration must have been quite sudden. We turned round. Fortunately the descent of the Grand Gendarme didn't seem as daunting as I had feared, and on our return to the hut, the guardian congratulated us on our decision. He had been watching our progress through binoculars. So the Lenzspitze would have to wait until another occasion.

That was, however, not the end of the 1988 season. With Pete and Margaret, we moved to Vicosoprano in the Bregaglia, an area of sharp granite peaks and towers straddling the Swiss/Italian border a few miles south of St. Moritz. From Vicosoprano, Les drove Pete and me round to Chiareggio in Italy to climb Monte Disgrazia, a vast, remote, glaciated peak which, despite its stature, only reaches a height of 3678m. Our ascent by the North-North-East Ridge, the Corda Molla Route, was one of the most splendid days of my whole mountaineering career. In his 1995 Alpine Club guide-book, Lindsay Griffin describes the ridge as 'a brilliant mixed route of a quality equal to any other of its standard (AD+) in the Alps … a classic undertaking for the middle-grade mountaineer'.

A long, rough walk with heavy rucksacks took us to the Taveggia Hut, a tiny metal bivouac shelter, where we spent the night. The silence of this isolated spot enveloped me like a comforting blanket and, though the bunk was hard and narrow, I relaxed into much-needed sleep. At 2.15 am the alarm rang and I breakfasted on the bread and honey I had brought with me. Then, long before daylight, we set out, having roped up just above the hut. Two Englishmen had come up the previous evening but, as there were only four sleeping places and we had already occupied three of them, they had continued to another bivouac hut some way beyond ours.

There was no sign of them when we passed by in the night.

As it was barely light when we reached the rock ridge, we waited a short while so we wouldn't need to use torches. The rough, red rock was delightful and it was a pleasure to scramble steadily along the many crests and pinnacles, moving together with only the occasional rope belay. My shoulder gave me no trouble at all, not even on a hand-traverse. Many hours after we'd left the hut, I began to feel the need for food and a rest, but Les was up front and determined to keep going. At last, beyond the fine snow crest of the Corda Molla itself, Pete demanded a halt and Les succumbed. By then, the Englishmen had caught us up, having soloed all the way.

After our short rest, we came to a steep snow slope requiring an ice-screw belay and delicate climbing on the front points of our crampons. I was amazed afterwards when I realised that my calf muscles had coped without a hint of pain, so absorbed had I been in the task of climbing safely on a 40° or maybe even a 50° slope. Next came a very steep crack, followed by several pitches of loose rock, and my shoulder began to hurt from wrestling with the holds. Visions of doctors slipped through my mind.

At last we stood at the top of Monte Disgrazia, rewarded with a clear view of Piz Bernina and the other summits of the Engadine. The sun was beating down and it was a relief to escape into the coolness of the immaculate modern bivouac hut which had been built at the summit. We were now by no means alone: a dozen or so other climbers were also there, having ascended by another route.

The first part of the descent required eight or so abseils, an activity I never enjoyed. I was especially thankful to Pete, whose presence I found very reassuring as he was a most experienced abseiler from his many expeditions underground in the Coniston Coppermines. He also kindly accompanied me on the long, exhausting walk down the Ventina Glacier to reach the Porro Hut, where we caught up with Les. He was sitting with the two Englishmen who, unlike us, had some Italian money. Half a bottle of beer was thrust into my hand: a welcome gesture, indeed. We had been out for nearly fourteen hours and all I had drunk that day was my breakfast tea at 2.30 am and the litre of cold water I carried in my rucksack.

PART SIX

Endgame

The greatest asset a mountaineer or traveller can have when embarking upon a difficult undertaking, more valuable than any amount of money, equipment or fine weather, is a companion in whom, both physically and morally, he has implicit confidence.

– E. E. Shipton[1]

The Schreckhorn, Lauteraarhorn and Finsteraarhorn

---

1 *Nanda Devi* by E. E.Shipton

1

DECISION

My return to alpinism in 1988 after the two-year hiatus had been enjoyable and successful. We had spent yet another summer holiday with Pete and Margaret Fleming and now, in the summer of 1989, we would be with them again. Les and Pete both hoped that I would continue to add as many of the missing Fourthousanders as I could to my own tally of peaks, and I was not averse to the idea. I was still reasonably fit and had proved myself capable of rock climbing without damaging my shoulder again. Of the 52 major mountains on Collomb's List, I only had seven left to do, but it had never been my intention to volunteer to climb either the Dent du Géant or the Aiguille Blanche de Peuterey.

I cannot recall how I came to agree to climb the Géant. Certainly, I was not coerced against my will, but I did allow Les and Pete to persuade me that I should give it a try. That was the first of two decisions I made in 1989. Without it, I would not have known that I could make the second, the most important one of all: the decision to attempt to climb all the Fourthousanders.

That summer we attended the Alpine Club meet in the Val Veni in Italy. As usual, we intended to do some climbing with Pete Fleming, and our Gloucestershire Mountaineering Club friend, Andy Hodges, joined us as well. After a training route on Mont Dolent, Les and I took the cable car yet again up to the Torino Hut. From there, we made an ascent of the South-East Ridge of the Tour Ronde, a magnificent viewpoint, where Les was able to take photographs for the new Mont Blanc guidebook which he was editing.

Sitting on the summit of the Tour Ronde, admiring the Brenva Face of Mont Blanc and the long, jagged Peuterey Ridge beyond, I had no inkling of the plan that was to be formulated a few days later. My immediate thoughts were with the Dent du Géant, which we were planning to climb the next day. All the previous afternoon I had sat at the Torino Hut looking dolefully at the peaks around us. I simply couldn't summon up any positive feelings as far as the Géant was concerned. I had always felt apprehensive about it, and now I feared it was the height of folly to punish my shoulders on such a long, steep rock climb. For the first time in my climbing career, I had a suspicion that I was being persuaded to do a route I didn't really want to do. Why hadn't I had the courage to say no? But now, at last, on the Tour Ronde, I began to smile. The scramble had boosted my morale.

That evening, Pete joined us as planned and I was so grateful for his presence the next day. The Dent du Géant merits its name: the Giant's Tooth. The Normal Route takes a line for over 100m up the Burgener Slabs on the South-West Face of this imposing pillar of rock. From many viewpoints the Géant looks just like a tall canine tooth: on all sides it is steep, even on its easiest face, and the sense of exposure is considerable. In my mind it resembled a mini-Matterhorn: one unprotected slip and the climber would fall to his doom. I had to steel myself to do what I had done on the traverse from the Täschhorn to the Dom: I had to ignore my doubts and press on with the job of scaling the rock face, then redescending as safely and as swiftly as I could.

This mental attitude paid off and the result was that my morale remained high all day. I performed well, kept moving whenever required and, when we reached the summit, was rewarded by the warm glow of achievement. As I crossed the final shelf to reach the Madonna, I smiled. There below me was the Rochefort Arête glistening in the sun. How much safer I would have felt down there on the snow, rather than perched on the top of this crazy rock tower! My thoughts turned to the descent, but I put the lid firmly on my doubts and took the abseils in my stride.

Timing one's ascent of the Géant is quite important. Arriving too early at the foot of the slabs means climbing in the shade on cold rock, but delaying one's start inevitably brings the unpleasantness of ascending the same line that earlier parties are already descending. Thick fixed ropes adorn the slabs, but I contrived to use them as little as possible. At the start, the rock to the side of them was quite superb for a considerable way, offering many little holds but, higher up, the gradient steepened sharply and I had no choice but to go up the fixed rope hand over hand. This was so exhausting that eventually I had difficulty in holding on to it. I was at the limit of my endurance and the tight rope from Les above me was essential to keep me in contact with the rock. There were several pitches to climb in this way, with belays at intervals, and just as we were waiting at one point, a party of two men and a very small boy came past us on their way down. It was difficult to believe that the little lad was enjoying himself: his feet were scarcely in contact with the rock and he was moaning about stomach pains. Poor little boy, I knew how he felt, but at least I had freely chosen to be there – or had I? Without the encouragement of my two companions, whom I trusted implicitly, I doubt if I would ever have had the courage to decide to climb the Géant.

The final part of the climb had a real sting in its tail. The slabs were behind us, but a short, steep wall awaited and there I was almost defeated by the strenuousness of the moves. Yet again I needed a tight rope: I was simply not strong enough to do the climb without assistance. Over a century earlier, Mrs E. Burnaby (Mrs. Aubrey Le Blond) had made the third ascent of the Dent du Géant, no doubt climbing with much greater ease than I did. She would also have had a much more peaceful descent of the mountain.

Our problem, as we returned from the summit, was more to do with the people who were still coming up, rather than the actual down-climbing. Reversing the steep wall after leaving the top, we became rather tangled up with a group of six Italian soldiers. Once we reached the slab pitches, however, it was simply a matter of abseiling. Here we bypassed a party of Swiss Germans. The young lady with them looked at me and expressed astonishment that we were going down already. It appeared that she could not believe that someone of my age had reached the top and then descended so quickly! I was amused. Did I really seem so ancient? At 47, I was probably older than her mother.

By the time we reached the base of the Géant, my heart was singing and we made a quick descent down the loose, rocky ridge to the glacier. Unroped, we trudged back to the hut and all around me the world seemed bathed in an ethereal glow. How could I find these peaks so grim and daunting, so unappealing on one day, and then, two days later, feel as if I were in heaven? Mont Blanc and all the surrounding summits shimmered enticingly in the afternoon light. Turning back to look at the Géant, I experienced all the feelings I had had after the descent of the Matterhorn. I remembered them quite distinctly: pride, satisfaction, awe and amazement.

We returned to the valley. In glorious weather we joined some other Alpine Club members on an ascent of the Gran Paradiso, a second ascent for Les and me, from the Vittorio e Emmanuele Hut. Visibility was excellent and from the summit we could see not only the Mont Blanc Massif, but also the Pennine Alps, the high peaks of the Dauphiné and finally Monte Viso, the mountain Will McLewin names in the title of his book about the 4000m peaks, *In Monte Viso's Horizon*.

Now came the moment of decision! Back in Val Veni, impressed by my performance on the Dent du Géant, Les and Pete both believed that I would manage without difficulty all the rock climbing on the Normal Route of the Aiguille Blanche de Peuterey. Motivated by the thought that

I could become the first British woman to climb all the Fourthousanders, they encouraged me to make an attempt on this, the most inaccessible of all the peaks on the List. I warmed to the idea, and to the idea of climbing all my remaining six peaks. It seemed such a pity to omit the last few Fourthousanders, when I had already done so many. Without my two partners, however, I neither could, nor would, have attempted to reach my goal. Without their support I would not even have achieved what I did.

2

The Aiguille Blanche
de Peuterey

At a mere 4112m, the Aiguille Blanche is one of the lower Fourthousanders, but its location makes it relatively inaccessible and it seems to me to be in a league of its own. Situated on the Italian side of Mont Blanc, it is one of the summits that form part of the Peuterey Ridge. When I was planning to climb it, I considered several different routes to reach the summit. None of my options presented any great technical difficulty but they were all serious, in that they were difficult of access and remote from the valley. Furthermore, it is not enough to climb a mountain. A safe return is just as important and the logistics of returning safely from the summit of the Aiguille Blanche should not be underestimated, any more than the choice of ascent route. Will McLewin[1] described this particular mountain as the most serious of the 4000m peaks to climb.

In the early 1980s, Les and Pete had climbed it by the Normal Route, taking the Schneider Couloir from the Frêney Glacier to the South-East Ridge. Whilst not technically difficult, this route is serious and remote, involving an approach from the Monzino Hut, situated at the relatively low altitude of 2590m above the Val Veni, then a long climb to the Col de l'Innominata, followed by an abseil down a loose couloir. Finally, you have to cross the extremely crevassed and constantly changing Frêney Glacier to reach the foot of the mountain itself. From there, it could take another four hours to reach the summit. By the end of the decade, the Frêney Glacier had become much more difficult to cross.

To the north of the Aiguille Blanche, the summit can be approached from the Col de Peuterey but this col, at 3934m, is high up on the steep, south side of Mont Blanc and is difficult to reach from the valley. Climbers have a choice of approach to the col, either by traversing the Upper Frêney Glacier from the Col Eccles, or by walking across the Upper Brenva Glacier from the Col du Trident. However, by the time I was considering my options,

---

1 *In Monte Viso's Horizon* by Will McLewin

rockfall and the closure of the Trident Bivouac Hut had rendered the latter strategy less feasible. In any case, we deemed this route too serious for me because of the very steep approach to the Col de Peuterey on that side. It is also possible to climb the Rochers Gruber from the Lower Frêney to the Upper Frêney Glacier but this is a route recommended for descent rather than ascent, as we unfortunately learned through experience. All these routes are subject to rock or ice fall, especially in the heat of the day. It is a very long way from these glaciers to the safety of the Val Veni below.

I considered climbing the mountain by each of these routes, and when I was at the peak of fitness, they were all reasonable targets. The Aiguille Blanche is, however, a mountain that I could only approach in a period of stable weather and with the right companions. Companions, plural. It is not a mountain I could think of climbing with only one other companion. It seemed too serious for that, especially in the days before climbers carried mobile phones.

The nearest accommodation is primitive and extremely remote. At that time, there was a choice between the bivouac hut at 3680m on the Col de la Fourche below the Brenva Ridge, or the two small shelters at 3850m near the Col Eccles, or the even tinier bivouac hut perched at 3490m on the Brèche Nord des Dames Anglaises. The latter is usually only used by parties doing the Peuterey Ridge Intégral, the lengthy route that can be climbed all the way from the Val Veni over both the Aiguille Noire and the Aiguille Blanche, and culminates in the ascent of the ridge from the Col de Peuterey to the summit of Mont Blanc. The Monzino Hut was the only relatively luxurious accommodation in the vicinity but it was situated so low down the mountain that I couldn't be sure of climbing the Aiguille Blanche from it and returning to it on the same day. It was simply too far away for the speed at which I was likely to travel. Other than those options, the only alternative is to take one's own bivouac gear and find a suitable spot to spend the night.

The Aiguille Blanche de Peuterey is only distinguishable as a separate mountain from certain viewpoints. If you approach the Mont Blanc Massif from the South, the Aiguille Blanche appears to be flattened out of recognition, sandwiched between the Brenva and Freney Faces; from the Tour Ronde to the north-east, the mountain simply becomes a snow crest between two rock points on the Peuterey Ridge Intégral, with the much spikier, but significantly lower, Aiguille Noire on one side and, on the other, the Upper Peuterey Ridge continuing to ascend another 700m or so to the snow dome of Mont Blanc. It is only from the village of Entrèves, near the Italian exit from the Mont Blanc tunnel, that I have looked up in awe at the Aiguille Blanche and felt convinced that the distinctive form high above me really is a separate mountain in its own right.

Because the mountain is such a challenge and because I had become so aware of my position as a female alpinist, I was interested to know more about the ascents of two of my early predecessors: Una Cameron and Dorothy Thompson.

Una Cameron, with her guides from Courmayeur, not only climbed the Aiguille Blanche, but also the Aiguille Noire and several other major routes on the South Face of Mont Blanc. Furthermore, in 1935, as we have seen, she made the first British female ascent of the Peuterey Ridge, with Dora de Beer and two guides. Dorothy Thompson, who had already descended the Peuterey Ridge two years previously, in 1933, made an outstanding traverse of Mont Blanc with two guides, including Joseph Georges. The traverse started at the Durier Hut, went up and over both the Aiguille de Bionnassay and Mont Blanc, before descending the Peuterey Ridge to complete the expedition at the Gamba Hut (now the Monzino Hut). It took them 34 hours. Una Cameron and Dorothy Thompson were indeed 'tigresses', as Cicely Williams[2] refers to most of the female alpinists I have mentioned in this book. I, on the other hand, was merely a 'moderate'.

It remained to be seen how I would fare on the Aiguille Blanche.

---

2 *Women on the Rope* by Cicely Williams

3

FIRST ATTEMPT

The Aiguille Blanche really is in a different league from all the other Four-thousanders. It requires a careful strategy and a period of stable weather. That August in 1989, we thought we had both, and companions at the Alpine Club meet were equally convinced. We were not alone in our objective: John Mercer, who was also on the meet, had only three Four-thousanders left to climb, so he and his climbing partner, Maz, were also determined to make an attempt on the Aiguille Blanche. We decided to join forces. Andy Hodges was persuaded to team up with Pete, and Les and I were the third rope in the party.

Pete, Andy, Les and I sent up our rucksacks on a service lift from the Val Veni to the Monzino Hut one afternoon in early August. The weather forecast was good for the following day but storms were predicted a few days later, so it was essential to complete the route and return to the valley as soon as possible. We four were all to bivouac that night on the glacier below the Col de l'Innominata but Andy seemed not to have realised this and brought neither sleeping bag nor karrimat, so he must have had a fairly uncomfortable night. John and Maz were to snatch a few hours' sleep at the Monzino Hut and catch us up the following morning.

We set off from the Val Veni, Les in front, then Andy and Pete, with me at the rear, far behind. It was quite a long walk through the woods and up the slopes beyond but eventually I arrived at the bottom of a steep cliff. There I made my way apprehensively up fixed chain after fixed chain, relieved that I wasn't carrying a heavy rucksack. The men had disappeared ahead of me, so I was alone with my doubts about soloing in this precarious situation. In all my years of climbing, I never did completely overcome my tendency to vertigo.

The tension I was under manifested itself in an angry outburst when I arrived at the hut. Somehow it was the last straw to have made such a daring ascent, which many mountain walkers would have found extremely daunting, only to find an orderly queue of people, all equipped with shampoo and towels, waiting to use the bathroom. I had never before come across an Alpine hut with a bathroom, and few with a plentiful supply of running water. I was so used to roughing it that this luxury seemed completely incongruous. The contrast was just too great but times were evidently changing.

A little later we sat down to a hut meal at vast expense: soup, chicken, salad and fresh fruit cost us each 28000 lire. Maz declined to join us. Then Pete, Andy, Les and I retrieved our heavy rucksacks from the lift, and headed for the glacier. After an hour or so, we found a suitable bivouac site on a stony shelf at the foot of the snow slope leading up to the cliff below the Col de l'Innominata. I slept fitfully, being fairly uncomfortable and a bit chilly on my bed of stones and snow, but despite all that was very pleased we had reached such a high point for the morning's start. The alarm was set for 3.30 am, but nobody seemed to have heard it, although we all awoke. We were away at four o'clock, with the torchlights of John and Maz rapidly catching us up from the glacier below. A steep snow slope and a rocky gully led us to the col, where the seriousness of our route was brought home by the various plaques commemorating the tragedy that occurred there in 1961. Seven climbers, including Walter Bonatti, his two Italian companions and four Frenchmen they had met *en route*, were caught in a ferocious storm on the Central Pillar of Frêney. Bonatti tried to save them but their retreat was hampered by the foul weather that continued for several days. Only Bonatti, one Italian and one Frenchman survived. Some members of the group died, exhausted, in the gully we were about to descend.

John and Maz had now joined us and it took some time for all six of us to abseil down the couloir to the Frêney Glacier. There we paused to take stock of the condition of the traverse we had to make to reach the foot of the Schneider Couloir below the Aiguille Blanche. It was now daylight and we could see that the tracks across the glacier, though complicated, did not appear to present any insurmountable obstacles. However, the route to the Schneider Couloir looked so tricky that the men agreed to abandon the Normal Route and head for the Rochers Gruber instead. This turned out to be a mistake, as the climbing was so serious that we had to pitch it all the way and, as we were so numerous, we held each other up. The Rochers Gruber is really only a descent route: it is very time-consuming in ascent and susceptible to snow and rock avalanching when the sun warms up the south-facing slopes.

At one point we climbed a grade III ice pitch up a gully to avoid overhanging rock. Two rock pitches beyond that, we came to a serious slab. At the top of this, Les suddenly announced that we must turn back, as it was by then 11.30 am. Both snow and rocks were beginning to fall down the couloir to our right.

The abseiling began. It was about a couple of hundred metres down to the glacier, which took quite some time. Back at the base of the couloir leading up to the Col de l'Innominata, we began the ascent of this cleft. It was most unpleasant. I found it strenuous and we all had to be careful not to knock the many loose stones down on our companions. Another slow abseil brought us from the col back down to the gear we had stashed at our bivouac site. Pete decided to make a brew, which I gratefully accepted, but Les, who never drinks tea, refused to stop for long. The two of us abseiled – quicker than climbing down – down wet rocks from there to the little Glacier du Châtelet, getting armfuls of water as we went. After putting my crampons back on for the last time that day, I set off as fast as I could in Les's wake but inevitably dropped further and further behind.

At the Monzino Hut we all met up again and, after a pause to drink a much-appreciated small beer, began the final section of the descent to the Val Veni. Once we had made our way down the steep cliff, Les disappeared into the distance again, carrying the only load we had between the two of us. (He had persuaded the hut guardian to send my rucksack down on the cable car the following morning.) So it was Maz who kindly accompanied me during the rest of the walk and I was especially grateful to him, as darkness had fallen by the time we reached the woods near the bottom of the descent. It was 10.00 pm when we arrived at the campsite, after being on the move for eighteen hours. All I had eaten during that time was a couple of packets of Dextrasol, some Cadbury's chocolate and a hunk of bread and cheese.

Although the outing had been a failure in some ways, it was one of the finest mountain experiences I had ever had, and left me all the more resolute about climbing my remaining six Fourthousanders. Early in the next millennium, Vicky Jack, a Scotswoman who modestly described herself as 'a high hill walker', would feel a similar determination. In 2002 she did her utmost to climb Everest, but had the good sense to turn back when she reached the point where her energy ran out. She returned the following year and so became, at the age of 51, the oldest woman to have climbed Everest and the first Scotswoman to complete the Seven Summits, the highest peaks on the seven continents of the world.[1]

I would return to climb the Aiguille Blanche.

---

1 *The Sky's the Limit* by Anna Magnusson

4

THREE FOURTHOUSANDERS
ON SKI

Another new decade! This one began with a great deal of feverish activity at college. My department was in the process of moving from the Further Education sector to a new Higher Education college and was preparing to deliver degree programmes for the first time. I was involved in a vast amount of preparatory work and had high hopes for advancement in my career. Optimism prevailed at work, as it did in my climbing plans. 1990 was to be the year in which I would make every effort to complete my list of 4000m peaks and Pete Fleming and Les both encouraged me in this aim.

After my return from the Alps the previous summer, I had started to learn Alexander Technique, which I thought would help to alleviate the neck and back pain that dogged me at that time. It did. Furthermore, it seemed to speed up my walking and that improved my general fitness. We spent a great deal of time in the hills of South Wales, North Wales and the Lake District during autumn and winter weekends and I would also do a gentle workout at the gym during the week. This was a fairly recent addition to my training, as such facilities had barely existed in our area before then.

In April 1990, I accompanied Les, Allan Brindley and Brian Cox on a ski-tour in Switzerland. Our main objective in the Bernese Oberland was to climb the Jungfrau, but first we acclimatised in the Western Oberland, making ascents of the Daubenhorn and the Wildstrubel. The weather began to deteriorate after this satisfactory start and our plan to move to the Lötschental was abandoned after consulting the weather maps in the local newspaper over breakfast the following morning. Instead, we opted for Saas Fee and two nights at the Britannia Hut. On a crisp, clear day I thus made my way up the Allalinhorn via its West-North-West Ridge, my third time on the summit of this Fourthousander. How very different the conditions were from the hot summer's day when I had last been there. This time it was so icy that there was little room to sit down and the bitterly cold north wind threatened to blow us off our feet. It was simply a question of hello and goodbye and back down again. We had left our skis at the Feejoch, from which we quickly skied back down through terrain interspersed with séracs and over the Fee Glacier until we reached the Saas Fee pistes.

By then, I was able to savour the views of the Täschhorn and the Dom, remembering our magnificent day on the traverse ridge in 1979, feeling yet again that sense of elation, achievement and wonder, that great feeling of satisfaction at having climbed well and successfully surmounted all the obstacles along the way. Once more, I gazed in awe at those two mountains, admiring the narrowness of their crests and the spikiness of their seemingly inaccessible pinnacles. I recalled their precipitous snow-covered faces, broken here and there by threatening séracs, and the blues and whites and greys of the crevasse-ridden glaciers. Even when we were perched up on that traverse, and certainly many times since, whenever I caught sight of the Täschhorn and Dom from another viewpoint, I marvelled at the fact that I had been so fortunate to climb in such a place.

'What an amazing life I've led!' I thought to myself as, surrounded by piste skiers, we sat outside a mountain restaurant drinking a well-earned cup of hot chocolate.

The weather the next day started just as fine, so we skinned up the Allalin Glacier to the Adler Pass. Back in the summer of 1973, Les and I had climbed the Strahlhorn in deep, fresh snow, yet now, in the spring of 1990, the same approach to the summit took us along a narrow ridge of hard ice. Having returned safely to the pass after this precarious little expedition, we put our skis back on and prepared to descend the steep slope on the other side. We had intended to continue to the Monte Rosa Hut but the weather was looking a little unsettled by then, so we opted for Zermatt instead.

A day of snowfall followed. We sat it out in a hotel cum bunkhouse in the little village of Blatten on the south side of the Bernese Oberland. Still determined to make an attempt on the Jungfrau, we went up the long glacier to the Hollandia Hut at the Lötschenlücke the next day, but the window in the weather turned out to have been brief. Once again, we found ourselves at this isolated refuge with further snowfall and high wind destroying the good work of the sun the previous day. Now the whole area was at high risk of avalanche. The Jungfrau was proving a most elusive 4000m peak.

Since our time was running out, we opted for the relatively safe walk further into the heart of the Bernese Oberland glacier system via the Konkordiaplatz. Here we turned south, heading for the Marjelensee and Kühboden, over the flanks of the Eggishorn: a familiar route, but long and in soft snow. The gradient of the glacier is so gentle that in those conditions it was impossible to slide downhill. So walk we did. The skis merely prevent you from sinking even more deeply into the fresh powder.

We returned home to a period of lovely sunny weather. My parents visited Gloucester briefly on their way back from a holiday in Devon. With them were two of my father's sisters and it was a very happy occasion. Little did I know that I would never see my father again: ten days later he died very suddenly of a heart attack. Although I had begun to perceive him as an elderly man – he was 78 – I was quite unprepared for the shock his death caused me. There I was, thoroughly immersed in exciting new work at college, and planning to return to the Alps at the half-term break to make another attempt at skiing the Jungfrau, and I was confronted by this devastating new experience. It was the first death in my family to affect me so profoundly. What was I to do? Could I really go away again on a hazardous expedition so soon after my mother had been bereaved? With the encouragement of all the family, I did just that. It was not an easy decision to make and it can't have been easy for my mother, but she never voiced any negative thoughts about it to me.

On 28th May, Les and I set out for the Jungfrau by the 7.00 am train from Lauterbrunnen. I had never imagined that I would use this impressive railway up and through the Eiger to the Jungfraujoch, but it was the only way to reach our target in a day from the valley. At ten minutes past nine we were ready to begin the descent on ski down the Jungfraufirn to the starting-point for the ascent of the mountain. There we fixed skins to our skis and moved easily uphill for a while, passing a young man sitting in the sun, unable to continue because his *harscheisen* had broken. Progress up a very steep slope, where I was to come to grief later in the day, proved awkward. I found that my fitness was such that I could move along steadily, but lifting my skis round the steepest turns as we zigzagged up was slow, hard work. The gradient eased and I continued to follow Les. Clouds were beginning to swirl up threateningly from the northern side of the mountains but otherwise it was still a beautiful day, with ever-improving views of the high peaks of the Oberland as we gained height.

The higher we climbed, the more my poor emotional state, general tiredness and recent lack of training began to show. I was irritable when Les tried to encourage me to move a little faster. It was three hours since we had left the Jungfraujoch and Les was becoming concerned about the time the ascent was taking us. Not only did the weather look as if it might affect our safety on the descent, but he needed to take some photographs for the new Bernese Oberland guidebook. It must have been frustrating for him that I was taking longer than expected but I was doing my best. I was not prepared to overreach myself, especially when I found, for the first time ever at high altitude, that I was experiencing attacks of slight nausea and dizziness. Moving across the wide, flat area just before the *bergschrund* at the top of the glacier, I suddenly had a sensation of vertigo. Without doubt, the rapid ascent from Lauterbrunnen at 1200m to the slopes of the Jungfrau at nearly 4000m was responsible for this unaccustomed mountain sickness. I had never previously suffered such symptoms on an alpine route, and it seemed weird to feel vertiginous on relatively safe ground.

On reaching the ski depot, we found we were not alone on the mountain. Above us, a couple of parties were already descending to the *bergschrund* that we were about to cross. Two more were heading in the same direction as us. Whilst we rested briefly, taking the skins off our skis and putting our crampons on our boots, the *bergschrund* and the steep slope above it became free for us to continue on our way unhindered. Les set off solo directly towards the col above. I followed but the steep gradient made me fear another attack of vertigo, so I yelled at Les to drop me a rope. This really was unnecessary, as the climbing was very easy but, in my fraught state, I wasn't keen to take any risks. We reached the Rottalsattel.

Above the col, we had to bypass several parties who were descending with extreme caution, but otherwise we proceeded without interruption to the summit, our only difficulty being our lack of acclimatisation. Les was also afflicted to some extent. It had taken us four and a half hours from the Jungfraujoch instead of the three hours we had planned. All around us the glaciers and peaks were gradually becoming shrouded in mist, so we didn't linger. After a few moments on the summit, we turned around and began the descent.

Having returned to our skis, we had a quick snack and set off in the wake of a couple of other skiers. I found I was skiing rather well, despite very poor snow. Using the icy trail, I turned very neatly and avoided most of the breakable crust to the side. Les muttered that he was finding the going rather unpleasant and I felt a bit smug. I shouldn't have forgotten the old maxim that 'pride comes before a fall' – literally! I took an unexpected tumble and had to put my left ski binding together again. Several turns later I sat down again, unscathed. I was becoming tired and we were skiing in the flat light that results from heavy cloud cover. The condition of the snow was worsening and the slope steepening rapidly. As we approached the area that I had found unpleasant in ascent, we discovered that the other descending parties had chewed up the snow even more. I lost my usual sense of self-preservation: normally, I would have made many more kick turns and would not have attempted to snowplough or make step turns.

I was being foolishly brave in soldiering on behind Les without due precaution. Then suddenly, splat! My left ski binding broke open again. I had possibly not fixed it quite correctly after my earlier fall. This time my right leg sailed on, skiing into a large lump of ice under the surface and coming to a sudden halt. I knew immediately that I had seriously torn my calf muscle and cursed aloud the fact that it would take at least six weeks to mend, jeopardising my training for the summer season.

In the meantime, my immediate problem was getting my left binding back together again. I hobbled down to Les, who managed to clear the ice away from the device, and then I continued skiing gingerly down the rest of the slope. I filled my long socks with snowballs to ease the inflammation and deaden the pain. Then slowly, doggedly, I dragged myself back from the foot of the mountain up the glacier to the Jungfraujoch. We just arrived in time to catch the 5.00 pm train down to Lauterbrunnen. At last I had climbed the Jungfrau – but at what cost?

5

PENULTIMATE FOURTHOUSANDERS

One less widely known lady climber of the 19th century was Mrs. E. P. Jackson. In *Women on the Rope*, Cicely Williams quotes Mrs. Le Blond's description of her as 'one of the greatest women climbers of her time'[1]. After a dozen or more active years in the Alps, Mrs. Jackson traversed the Jungfrau in January 1888 and suffered a far greater setback than I did in May 1990. Starting from the Bergli Hut, she and her party reached the summit via the Rottalsattel, then took the Guggi Route in descent. Although it had been perfect weather all day, the party was delayed by difficult conditions on the descent from the Schneehorn and became benighted before they could reach the bottom of the ice fall above the Guggi Glacier. They spent the night in a snow cave, where Mrs. Jackson enjoyed the beauty of her surroundings so much that, in the account she wrote afterwards, she ignored the unfortunate consequences of the escapade, as recorded by Cicely Williams:

As a result of the night in the ice-cavern she suffered severe frostbite of the feet; this caused her much suffering and the eventual amputation of several toes, which brought to an end her magnificent climbing career.[2]

In the case of my own injury, the calf muscle took four weeks to mend to the stage at which I could go hill walking again. I then managed a couple of brief rambles in the Lake District before setting off for the Alps in mid-July. This training was quite insufficient to make me fit enough to enjoy the huge expeditions we had planned, but it did suffice to get me up and down the mountains again. For once, the sun shone almost every day: in the entire four-week period of our visit to France and Switzerland, we had no more than two days of poor weather. For the rest of the time, there was a

---

1 *Women on the Rope* by Cicely Williams
2 ibid.

heat wave. This made conditions particularly hazardous, with a great deal of stonefall, especially in the Mont Blanc Massif. Moreover, the snow, lacking because of three successive poor winters, rarely froze at night to the desired degree and by midday was extremely soft. In the Bernese Oberland, however, during the last two weeks of July, we experienced reasonable conditions and didn't feel that our safety was at risk.

At the start of our holiday, Les and I spent several days relaxing, first in the Alpes Vaudoises and then in the Rosenlaui area of Central Switzerland. After that, we had a few days acclimatising on some easy routes near the Oberaar Hut at the eastern end of the Bernese Oberland, where the guardian made us extremely welcome. When we stayed at this hut on our ski-tour in 1981, he had not been in residence and we had had to make do for ourselves.

The time had now come to start our assault upon my remaining Four-thousanders. This year we had no companions. On 20th July we bivouacked discreetly near the Grimsel Pass in order to make an early start and, next morning, drove up to the Grimselhospiz Hotel and left our car in the car park. My wristwatch showed exactly 7.27 am when I shouldered a heavily loaded rucksack to set off on our long walk. Already rock climbers galore were heading for the massive slabs of Eldorado and other crags. To my astonishment, people were lying in sleeping bags all over the place and, when we passed the slabs two hours later, some climbers were already half-way up the routes. After seven and a half hours of hard work, I reached the Aar Bivouac Hut and was pleasantly surprised to find a lovely modern building with excellent facilities, clean, dry and cosy. The hut had room for about twenty people but there was only a small group there that night, apart from ourselves, so we were very comfortable. The following night we were alone.

On 22nd July, our 21st wedding anniversary, we climbed the Schreckhorn. We were up at 2.30 am and away in forty minutes, a record for me. It was a perfect starry night, followed by a perfect sunny day. I started off badly, however, by falling through some old snow below the hut into a small crevasse on the otherwise dry glacier. There were no serious consequences but I felt stupid and was annoyed with myself, and so found the trudge up the moraine even more gruelling than it would otherwise have been. By the time I reached the head of the glacier I was demoralised and Les was displeased that I was moving more slowly than he had hoped. Daylight arrived in time for our ascent of the snow slope up to the Strahlegg Pass. Beyond that, a tiring but pleasant climb up the Schreckfirn Glacier brought us in a leftward curve to the foot of a wide couloir descending from the shoulder of the South-West Ridge of the Schreckhorn.

I was carrying my new ski-touring rucksack, somewhat larger than my usual climbing one, and I found it uncomfortable and cumbersome. When we arrived at the shoulder, we dumped the offending article, adding to it some of the contents of Les's sack, and continued up the ridge, Les carrying a lighter rucksack, whilst I had no rucksack at all. Thus unfettered, climbing became so much more enjoyable and we made faster progress. The rock was mainly excellent, even though there were enough loose stones here and there to ensure that we moved cautiously. Approximately six and a half hours after leaving the Aar Bivouac Hut, we reached the summit of the Schreckhorn. What a situation! The views were magnificent and the Eiger looked especially enticing. How I wished that I could climb that too. A decade ago, we had intended to climb it via the Mittelegi Ridge but stormy weather had prevented us from setting out from the valley. Now I suspected that my shoulders would not appreciate such a strenuous ascent. The upper part of the ridge is particularly steep, and I had heard too many stories about the unpleasant looseness of the rock on the West Flank to be enthusiastic about climbing the Eiger that way. For the time being, I was in any case concentrating purely on collecting my remaining Fourthousanders. The Eiger would have to wait.

Once again, we were not completely alone on our route: as we reached the summit, one rope of two was starting to descend. Another pair had just arrived from the direction of the Lauteraarhorn. They stayed long enough at the summit to be behind us as we started on our own descent back down the ridge. We abseiled most of the way to the shoulder and then continued abseiling down the buttress towards the glacier. This was not strictly necessary but I preferred this means of descent as it put less strain on the knees than climbing down. At last we came to the bottom of the rock, but here we had to cross the couloir again. It was with considerable trepidation that I scooted across the path of the little rocky missiles that were already falling in the warmth of the midday sun. Carefully avoiding crevasses, we continued steadily down the softening snow of the glacier until we reached an icy slope where we considered it prudent to put crampons on again. Back at the pass, we stopped for a short break before embarking on the descent to the Strahlegg Glacier.

Even at the time, we knew that we were much too late to be descending this section; in retrospect, it was all too apparent. The snow was absolutely rotten and the alternative rock descent was covered in grit, making that very dangerous. We kept mainly to the snow, facing inwards, carefully using ice axes as a prop. With relief, I reached the lowest part of the gully and we moved leftwards over an easier-angled slope towards the snow bridge over the *bergschrund*.

It was there that Les slipped, a snow step simply crumbling beneath him. To my horror he was unable to prevent himself being carried with the little avalanche and he continued to slide. My hurried attempt to arrest us failed completely. When the rope came taut, the ice axe I had swiftly rammed into the snow was jerked out and I started to slide as well. We picked up momentum and the next thing I knew was that I had landed on a narrow snow bridge just inside the lower edge of the *bergschrund*. For a second or so I panicked, smothered in the snow that had slid down the slope with me. Then I used my left hand to ensure that my nose had some air around it and, a few moments later, managed to release my head and, finally, my right arm, still holding my ice axe.

Meanwhile Les had apparently had the wit to flip himself over as he slid, so that he was facing outwards in a position to jump over the *bergschrund*. This he had done successfully, landing on the lip on the lower side. I now saw him making his way towards me, unharmed, from a few metres away. With a little effort and a helping hand, I managed to extricate myself and took in the frightening fact that I had flown over a gaping hole, airborne for perhaps four or five metres, and landed in deep soft snow, narrowly missing an area of bare ice. In shock and with a badly bruised arm, but otherwise unscathed, I followed Les back to the hut. This was the first accident we had ever had and we were fortunate to escape, isolated as we were on this remote glacier. What a way to spend a wedding anniversary.

Despite my bruised arm and weariness after such a long day out, I had no intention of opting out of the opportunity to climb the Lauteraarhorn from the Aar Bivouac. I had no wish to make an arduous return trip to this remote place. So, the next day, we set out at 4.00 am to ascend the South Face Couloir. Repeating the same glacier approach as the previous day, I was pleased to find myself moving really well. Then I noticed that clouds were building up and for a moment I panicked that we might not be able to do the route after all. Fortunately, the sky cleared as we approached the lower slopes of the Lauteraarhorn and we continued up the steep snow of the South Face, moving together all the way. About two thirds of the way up, I began to tire and insisted on frequent short rests. That was how we noticed a large party a long way below us, gradually catching us up.

There was nothing particularly difficult about either the various rock bands or the longer snowfields between them, but the face route starts at about 3000m and ascends 900m before you reach the South-East Ridge of the Lauteraarhorn. The highlight of the route is the last 100m up excellent rock to the summit. I was unable to enjoy the ridge to the full, as the events the previous afternoon had had their effect on my nerves and I felt uneasy on the airy crest. At the summit we searched in vain for a pencil to write our names in the book but there was none there, and mine was in my rucksack that I'd dumped at the spot where we had reached the ridge.

As we returned to that spot, the party of seven climbers we had noticed earlier passed us on their way up to the summit. On our way down the face, we kept as much as possible to the rock rib on the western edge, avoiding the soft snow, which was inclined to avalanche. Indeed it did so just after we had carefully tested it at one point. The rib was little better than the snow, however, as it was covered in loose rocks and grit. It was a most unpleasant descent. The other people, who seemed to be with a guide, were soon following. When they passed us, Les urged me to keep closely behind them, as they appeared to know exactly which line to take. This worked well and we eventually came to an excellent gully that led to the final snow slope and the glacier below.

My journal summarises how I felt:

It was a relief that we could spend a third night at the Aar Bivouac Hut, before making the return trip to the Grimsel Pass. These three days had been so gruelling.

The Schreckhorn and the Lauteraarhorn had definitely taken their toll. These two Fourthousanders are remote from the valley bases and although neither of our routes, each graded AD, is particularly difficult to climb, a great deal of stamina is essential for such a lengthy expedition.

It was now the end of July and the F&RCC had begun to set up camp in Randa. There Pete and Margaret Fleming joined us once again and, whilst Pete acclimatised, Les and I went to the Lenzspitze. This was my final Swiss Fourthousander. It should have been an easy day out on a PD route but my lack of fitness and increasing timidity, combined with insufficient rest after the Bernese Oberland expedition, resulted in another very long outing.

Having already climbed all the interesting rock on the East Ridge of the Lenzspitze, we decided this time to approach the mountain from the Dom Hut above Randa. Our route would take us to the summit via the South Ridge from the Lenzjoch and initially we hoped to continue along the Nadelgrat and return to the hut from the Stecknadeljoch. However, by the time we had talked to other people and seen for ourselves the bare state of that descent route, neither of us seriously considered doing anything other than a straight ascent and return via the South Ridge. In fact, I was moving so slowly that day that nothing else would have been feasible.

There were many other parties on the glacier above the Dom Hut and we were overtaken time and time again. Most people were heading for the Dom.

We had had a crowded night at the hut and now, after our peaceful days in the Oberland, the mountains seemed cluttered with humanity. At the approach to the Festijoch someone pushed past Les and stood on our new rope. Les was furious and it was probably only the icy slope where we were all standing that prevented the argument from deteriorating into something more serious. It is unforgivable to spear someone's rope, old or new. Lives depend upon it, as I proved later that same day.

As we ascended the rock below the col, we suffered a shower of grit, stones and dust from climbers above us. I was glad to cross the Festijoch and reach the snow on the Hohbärg Glacier. For a while we continued on the same route as the parties heading for the Dom, but further up we turned off towards the Lenzjoch. We had expected to climb directly up the slope below this col but the gradient looked so steep that we opted for a slope to its right which offered a much more pleasant approach to the ridge. Confronted with an awkward descent to the Lenzjoch, I led the way over a delicate snow bridge to a point where I could drive in an ice screw and belay Les as he climbed down to join me.

After the col, Les took the lead up the rocks on the South Ridge of the Lenzspitze. Sometimes we kept to the crest, at other times it was preferable to resort to the flank, but the crest presented us with loose blocks and the flank was covered in scree. Each block had to be tested carefully before we could risk entrusting our lives to it – a slow process. On one occasion I had a lucky escape: whilst traversing round a block, I made a clumsy move and fell. I must have been more tired than I realised. Suddenly I found myself swinging like a pendulum into space but fortunately Les was belayed. As I landed back on the ridge below him, the rope tipped a stone on to the back of my head. Unaware of this, I moved to follow Les once more, only to feel the stone falling off the back of my neck! I was lucky to escape with nothing more than a bruise. Somewhat shaken, I continued up a gully and over the final shattered slopes to the summit. It was by then 11.30 am, seven hours or more since we had left the Dom Hut.

Sitting on the top of the Lenzspitze, I was so exhausted and so nervous about having to reverse our route, that I was barely able to enjoy the fact that I had just climbed my last Swiss Fourthousander. In fact, I silently vowed that I would never return to the high peaks, that I would leave the final two Fourthousanders alone and be satisfied with what I had done. I would tempt fate no more. I hope Mrs. Tromp-Tromp, a member of the LAC, felt rather more exhilarated when she reached her final Swiss Fourthousander, the Aletschhorn, in 1932.

My immediate concern was with our safe descent. To reverse the South Ridge, we abseiled several times, taking great care not to knock stones down.

It took us two hours to return to the Lenzjoch. Back on the glacier, the snow was surprisingly crisp, despite the fact that it was now afternoon. The Festijoch, however, proved even more unpleasant in descent than it had been on the way up. We considered abseiling from the sling *in situ*, but feared our rope might be too short, so we climbed down at least half of the cliff. This was a horrible experience, as the rock was covered in slippery dust. Eventually we reached a Swiss guide who had been lowering his clients down the crag and he kindly allowed us to abseil the last 100 feet on his rope.

Wearily I followed Les down the lower glacier slopes and finally reached the hut at 5.00 pm. My morale was very low indeed and the next morning I creaked my way down to Randa with very painful knees. Yet I was already weakening and beginning to consider continuing the quest. First of all, however, a total rest was required to allow me to recover from this hectic fortnight, so Les and Pete left me in the valley with Margaret and the F&RCC meet, whilst they climbed the Kanzelgrat on the Zinalrothorn. I wandered about, practised my drawing skills and visited Zermatt. The weather continued to be perfect, a most unusual summer.

When I had recovered, we left the Zermatt Valley and travelled across the border to Argentière, with the intention of climbing first the Droites and then the Aiguille Blanche de Peuterey, the last two peaks on my list. Leaving Margaret in the valley, Pete, Les and I went up to the Couvercle Hut for the night. We were allocated bed spaces in the same dormitory we had used in 1981, when the three of us had climbed the Aiguille Verte. There were intermittent disturbances throughout the hours we lay there dozing. At 2.00 am we rose, quite unaware of the tragedy that had befallen a party of Swiss climbers in the Whymper Couloir whilst we attempted to rest. Four men died, crushed and swept away by stonefall. Fortunately for our peace of mind, we didn't learn this until we had returned from our route the next day.

We left the hut on a clear, starry night, made our way up the Talèfre Glacier, climbed the Droites by its South Ridge and sat on the summit, savouring the fact that this was my final French Fourthousander. We commented on the amount of helicopter activity in the surrounding area and speculated about the objective of their search, if that was what it was. Two other climbers were at the summit with us, having ascended from the other side of the mountain, and they thought it possible that their friends had sent out the Mountain Rescue to look for them. Apparently they were a day late returning to their base. As we turned our thoughts to the matter of our own descent, we had no premonition that only a couple of hours later, we too would be in the sort of situation that might trigger a search party.

We carefully reversed the route we had just climbed, down the ridge and then the gully. Wasting no time, we headed back across the Talèfre Glacier and made our way downhill. We had descended about two-thirds of this long slope when the incident occurred. Somewhere at the top of the snow face above us, part of a cliff shattered, sending countless huge boulders and all manner of debris cascading directly towards our path. As I cowered against the only possible shelter I could find, I was only too well aware that our last moment might have come. Then the noise of the rockfall died away and, utterly astonished, I realised that I had not been hit. Neither had Les – but what had happened to Pete? I shouted his name. There was no reply. Thoughts of disaster flashed through my mind. Was he still alive? Then, at last, came the unmistakable, reassuring voice from somewhere below me:

'I'm here!'

The sense of relief was palpable as Pete stepped out from a snow hollow at the foot of the rock where I was still standing. He had been sheltered from the falling debris and had been able to watch the whole event, his chief danger being the possibility of one or both of us falling down the mountain and the rope dragging him out from his relatively safe position. Astonishingly, we had all emerged unscathed from the onslaught. The mountain had fallen apart but none of us had been hit by so much as a pebble. It had been an unpredictable act of Nature and we were fortunate indeed to escape with our lives. Subdued and silent, each wrapped up in our own thoughts, we returned to the Couvercle Hut, where we were to discover that the Swiss party on the Aiguille Verte had not had such good fortune.

When an accident happens, you try to rationalise it and possibly apportion guilt. Was I to blame for moving too slowly? If we had been descending the slope earlier in the day, it wouldn't have been so warm and the cliff would not have split at the moment when we passed by. On the other hand, perhaps it was just a freak accident that could have happened at any time of day or night, and at any temperature. Over the many years we had been climbing in the Alps, we had learned of incidents of equal magnitude and unpredictability. It was a phenomenon of Nature that we accepted as a possibility, but which doesn't really hit home until you experience it at first hand.

Perhaps I simply wasn't meant to climb all the Fourthousanders. Perhaps there was such a thing as Fate. Perhaps this was a warning?

'Nonsense,' I thought to myself. This was not my philosophy at all. As long as we took sensible precautions and climbed carefully, there was no reason to abandon Alpine climbing, now or in the future. I had always accepted that risks existed but believed that we should remain true to ourselves, continuing to climb mountains if we wished to do so. We would do our utmost never to court danger and put the happiness of each other or our close friends and relatives at risk, any more than if we were driving on a crowded motorway. Nor did we wish to bring the 'sport' of mountaineering into disrepute.

The 1990 summer season was coming to a close. We still planned to make an attempt on the Aiguille Blanche, despite everything that had happened, but Nature made the decision for us. The weather turned and storms came in. So the season ended for me and I summed it up in my journal thus:

A season of epics, terror and frustration, dissatisfaction, yet satisfaction that I had completed all my plans except the last one … the Aiguille Blanche de Peuterey is no mean task. We shall have to see.

6

SECOND ATTEMPT

Within a few weeks of our return from the Alps in the summer of 1990, I was putting on my jacket to go to work one morning when there was a sudden shooting pain down my right arm. From that moment onwards, my intention of soon returning to the Aiguille Blanche was thwarted. Further spasms ensued over the following weeks, despite the care I took this time not to mistreat the apparent injury, but once again I found myself having to resort to surgery. Just before Christmas I was admitted to hospital and underwent a coraco-acromioplasty and excision of the distal end of my clavicle. The expected three weeks of discomfort afterwards turned into three months of pain and 1991 was a totally inactive year as far as moun-taineering was concerned. Both skiing and climbing were written off. By September, I had recovered enough to go mountain walking again, but then my back began to give me problems.

It was 1993 before I was ready to go alpine climbing again. In January, February and March that year, unusually warm weather permitted a return to rock climbing, with an initial scramble on Middlefell Buttress in Great Langdale, followed by old favourites such as Crackstone Rib and Spiral Stairs in the Llanberis Pass. Easy routes these, but an excellent way to complete the rehabilitation of my shoulder. Throughout the winter, spring and early summer, we also walked on the hills of the Lake District, Snowdonia, South Wales and Scotland at every opportunity. College work was strictly confined to weekdays. So my progress to a high level of fitness continued unabated until our departure for the Alps in mid-July.

Our first destination was Arolla, the village in the Swiss Valais where we had been based a couple of times in the early 1970s and a starting point for various suitable training routes. We then moved to Italy, to meet Pete and Margaret Fleming in Courmayeur and to be in position to make another attempt on the Aiguille Blanche de Peuterey. First, needing to acclimatise further, we decided to climb in the Gran Paradiso area. Our hopes of making an ascent of Ciarforon were immediately dashed when we phoned the

Vittorio e Emmanuele Hut and discovered that it was full. So we went to the Rifugio Chabod instead, which gave us an alternative route to the Gran Paradiso itself. The next day, crisp, clear conditions gave us wide-ranging views from the summit. It was the third time Les and I had stood there and on every occasion we could see from one end of the Alps to the other.

That summer also saw a group of friends from the Gloucestershire Mountaineering Club setting up camp in the same site as us in the Val Veni, below the south faces of the Mont Blanc Massif. It was with three fellow club members that Pete, Les and I set out for our next climb, the Aiguille de Bionnassay. They were extremely fit and enthusiastic young people in their thirties, who had been members of our club for a few years. Bill and Fiona Turner had climbed at university and then with the Croydon Mountaineering Club. They both worked hard – Bill in the nuclear industry and Fiona in business – and devoted most of their spare time to outdoor activities, running competitively as well as climbing and walking in the mountains.

Similarly, Alan Jonas devoted every possible spare moment to outdoor pursuits. He worked for an industrial firm in the Forest of Dean, not far from Gloucester, and the easy access to the crags of the Wye Valley gave him ample opportunity to hone his rock climbing skills at weekends and in the evenings. He was an excellent companion, who climbed at a slightly higher grade than Les would normally lead, and would frequently phone Les and other friends at short notice, hoping to snatch an extra few hours on the rock with suitable climbing partners. 'Can you spare your hubby …?' the conversation would begin, and I would always say yes. I wanted Les to make the most of his opportunities to climb at a harder grade than he could with me. After all, he encouraged me to climb more technical routes than I might otherwise have done and I gained considerable satisfaction from that, even though I had been such a nervous learner. Thus Les and I both climbed more or less to our own limits.

Out in Italy, these three friends were all very competent mountaineers but had much less Alpine experience than us. They were all, however, far better rock climbers and much faster on foot than me.

After driving up the Val Veni as far as we could, the six of us embarked on the tough walk to the Gonella Hut. It took me five hours of toil up a stone-strewn glacier, followed by a snow field and, finally, a steep cliff equipped with fixed ladders, cables and chains, to reach the yellow building which had been mocking us from a distance long before we arrived. To my astonishment, when I was within about 30m of the hut, Les suddenly appeared and I gratefully allowed him to shoulder my rucksack and carry it up the final few steps for me. I was the butt of a few jokes when I arrived.

How embarrassing to be proved so weak – this really was almost the only occasion I can recall having received such assistance, so I hoped our young friends were simply impressed by Les's chivalry!

At the hut, it was difficult to relax because it was so cold. The sun went down not long after my arrival and we were forced to retreat indoors. My journal noted:

I have rarely been so cold at a hut in the summer. It was perishing in the living room and perishing in the dormitory.

It reminded me of similarly bitter conditions at the Hollandia Hut in 1973. By morning I was showing signs of developing a throat and chest infection, probably acquired in the Rifugio Chabod, where someone on the bunk above us had spent the night coughing and sneezing. Dinner was rudimentary. Since the hut food was expensive, we dined on soup and stale bread followed by fried eggs, which I found hard to digest, and I had a very poor night. At 1.00 am we were rudely disturbed by the majority of the hut occupants, all bound for Mont Blanc, and at 3.00 am we rose ourselves.

We were in three ropes of two: Bill and Fiona, Pete and Alan, Les and me. I was feeling quite fragile after my bad night and my chest felt tight, but there was no turning back now. The glacier above the hut was intricate and unrelentingly steep but there was a clear trail to follow as far as the Col des Aiguilles Grises. From there, we continued up the ridge a little, then branched off leftwards over the steep slope towards the Col de Bionnassay. I had been expecting a more daunting experience and was glad to find instead that the slope was steep enough to be interesting, yet easy enough to be enjoyable.

Les and I had climbed the Aiguille de Bionnassay in 1975 with Colin Wornham and my recollections of the East Ridge leading down to the col where we now stood, were happy memories of an easy, undemanding descent. Pete had also climbed the Bionnassay that year and his impressions corresponded with ours. Thus we were all three taken by surprise to find that this time the ridge lived up to its traditional reputation: a delicate climb along a knife-edge of snow requiring considerable concentration and care. Sometimes we walked along the snow crest itself. Then it would become too narrow, so we shuffled along crabwise on one side with the axe in the top of the crest. We frequently changed from one mode to the other and from one side of the ridge to the other.

It was a fine situation, but the only emotion I felt was a slight nervousness.

It seemed almost uncanny to look down at the familiar Arve Valley 3000m below us on the French side. The greenness and the towns and villages were strangely remote from our narrow snow crest overlooking the precipitous drop to the glacier. I felt unsure, as if I no longer knew to which world I belonged. Not for the first or the last time in my life, I was having a momentary 'out of body' experience, feeling that I was observing the earth and all those on it from a great height. In this instance, however, I really was literally a very long way above the valley.

We arrived at the summit just four hours after leaving the hut – a good time – and sat in a row facing the south, contemplating our descent. We intended to traverse the mountain by going down the South Ridge to the Durier Hut and thence to the Val Veni and, as a few clouds had started to build up around Mont Blanc, we were soon on our way. None of us realised it was going to take so long.

Les and I led off down the broad snow slope and I was just moving confidently and quickly, when one of my crampons came adrift. A temporary repair was effected and we carried on, but my confidence was now accompanied by wariness. Would the crampon disintegrate again? It was not long before we reached the top of the rocky section of the ridge and soon were at the point where it is too steep to walk. An abseil was set up, but the rock was littered with loose stones and great care had to be taken. Worse still, we were unable to reach the snow slope below without making a second abseil. I spent a long time on a very small stance in what seemed a precarious position in direct line of fire from the stones above. It was late morning by the time we reached the slope leading down to the Durier Hut and we had to descend extremely cautiously because the snow was rapidly softening and becoming unstable. To avoid sliding on our heels, we faced inwards and that took up more precious time.

Regrouping on the rocks outside the hut, we were able to seek advice from a French guide about the descent of the glacier below. Despite his description, it wasn't easy to find the safest way down. Soft snow in the heat of the day, crevasses, loose rock and the steep gradient all contrived to make this a difficult descent. It was slow, tedious and probably dangerous. I was particularly concerned about rockfall from above and simply could not believe that we had put ourselves into a situation so like the descent from Les Droites in 1990! I therefore raced downhill as fast as my legs would carry me, plagued by the fear that at any moment rocks would come hurtling towards us. None did and we survived.

Down in the glacier basin, far beyond the potential dangers, we all met up again and unroped. It was a long walk down to the Val Veni, but eventually we came to the roadhead. A little bar was still open and I sank with relief into a deckchair to drink a most unexpected, but very welcome, beer. After that, I 'floated' down the road to the car.

A day's recovery or more was now essential for me before Pete, Les and I attempted my final Fourthousander. We were all confident that it could be done. However, my chest infection intervened and it was obvious that I needed a longer rest than planned. There was also the matter of the weather: it was excellent, but liable to become stormy in the next few days, so it was not ideal for an expedition that would take me three days. Les and Pete therefore took themselves off to do another route, whilst I relaxed in the valley with Margaret. It was not until Sunday, 1st August that we set out for my second attempt to climb the elusive Aiguille Blanche de Peuterey.

When the men came back from their route, we went to the guides' office in Courmayeur to check the weather forecast again and ask about snow conditions in the area where we wanted to climb. Five days of *bel tempo* with good mountaineering conditions were predicted, so Pete, Les and I made our preparations. Before we left the campsite, our GMC friends wished us all the best for a successful ascent, Alan Jonas enthusiastically encouraging me to look forward to a celebratory barbecue on the Friday night before everyone packed up and left for home.

This time, we planned to approach the Aiguille Blanche from the Col Eccles, near the top end of the Innominata Ridge between the Brouillard and Upper Frêney Glaciers. Two tiny bivouac shelters, at 3850m, are situated just 150m below this col. Having spent the night there, we would cross the Upper Frêney Glacier to the Col de Peuterey, 3934m, and then climb the North-West Ridge of the Aiguille Blanche to reach the summit at 4112m. There would therefore be less than 200m difference in altitude between our starting point on the day of the climb and the summit. Such an advantage was very attractive. Our aim was to walk up to the Monzino Hut, spend one night there and then continue to the Eccles Bivouac the following morning. On the third day we would make our attempt on the Aiguille Blanche, and return to the Val Veni via the same route. This plan, we thought, would be much more efficient than the one we had adopted in 1989.

As on that occasion, we had our rucksacks sent up in the cable lift that services the hut. Thus unencumbered, we walked up to the Monzino Hut and this time I found the steep buttress much less daunting than before. I was full of confidence that within two days we would be standing on the summit of the Aiguille Blanche, which now looked tantalisingly close and, compared with Mont Blanc, not so very far above us. The by now familiar snow crest of the Blanche seemed to beckon to me but this happy illusion didn't last. As we whiled away the remaining hours of the day at the Monzino Hut, clouds began to roll in across the mountain-tops and gradually obliterated everything above us.

The hut was not very busy, probably because it had been closed at short notice for a few days following the unexpected death of the guardian. Amongst the other guests were two Englishmen who were attempting to climb all the Fourthousanders in one season. They did not succeed in their enterprise, unlike Martin Moran and Simon Jenkins, who not only completed the whole List and more, just a few days later that summer, but also cycled between the different mountain areas.

Also at the hut that night were two Dutch boys who were, like us, planning to continue the next day to the Eccles Bivouac Huts. The Englishmen, however, said they intended to climb the Aiguille Blanche by the classic South-East Ridge and, when we rose at 3.30 am, we believed that they had already set off for the Col de l'Innominata sometime in the night. We breakfasted on the landing outside the dormitory, where the new guardian had put out flasks of hot water for us. The two Dutch boys were not far behind when we started to walk up the moraine behind the hut and they soon overtook us.

Despite the dense cloud cover, we remained optimistic that the poor weather was only temporary. When we reached the snow on the Brouillard Glacier, we roped up. Conditions underfoot were good at first, but much higher up the mountain the snow deteriorated and we began to sink in more and more deeply. Although we appeared to be in no danger, there was a continual sound of stones crashing down on the other side of the glacier.

The higher we climbed, the less visibility we had and the worse the snow became. At the head of the glacier the slope steepened and we made our way up rocks until a tiny bivouac shelter appeared out of the fog. As we approached, we became aware that this hut was occupied. To our surprise, we heard the voices of the two Englishmen. Apparently they had abandoned their climb to the Aiguille Blanche via the Col de l'Innominata and had decided to use our approach route instead. They did not encourage us to share their tiny six-person bivouac but instead assisted us to climb down the steep rock step to the lower hut, which was set up for nine people.

The threshold of our metal shelter was only large enough for two or three people to stand side by side. It was perilously icy underfoot and there was absolutely no other flat ground nearby. Paying a call of nature here was going to be extremely hazardous. Indeed, the first time I went out, I set up a belay. Later, I became more courageous.

On entering the hut, we found not only that the two Dutch boys were in residence, sitting at the table making a brew of tea, but there were also signs of occupation by two other people, who were presumably somewhere out in the fog. That left little speculation as to which of the remaining five sleeping spaces we would have, and three of them were on the floor! By the time Pete, Les and I had all inched our way into this little cabin and found somewhere to put our gear and clothing, there was no space left at all. I sat there for a long while trying to keep warm. We melted snow over our tiny stove and had a brew or two.

Then the two absent Italians came in and I retreated to my sleeping bag, temporarily ensconced on the central bunk at the end of the room. The Italians were carrying a cellular phone, a fairly heavy contraption – it was the first time we had ever come across an alpinist with one. In 1993, the mobile phone was not the ubiquitous device it is today. One of the men decided to call a friend at the Torino Hut to obtain a weather forecast. Their report encouraged us to think that the cloud might soon lift and the temperature would fall below zero, giving us suitable conditions for the climb.

However, that was not the end of the phone call. Once the Italians had received an answer to their question about the weather, their friend at the other end of the line dropped a bombshell: there had been a major sérac fall on the Normal Route of the Grandes Jorasses that morning. Eight climbers had lost their lives. Of these, it transpired, three were friends of our Italian companions. Tears flowed, bags were hastily packed, and despite the unpleasant conditions, the two men set off within the hour for the Val Veni.

I sat on in the hut, chilled to the bone at the thought of what had happened just a few miles away, on a route I had previously climbed. To add to my discomfort, Les and Pete decided to go outside to reconnoitre the route for the following day. The noises which accompanied this foray were quite terrifying. Every time any snow was dislodged, it came crashing down upon my tin shack, giving the impression that the mountain and anyone on it were about to be swept away for ever. Fortunately, at the time, I was unaware that in July 1952, Jocelyn Moore, a member of the LAC, and her companion were killed when a large block fell from the ridge above the Eccles Bivouac, crushing the hut and its inmates, and precipitating everything except the floor down the cliff, to land on the Brouillard Glacier below.[1]

At last Les and Pete reappeared, having abandoned their efforts as the way to the Col Eccles was none too clear, the rocks being smothered in

1 LAC Yearbook, 1953

snow and wreathed in mist, but they were none the worse for their little expedition, and a sensation of relief burst warmly throughout my body. That particular tension was eased. I calmed down and moved my mind back into acceptance mode, to deal with the minutiae of living in these cramped conditions so far from civilisation. Had it not been for the uncertainty about the weather, I would have been a very happy person. A brief period living in a bivouac hut amongst the high mountains was usually a situation guaranteed to make me feel totally at ease, at peace with the world. It was surprising how living at such close quarters with one another didn't lead to friction. Not only were we in tune with our surroundings, but we were also in tune with each other.

A difficult night followed. Our rest was constantly interrupted by our attempts to ascertain the state of the weather. The two Dutch boys did go out at 2.00 am, but came in again towards dawn and departed soon after for the valley. We finally arose at 8.00 am and went out to test the conditions beyond the hut, thinking that we might stay another night in the hope that it would be possible to climb the following day. It was immediately apparent that we would achieve nothing by remaining there. Indeed, it would have been sheer folly to venture on to the mountain above in the unconsolidated, soft snow. We too packed our bags and left. The other Englishmen had long since disappeared, presumably downwards.

The descent was long and gruelling. The snow was inclined to avalanche and full concentration was necessary. Disappointment was postponed: the only thought in my mind was the business of escaping safely. On our way up to the Monzino Hut two days before, the summit of the Aiguille Blanche had looked so close. I had felt so certain that we would make a successful ascent; now we were defeated. All we had seen from the hut doorway was an occasional glimpse of the Aiguille Noire further down the Peuterey Ridge. The Blanche, further up, was hidden under the clouds.

Back in the valley, we looked up as the weather improved a little, and there, once again, the Aiguille Blanche came into view. Frustration bowed to reason: despite clearer visibility, the snow conditions would still not have been safe enough for the climb we had envisaged. A much greater drop in temperature at night would be required. Ironically, Martin Moran and Simon Jenkins spent the following Saturday night at the Eccles Bivouac[2] and were successful in climbing the Aiguille Blanche on the Sunday by the exact route that we had planned to take. In contrast to us, they had perfect snow conditions but they only just caught the mountain

---

2 *Alpes 4000* by Martin Moran

in time. A storm rolled in an hour after they had reached the Val Veni on their return from the summit.

I was too tired now to contemplate another effort and my chest infection had returned to plague me, so we relaxed in the valley the following day. Pete and Margaret were almost at the end of their holiday, which meant there were no more plans to attempt the Aiguille Blanche that summer. It would have to wait.

As the four of us sat in our tent that evening, drowning our sorrows in duty-free spirit, one of the Gloucestershire people turned up at 10.00 pm, just back from the hill. He reported to us that two of the men had gone to climb the Triolet that morning and had not returned to the hut. Apart from telephoning the guardian to ascertain that Alan Jonas and Bill Turner were still missing, there was nothing more that we could do till morning. Fiona, Bill's wife, was still at the hut, alone, and the guardian could not be persuaded to bring her to the phone.

After considerable hassle with the telephone and a whole morning's wait, we finally obtained news the following afternoon that Bill had been found alive, but seriously injured, and flown by helicopter to the hospital in Aosta. Alan was not found until a day later, a boot sticking out of the snow, his body in a crevasse, having fallen down the gully they had been climbing. A rockfall had simply swept him away, severing the rope as it went. He was only 36 years old.

There was no question of climbing again that summer after such a tragedy. We left for home, subdued and shocked. Alan had been a delight to know, trustworthy, kind and such good fun. Meanwhile, Fiona stayed on in Italy for another week or so and accompanied Bill home by air. After a considerable period of rehabilitation, he recovered from his injuries and continued to lead an active life, rock climbing, skiing and running.

The following year, I wrote in my journal:

During the twelve months which had elapsed since the 1993 summer season, I had not been able to keep as high a degree of fitness as in the previous year. Persistent back and knee trouble prevented more than a couple of afternoons piste-skiing over the New Year in Switzerland, and thus I didn't even attempt to go ski-touring with Les at Easter. By May I was able to jog a little on grass, but even that was rather dodgy for my knees. So when we went away in July, I was none too sure whether I really wanted to push for the Aiguille Blanche again. I had a 'wait and see' attitude this time. Thus when the weather and snow conditions militated against us in early August, I was really not particularly disappointed.

Yet I followed that statement up by saying that the inclination still lingered. I had not fully given up on the idea of completing my list of Fourthousanders.

Only two of the Alpine climbs that we did that summer merit a mention here. The first, on our Silver Wedding Anniversary, was the Montagne des Agneaux, a low peak in the Dauphiné, not far from Briançon. The Glacier Blanc Hut being already fully booked, we decided to bivouac nearby. Although this meant that we had heavier loads than usual, it wasn't very far to carry them uphill, but we were astonished at the number of tourists on the path leading from the Pré de Madame Carle beyond Ailefroide. I figured that on that one day, there must have been about 3000 people heading in the same direction as us: men, women, children, even babies and dogs, but very few alpinists. We were well prepared with all the items we needed for a comfortable night, and our bivouac was a delightful experience; there was water nearby and the ground was amenable to a little hollowing out to the shape of my body. It was a lovely warm evening, too, and I was able to use some of my extra clothing beneath me to give me a comfortable 'mattress'. When we turned in for the night, the sky was a little cloudy, but by 3.30 am, when passers-by woke me, it was completely clear, with a full moon. I had slept like a log. This was the kind of bivouac that Will McLewin rated so highly.[3] It really was an occasion to commune with nature.

The second memorable climb was with Pete Fleming, on Monte Viso. We had long been aware of this peak, drawn to our attention by Will McLewin's book about the Alpine Fourthousanders and chosen for his title, despite not reaching 4000m. He calls Monte Viso a distant 'sentinel'[4] because, on a clear day, it can be seen from many Fourthousanders, standing out 'mysterious and intriguing' on the far horizon in Italy. He says: 'Eventually you will succumb and go there to look in the opposite direction.'[5] We did.

To reach Monte Viso, on the Italian side of the French border beyond the Queyras Hills, we drove through spectacular gorges and over a steep pass down to the quiet little village of Castello. From there we trudged in the hot sun to the Rifugio Sella, passing through varied terrain: green pastures, steep hillsides, stony screes, and great expanses of barren landscape with little lakes and delicious, clear streams which provided a welcome drink for parched tongues. Finally, after four or more hours of toil, the path levelled off and we walked across a scree slope covered in the most splendid carpet of Alpine flowers that I had ever seen.

3 *In Monte Viso's Horizon* by Will McLewin
4 ibid.
5 ibid.

After a night at the hut, we set off with numerous other parties to climb the mountain. Tiredness slowed me and I took almost five hours to reach the summit. When I did arrive, however, I was overwhelmed and tears welled up in my eyes. The panorama was breathtaking. Monte Viso stands apart from the Alps and Will McLewin was right to draw attention to this viewpoint. I felt privileged to be there and privileged to have stood upon so many of the summits laid out on the horizon before me. Whether we turned westwards, northwards or north-eastwards, we could see mountains that we had climbed, 'old friends', and the stuff of grand memories. If Monte Viso turned out to be the last major peak I ever climbed in summer, it would be a fitting finale.

A few days later, in Courmayeur, Les and I considered the possibility of climbing the Aiguille Blanche with a guide. Pete didn't have time to stay any longer in the Alps and Les and I were not keen to try an ascent without a third person in the party. The weather was the deciding factor, however. It was simply too hot. At night nothing was freezing below 4000m, so the approach to the mountain would have been very dangerous by any route. It was probably for the best that we abandoned the idea: I really wasn't fit enough that year to enjoy it. Yet again, it would have to wait.

7

AFTERWARDS

Life continued much as normal throughout the following autumn and winter. In the spring of 1995, for the first time in several years, I was fit enough to join Les, Brian Cox and another friend, Ian Inch, for an easy ski-tour in the French Vanoise area. We had made Ian's acquaintance through some of our Gloucestershire friends who had known him from Croydon Mountaineering Club days. As he already had some experience of ski-touring, he was a very welcome addition to Les's team, even though he could only be with us for the first week.

During the month before the ski-tour, I noticed a few twinges in my right hip and leg, usually when I had been sitting for a while at the computer. Otherwise, these new sensations didn't hamper my outdoor activities and it never occurred to me that they were the warning signals of a serious condition. I had, after all, had so many minor niggles in my back over the past three decades, although these pains were different from the usual ones. During the tour I had no problem skiing or walking uphill and, although I was unable to keep up with my stronger companions on the way up to huts, on the descents I was skiing very well indeed. It was in the evenings that I suffered. There was a daily deterioration in my ability to sit on the hard wooden seats in the huts, and the pain in my lower back finally became intolerable on the last evening in the living room at the Carro Hut. Only by sitting on a stool with my back to the stove could I relieve the discomfort, and after dinner I was forced to retire to the freezing cold dormitory so that I could lie down.

Perhaps it was the rough scramble through avalanche debris the next morning that upset my leg, or maybe it was my struggle a little later through the only breakable crust of the whole tour, but something triggered the serious spasms that manifested themselves on our downhill run to the valley. Until then, I had had no problems of that kind during the tour. Even here, fortunately, I only had a few nasty moments as the pain shot down my right leg and I was able to enjoy most of the descent. It was the final run of the holiday; we had had splendid conditions throughout the trip and I felt that I had never skied so well.

Just three weeks later, therefore, it was ironic to find that my spine let me down completely: I could no longer walk, sit or stand and found myself in hospital again. This time there was absolutely no choice: I was whisked in without delay for a discectomy and it was not until the beginning of August that I could walk beyond the confines of our village. From then on, although I made a good recovery, and for several years kept hoping I might be able to return to Alpine climbing, it became increasingly obvious that I would never be able to carry a heavy rucksack again. Gradually, the realisation dawned that a successful attempt on the Aiguille Blanche de Peuterey was just a dream. My luck had run out. From the womb to the last breath, luck plays a part in all aspects of our lives, not least in mountaineering. I was not destined, after all, to become the first British woman to climb all the Alpine Fourthousanders.

Twice I had attempted to climb the Aiguille Blanche. On each occasion I had to turn back. 'White needle' it may be, but this mountain was undoubtedly my *bête noire*. It seemed to mock me whenever I gazed at it. It beckoned me, it looked so near, so insignificant against the huge mass of Mont Blanc, yet it eluded me.

I had not climbed all the Fourthousanders but I had climbed them all but one. As far as I know, it was not until August 2009, nineteen years after I stood on the summit of the Droites, that my achievement was superseded. Kate Ross, a member of the Alpine Club and the Ladies' Scottish Climbing Club, summitted the Täschhorn, completing her tally of 4000m peaks.[1] She had already climbed the Aiguille Blanche some years previously. Kate, an experienced lead climber, well deserves the title of 'First British Lady'.

---

1 The Alpine Club Newsletter, 3/2009

EPILOGUE

I have regretted the loss of mountaineering more than most things. It was the key of a world a little above the human world and beyond it, where one could always find a refuge from friction and time.

– FREYA STARK[1]

Mont Blanc, the Aiguille Blanche and the Aiguille Noire de Peuterey

1   Quoted in *Women on the Rope* by Cicely Williams

THE CHALLENGE

We climb mountains for many reasons. For me, above all, it was to enjoy the ever-changing panorama of peaks and pinnacles, ridges and valleys, rock and snow, sometimes beneath a clear blue sky, at others shrouded in swirling mist and clouds that added a sense of mystery to the rugged environment. Just to feel the rock beneath my hands, or the snow crunching under my boots, would be enough in itself. Sometimes, however, it is fulfilling to invent a challenge. Purists may believe that 'collecting peaks' demeans the very essence of mountaineering but that is simply a personal opinion. Other mountaineers, like Les and me, relish such a challenge. For us, although mountaineering is essentially a way of life, not a competitive sport, it was sometimes motivating to set ourselves a target, and we derived great satisfaction if we succeeded in achieving our aim. Les, especially, loved any challenge related to speed, as he was naturally so swift of foot. I was certainly influenced by this but, being unable physically to match his pace, I would set my own at a level I found comfortable. It was always satisfying to complete a route, whether a walk or a climb, in 'guidebook time' or less, because this gave me a feeling of competence, but speed for its own sake was hardly ever my overriding concern.

Climbing all the Fourthousanders is one of the mountaineering challenges of the West European Alps. There are now several lists of 4000m peaks, most of which were published after my last attempt to climb the Aiguille Blanche. Long before that, however, towards the end of the 19th century, an Austrian oculist, Karl Blodig, set about climbing as many 4000m peaks as he could. To this end, he drew up a list of mountains and subsidiary tops over that height and, in the many years that followed, this list gave other climbers a basis for their own challenge. Then, in 1971, Robin Collomb, the Alpine Club guidebook editor at that time, published his comprehensive table of summits over 3500m[2] and, within the first 79, specified 52 separate mountains that reached an altitude of 4000m or more. To that number, he added a further twelve subsidiary tops that met the same criterion. The remaining fifteen 'summits' were simply deemed 'notable points'. It was Collomb's list of separate mountains that Les, Pete and I used.

WOMEN IN A MAN'S WORLD

In the Victorian era and at least until the First World War, the biggest question for women who wanted to climb was simply whether they should climb at all. As we have seen, climbing was considered a man's activity.

---

2 *Mountains of the Alps, Vol. 1, Western Alps* by Robin Collomb

Mrs. Le Blond, however, confessed to having been completely ignorant of public opinion when she started climbing. She didn't seem to realise that a female would be considered 'most shocking'[3] if she slept at a hut or bivouac without the presence of a father, brother or sister. After she had had her first book published, she suddenly discovered she had offended social mores. An early-Victorian great-aunt was so appalled that she did her utmost to persuade other relatives to stop the young woman from indulging in such indecent behaviour. This advice was ignored and she carried on climbing for many more years.

Mrs. Le Blond also defied that other strong convention, that women shouldn't be seen to wear 'men's clothing'. But, although she climbed in knickerbockers, not even she was prepared to walk into Zermatt without having covered them with a skirt. About fifty years later, she described one unfortunate occasion when she actually appears to have been embarrassed:

I had one awkward experience connected with climbing dress, however, for having left my skirt on the top of a rock with a heavy stone to keep it in place, a big avalanche gaily whisked it away before our very eyes, as we descended that afternoon. Unwilling to venture across the couloir so late under a hot sun in search of it, I came down just as I was till close to the village, where I remained concealed behind a clump of trees while Imboden [her guide] *fetched a skirt from my room at the hotel. I had carefully explained to him exactly where he would find a suitable one, but, to my horror, he appeared after a long interval with my best evening dress over his arm! There was nothing for it but to slink in when he gave the word that all was clear, and dash up to my room hoping I should meet no one on the stairs!*[4]

One exception to the men-only nature of early 20th-century climbing associations was the Fell & Rock Climbing Club, founded in 1906, which accepted female members from the start, though it was chiefly the men who led the rock climbs. This must have seemed their natural role at the time, and, perhaps, for some men, it still seems so today, even in these times of greater equality of the sexes. Certainly, this assumption persisted to a considerable extent in the 1960s when I started to climb. I was by no means the only female climber who held back from leading when a member of the opposite sex was there to assume that role. It wasn't for another decade that I realised that I had unwittingly assigned myself a secondary status.

---

3 'Then and Now', article by Mrs. Aubrey Le Blond, 1932, reproduced in the LAC Yearbook, 1975
4 ibid.

As a university student I had the impression, based purely on hearsay, that the climbing club was chiefly the preserve of males. Many years later, an item in Shirley Angell's history of the Pinnacle Club gave my theory about student climbing clubs some credence. Helen Jones, a young, single student in 1962, joined the mountaineering club at the university in Bangor, where she encountered the attitudes I had suspected:

Girls were not welcomed in the mountaineering club. Not only was no allowance made for their lack of speed but they were also expected to endure the foullest crudities of songs, speech and behaviour. The technique of acquiring climbing partners, apart from boyfriends, was difficult. One had to wait till the monsters were weakened mentally by alcohol, get them to agree to climb with you in front of witnesses, and hold them to it.

No amount of such unsubtle persuasion could make them allow me to join them in the Alps.[5]

Only a tough girl was likely to blossom in that environment. Certainly, Helen did, and so did Janet Cox at Birmingham University a few years previously, but I was much too shy and nowhere near physically strong enough.

Despite Helen's difficulty in persuading her climbing mates from the university club to allow her to climb with them in the Alps, she eventually struck lucky when one of the older students told her about the Pinnacle Club and introduced her to the Evans family:

He bundled me into his van and dragged me off to the Evans' house. He dropped me off at the gate, and told me to go and knock on the door and to ask Denise Evans if she could help me to join … I was immediately welcomed, put at my ease and given lots of useful advice.[6]

Denise's mother, Nea Morin, was also there that day, sitting in the garden, and she advised Helen to go to the Dauphiné, where she could climb in the Alps with a French organisation. Once her fellow students discovered that Helen was 'Nea's friend', she was warmly welcomed into their group. It wasn't, however, until they knew this that they accepted her so readily.

The Ladies' Alpine Club (founded precisely because of the deliberate exclusion of females from the Alpine Club), the Ladies' Scottish Climbing Club, also founded in the first decade of the 20th century, and the Pinnacle

---

5 *Pinnacle Club, A History of Women Climbing* by Shirley Angell
6 ibid.

Club were the lynchpins of progress in independent female mountaineering, but it took a long time for attitudes to change. When Nea Morin was presiding over the LAC Annual Dinner in 1944, she was most surprised to hear their guest, Mr. Amery, the President of the AC, state his belief that one day the two clubs would probably join forces:

At that time, and still for many years afterwards, this was considered an outrageous suggestion. But L. S. Amery had more foresight. True, he reminded us of the 600 years it had taken women to get into Parliament and suggested we should no doubt have to serve a suitable period of probation for the Alpine Club! Certainly I never expected it to come about in my lifetime.[7]

Why was it that men took the leading role so often, and why did so few women challenge that situation? The earlier women mountaineers had mainly been financially independent and had usually climbed with guides, as did men too in those days. In the period between the two World Wars, they often came from well-to-do family backgrounds where hiking and scrambling had been encouraged when they were children. Then came the period after the Second World War, when rock climbing and, to some extent, Alpine climbing opened up to a much wider section of the male population. In *Unjustifiable Risk*, Simon Thompson discusses the 'great proletarian revolution':

Before the war, middle-class women had climbed with the leading climbers and the best guides of the day, albeit generally as seconds rather than leaders. In the 1950s and 1960s as the climbing scene was increasingly dominated by the heroic, macho culture of the working-class men and their middle-class imitators, women were reduced to the role of camp followers. At the time, there was an assumption that 'birds' were simply not physically capable of climbing at the new standards of difficulty ... The rather limited achievements of British female climbers during these decades appear to have been almost entirely due to social conditioning.[8]

This was exactly my own experience between the mid-1960s and the mid-1970s. Brought up, as I mentioned in the Introduction, with the expectation of following in my mother's footsteps as a potential 'lower-middle-class' housewife and mother (after a few years of secretarial work, or something similar, in a subservient role with male bosses), I received a serious

7 'Past, Present and Future', article by Nea Morin, LAC Yearbook, 1975
8 *Unjustifiable Risk* by Simon Thompson

culture shock when I arrived at university. At that time, Birmingham University prided itself on its tradition of being open to students from any social background, and was at the forefront in encouraging young people from the working classes to study there. I therefore met a far wider section of society than I had done previously and, looking back, it is easy to see how many of the 'middle class' students, subconsciously perhaps, emulated their 'working-class' counterparts. There was a desire to shake off the trappings of middle-class culture that had surrounded us from birth: the accent, language, clothes and manners of our parents. Socialism, equality, these were the buzzwords, and yet, for all that, we girls had few career opportunities, and still accepted that when we married, the man's career would come first. We had indeed been 'socially conditioned'.

Of course there were exceptions. A minority of my university classmates became very successful careerwomen. Almost all became mothers, and a few were both. One is now, fifty years later, not only a grandmother, but also a University Pro-Chancellor. My own experience as a very young graduate in the business world of the mid-1960s convinced me that I stood very little chance of career success in export sales. Not only did I lack the appropriate training, but sexism was rife. In both the firms that employed me, I was expected to be a glorified secretary. Working for a textile firm, I was sent abroad to a trade fair and expected to wear the fabrics that my company produced. I was so penniless at that time, that I cheerfully accepted the free clothes and I was still so socially conditioned that I didn't realise this was a form of covert exploitation. I doubt if the men who organised this little diversion from the otherwise monotonous office work even realised that they were exploiting my femininity. I was simply assigned a role they deemed appropriate for a young woman.

Perhaps I should have been wiser at the age of 23 than to accept a post in a heavy engineering firm. By the time I realised that there really was no future there beyond organising the export sales administration from the office, I had become quite skilled at my work and was encouraged to stay on when I tendered my resignation. In the interim period, however, I had had to learn how to deal with numerous forms of 'sexual harrassment' – not that I had even heard of the expression at the time. It was several years before it became the subject of a legal framework.

Joining the teaching profession led to much more job satisfaction in a much less uncomfortable environment. In my new life as a college lecturer, I rarely ever had any of the hassle of being pestered by men that I had experienced in the business world. Sex discrimination was another matter. Opportunities for promotion were few and far between for females.

In the department I joined in 1969, there were approximately twenty full-time lecturers, of whom barely a quarter were female. Part-time staff, most of whom were women, did a considerable proportion of the teaching. During the following decade, even though the ratio of women to men employed full-time increased, only one woman was employed on a level above the basic grade, compared with at least half of the men. Despite the fact that female students had outnumbered male students by three to one in the languages department at my university, in the technical college modern languages section, I was outnumbered two to one by men. Our language students were, however, predominantly female. Most of the younger students were training to work as secretaries or shorthand-typists. Only in the special classes we ran for local businesses was our clientèle almost entirely male, many of them in quite high-ranking positions.

These gender imbalances were mirrored in my mountaineering life. As time went by, the 'birds' succeeded in finding their 'mate' and 'flying the nest' to become housewives and mothers, or they drifted off elsewhere to find a more suitable partner than a dedicated climber. I was aware from the beginning of the 'camp follower' mentality, prevalent amongst both sexes. Probably subconsciously, many male climbers didn't want the girls to out-shine them as leaders, and the girls were either too timid or too accepting to challenge the men. So we climbed mainly as seconds in this predomi-nantly male world. It was unusual for more than three or four young women to be on a weekend meet with the dozen or so males in the group. I had joined the GMC in order to walk and climb in the mountains. At the age of 24, I had decided that this was what I wanted to do, first and foremost. It had not occurred to me that it was in the mountaineering club that I would meet a potential husband – but that was precisely what happened.

In both my professional life and in mountaineering, therefore, I was in a secondary role: I climbed as a second, and I worked at a low level in the college hierarchy. I was by no means the only woman of my generation to be in such a position, whether as a college lecturer or as a mountaineer but, although I had been socially conditioned to accept my lot, it wasn't long before the inequality of the situation dawned upon me. In my professional life, in particular, I became very disenchanted by the increasingly out-of-date attitudes to women. As far as climbing was concerned, it was somewhat longer before I began to hanker after more independence.

This was how adult life began for me and for many young female gradu-ates in the mid-twentieth century. By the end of the 1970s, I had begun to move on and establish myself in a less secondary position in my career and in my mountaineering activities, and since then enormous progress has been made by women in both these domains. Leading climbs and expeditions is no longer the preserve of the LAC, long ago merged with the Alpine Club, or the members of the Pinnacle Club (though this society still flourishes and fulfils a role for many women, as does the LSCC). Men are still in the majority in the climbing world, and probably always will be, just as women are still the predominant parent in many families. It seems that even today in the UK 'women still have to take the primary responsibility for raising children'.[9]

Motherhood is indeed the key issue. During my mountaineering years, I knew few women who carried on climbing whilst they were bringing up small children. There were the practical issues of childcare but there were also, and always will be, the moral and emotional issues. At the time when I was of childbearing age, I knew that for me there was no question of continuing to go Alpine mountaineering at the same time as raising a family. I didn't see how serious mountain climbing could be compatible with family life. Perhaps if I had had more self-confidence in my climbing ability, and therefore felt certain that the risk was minimal, I might have come to a different conclusion. But I married Les in order to live my life with him, not in order to become a mother. Above all, I wanted to continue to climb in the Alps and I wanted to do that with him, and he with me. I felt I had already lost so many years of my youth when I could have been in the mountains, and I didn't want to abandon the lifestyle I had now adopted.

Since, in those days, I scarcely knew of the existence of the Pinnacle Club – and it didn't occur to me to consider joining it until a few years after we had made our decision about having children – I was unaware that there were women in the climbing world in the 1970s who found ways of combining family life with mountaineering. Their solution was often to join forces to share childminding. At the club hut in North Wales, they would introduce their children to the mountains and to rock scrambling and climbing. Rock climbing itself, especially in Britain, has become much less hazardous over the years, and there are few objective dangers. Alpine climbing is another matter; it is subject to loose rock and avalanche, but some Pinnacle Club members took their children mountaineering there despite such uncertainties. They were undoubtedly bolder, more skilled climbers than me.

Few climbers are obliged to climb. There are, however, exceptions. Professional mountaineers must continue to earn their living by climbing, or change their profession. There are many male examples of professionals,

---

9 *Shattered* by Rebecca Asher

from the guides who took Lucy Walker and all the other amateurs up Alpine peaks to the modern-day instructors in climbing centres, and those who earn their living by writing about their exploits, or filming them. From the mid-20th century onwards, a few women have also earned their living through mountaineering. In 1953, Gwen Moffat was the first British woman to become a mountain guide, even though she was by then the mother of a young child. Brede Arkless became the second female British mountain guide in the 1960s, and she was the mother of eight.

Many years later, in 1992, Alison Hargreaves set herself up as a professional climber, obtaining financial sponsorship to solo six classic North Faces in the Alps within a combined time of 24 hours.[10] Whilst pregnant with her first child in 1988, Alison had already climbed the North Face of the Eiger. I recall feeling very uneasy at the time. Was it really morally acceptable to take an unborn child on such a hazardous adventure? However, by 1995, Alison had become the chief breadwinner for her family, her husband's business having failed. Their two children were still quite young, but Alison had to leave them at home whilst she went on expeditions in the Himalaya and other parts of the world. If she was to make a success of her climbing career and earn a good living out of it, she simply had to sacrifice a substantial part of motherhood, whether she wanted to or not.

Alison Hargreaves' penultimate expedition was her successful solo ascent of Everest in May 1995, using no oxygen, the first woman to do so. In the middle of August she reached the summit of K2, at 8616m the second-highest mountain in the world, but failed to return to Base Camp. Her body was spotted at a height of 7000m. Alison appeared to have fallen from about 200m below the summit and her children were now without a mother. Back in 1865, Edward Whymper had been castigated for the fateful accident on the Matterhorn but, since then, the press had become less critical about the tragedies that happened to male mountaineers, even if they were fathers. Now, however, they were only too keen to deprecate a young mother for her selfishness towards her children, regardless of the fact that she was, like many men, simply trying to earn a living through her climbing. Attitudes to male climbers may have changed since Victorian times, but even in the 1990s, women were still expected to be the primary carers for their children. Mountaineering was only acceptable if a mother survived unscathed.

As discussed earlier, the conflict between the demands of motherhood and mountaineering did not arise for some of the pioneering women

---

10 *Savage Summit* by Jennifer Jordan

mountaineers mentioned in this book. Lucy Walker, Katy Richardson, Gertrude Bell and Dorothy Thompson were spinsters with no children. Mrs. Le Blond belonged to the upper classes, who tended to have nannies and governesses, leaving mothers free to live their own lives, and Dorothy Pilley Richards had no children. Nea Morin, on the other hand, brought up two youngsters after the death of her husband, and actively encouraged them to climb. There is no simple answer to the question about motherhood and mountaineering. Where there is a choice, a woman has to find her own solution to the conundrum.

Much has changed since Victorian times and much, also, since my early days, yet even today men still predominate in Alpine climbing and in mountaineering in the Greater Ranges of the world.

The key to a woman's ability to climb successfully is self-confidence. This is what makes the difference between a 'tigress' and an 'ordinary' mountaineer. Although natural athleticism is a great advantage, with self-confidence, this is not essential. The skills can be acquired. Determination is the other vital factor. For Alpine mountaineering, a considerable degree of stamina is necessary, but without determination there will be failure to complete a demanding expedition successfully. You have to be prepared to submit yourself to long hours of toil, to the vagaries of the weather and the snow conditions and, not least, to endure the hardships associated with living at high altitude. All the women I have written about were exceptionally successful at doing just that, and none of us could have achieved what we did without the essential combination of self-confidence and determination. However, it is self-confidence above all that underlies the ability of a climber to push herself to the limits of her comfort zone and beyond.

THE FINAL ANALYSIS

You, the reader, will think what you will of my tale. You will make your own judgment about my reasons for sharing my thoughts and memories with you. Maybe you will think that I have exaggerated my achievements or, on the contrary, been too modest. From time to time I have drawn your attention to other British female alpinists, particularly those from an earlier era, knowing that many of these women were much braver and more skilled than I can claim to have been. Maybe you believe that I should have abandoned climbing for motherhood, or attempted to combine both. One thing is clear: if I had not joined the Gloucestershire Mountaineering Club in 1966, my life would have taken a very different course.

Whereas I was just an ordinary climber, my predecessors were 'tigresses', as Cicely Williams described them. I feel humbled by their achievements and I consider myself privileged to have followed in their footsteps. Other women, my contemporaries as well as those who have succeeded us, have also proved themselves extremely competent in the mountains – but that is their story and I will leave it to them to tell if they wish.

Why did I climb, I, who was so lacking in temerity and strength? There was a point in my life when I suddenly understood something fundamental about myself. I was 24 years old. I wanted to throw away all forms of artifice and get to grips with the elemental world around me. This was the moment when I knew I had a compelling need to be true to myself. I had already joined the GMC, but had only been on a few meets. Now, suddenly, I knew that, above all, I wanted to get involved in the outdoor world. As time went by, I realised more and more that it was in the mountains that I really came alive. There I felt free and there I found a great sense of peace. Even in bad weather, I would often experience a feeling of well-being, especially when I was safely inside a tent or a hut, listening to the wind howling outside, the rain lashing down and the thunderclaps echoing across the mountains. There were moments of fear as well, of course, but they were part of the challenge I accepted.

If I had not joined the GMC, I would probably never have met Les, and perhaps I would not have had the courage to persevere with climbing. Perhaps I would not have thought of pursuing my career in further education either. Les was already working at the local technical college and it was his experience of taking a specialised teacher-training course for the tertiary sector that gave me the idea of doing the same. After a year teaching in secondary education, I left Gloucester to train at a college in Lancashire, unaware that I would have decided by the end of the academic year to return south and marry Les.

In Lancashire, I did everything I could to continue learning to climb. My visits to the GMC hut in North Wales continued and it was there that Les and I met frequently and quite soon decided to commit ourselves to a life together. I never looked back. Most of my mountaineering activities were carried out with him and our mutual friends and this was absolutely what I wanted. It is true that there were occasions when I followed Les where he wished to go, rather than taking an easier option, but it was my choice to do that. I never regretted it. We have had so many wonderful times together.

Now, several decades later, I still don't regret the decisions I took. The choices I made allowed me to enjoy both an Alpine career and a professional life, both of which gave me great satisfaction, despite all the difficulties and setbacks. I sometimes wonder if I would have had the stamina and patience to deal with the incessant demands of a family and the endless emotional seesaw that the love of a child brings. Motherhood offers great joy but it is also accompanied for evermore by underlying anxieties. No doubt I would have coped, just as most mothers do, but perhaps mountain climbing was the easier choice, even though it too comes with its contrasts of happiness and grief.

Reactions to my choice of lifestyle differ. Many years later, after my climbing years were over, I found myself more often than previously in the company of women. I hadn't realised until then that a number of other women at work had noticed me and, beneath their astonishment at how I apparently spent my free time, actually felt twinges of envy. This came to my attention one day when, by chance, I met an old colleague from the distant past. She said it was the freedom I appeared to enjoy that attracted their notice. The aspects of domesticity that they considered a constraint didn't hamper me. I didn't have to deal with the constant demands of children and I had a full-time job that paid a full-time salary, whereas many of the other female staff were employed on the relatively poor part-time scale, with far less attractive conditions of service than mine. By contrast, a woman I once met at a mountaineering club dinner, the wife of a mountaineer but not a climber herself, expressed shock when I told her I had no children: 'Oh, how sad,' she said.

The life I led amongst the high mountains was wonderful, and it still seems a privilege to have climbed amongst the highest Alpine peaks. Some memories will remain forever ingrained in my mind: the thundering cascade of water in a gorge as we passed by on the way to the refuge higher up the mountainside, the crampons crunching into the firm snow of the glacier as we set out in the night, sometimes with the full moon lighting our way, dark shapes of cliffs and pinnacles looming up like cardboard cut-outs, the sparkling white dome of a summit high above, the creaks and groans of the ice in an otherwise almost silent world, the blues, greens and turquoise of an ice fall, the comforting feel of a solid rock handhold, the sudden dazzle of a patch of white quartz, the intensity of the colour of an Alpine flower growing in such hostile terrain, the joy of moving on ski through the white 'desert', the sun, huge and orange, as it emerges above the horizon at dawn, or deep crimson, as it casts a pink glow across the snow at sunset, and the vast panorama of the Alps laid out before us as we stood on a summit on a clear day. These are just some of the experiences that stir the emotions, even in memory. Somehow, time tends to dampen down the pain of the difficult moments.

There were also the many friendships. Climbing is a potentially dangerous activity. Roped together, we rely on each other. There is a bond of trust.

We respect the mountains, and we respect our companions. Our safety is in each other's hands and we share unique experiences. I am grateful to every person who has climbed with me and to all those who spent time with me in the mountains.

All this, and more, has been my experience and I hope that you, the reader, have enjoyed sharing it with me. The choices we make in life are often influenced by circumstances. Luck also plays an important role. My own circumstances and my own luck, combined with my own choices, are what underlie the story of this book. In the end it doesn't matter that I was unable to climb the Aiguille Blanche de Peuterey and didn't complete Collomb's List of Fourthousanders, nor that I rarely led the routes myself. I did what I could.

On 30th June 2000, Les and I stood on the summit of Ben Bheòil, the most easterly of the mountains in the Ben Alder group in Scotland, and celebrated our completion of the Munros. Time seemed to be running out. Long days on rough terrain were taking their toll on our knees, even though my spine had become less troublesome. It was by using mountain bikes on the approach routes that we were able to reach the remotest of the Munros we climbed towards the end of the 1990s. Our friends, Pat and Andrew Reynolds, who had climbed in the Alps with us in my first season, were with us on Ben Bheòil, accompanied by Roger Chappell. Roger had spent numerous days with us in the British mountains over the previous three decades. Thus my most active years gradually came to a close and the completion of the Munros compensated to a certain degree for the disappointment at not quite succeeding in my mission to climb all the Fourthousanders.

The clouds came down after we reached our final Munro summit. Perhaps the 'gods'[11] were drawing a veil over my mountaineering career. Since then, I have still walked and skied in the Alps, and enjoyed the British hills, but I no longer feel compelled to reach the highest summits. It is better to look back with joy and gratitude for all the wonderful experiences we had, than with regret about the mountains and routes we didn't have the good fortune to climb.

Seven years after completing the Munros, Les and I were in Switzerland for an event that Stephen Goodwin described in his Foreword to the 2007 Alpine Journal:

---

11 'As flies to wanton boys, are we to the gods.' William Shakespeare, *King Lear,* Act IV, Scene 1

Alpine Club members present at the gala weekend in Zermatt last June will not quickly forget the moment when a helicopter hovered between the Grand Hotel Zermatterhof and the parish church and hoisted the cover from a sculpture marking 150 years of friendship between the AC and the Valaisian resort.[12]

This wasn't the only memorable moment for me. The following evening, we joined a large gathering of AC members and their guests for a celebratory dinner at the Riffelberg Hotel. There I had the privilege of meeting Walter Bonatti, the legendary climber who had tried to save his companions when trapped by a storm on the Frêney Pillar. Bonatti, unable to speak much English, and I, lacking the necessary skills in Italian, conversed in French, our *lingua franca*, as we stood in the chilly evening air on the terrace in full view of the Matterhorn. It was indeed a very special occasion. In the presence of this great mountaineer and that awe-inspiring peak, I experienced an overwhelming sense of humility.

---

12 Foreword by Stephen Goodwin, The Alpine Journal, 2007

GLOSSARY AND CLIMBING GRADES

Abseil *(Ger)*   Roped descent controlled by friction.

À cheval *(Fr)*   Straddling a knife-edge ridge with one leg on each side.

Aiguille *(Fr)*   Rock spire (needle).

Ascensions secondaires *(Fr)*   Routes without the difficulties or duration of *grandes courses*.

Belay   A means of attaching a climber to the mountain; to secure oneself or one's partner to the mountain.

Bergschrund *(Ger)*   The gap between the glacier and the mountain.

Brèche *(Fr)*   Narrow gap in a rock ridge.

Brocken spectre   The observer of the 'spectre' is near the edge of a mountain ridge or summit. His shadow, partially surrounded by an aura of rainbow colours, is cast on to a layer of cloud below.

Caisse *(Fr)*   Cash desk.

Chock(stone)s   Metal devices placed in a rock crack to secure the rope and protect the climber. (Natural chockstones, ranging from pebbles to boulders, are still sometimes used.)

Cirque *(Fr)*   Mountains arranged in the form of a crescent.

Col   Mountain pass.

Crampons   Metal spikes attached to the sole of boots to prevent slipping on ice.

Dièdre *(Fr)*   Rock groove.

Gendarme *(Fr)*   Rock pinnacle.

Grandes courses *(Fr)*   Very serious routes often taking more than one day to complete.

Note: routes that may have been considered *grandes courses* in the past, may no longer be rated as serious enough for this category.

Harscheisen *(Ger)*   Metal spikes attached to the sole of a ski in order to prevent slipping when climbing a steep, icy slope.

Karabiner *(Ger)*   Metal clip with a spring-loaded gate.

Madonna   A statue of the Virgin Mary sometimes placed on the summit of an Alpine peak.

Matratzenlager *(Ger)*   A long, communal bunk in a hut dormitory.

Moraine   Debris, often in the shape of a ridge, created by glaciation.

Névé *(Fr)*   Firm, old snow.

Nuts   Metal wedges used with a sling and inserted into rock fissures for protection when climbing.

Pitch   A section of a rock climb, often a rope's length; to climb a section at a time, with one climber in action, whilst the other climber is belayed.

Prusik loop   This loop of cord is tied to the climbing rope with a knot that slides upwards, but locks in place if there is a pull downwards. Using two prusiks, the climber puts one foot in the lower end of each loop, and pulls each cord in turn up the rope in order to climb out of a crevasse as on a ladder.

Schuss *(Ger)*   To ski, making no turns.

Sérac *(Fr)*   Unstable ice formation usually found on the steepest slopes of a glacier.

Skins   Brushed nylon fabric temporarily attached to the sole of a ski to prevent slipping backwards on ascent. (Originally fur.)

Sling   A short length of rope or nylon tape tied in a loop.

Stance   A ledge or foothold large enough to stand on when belaying.

Transceiver   Electronic device used by ski-mountaineers to locate a person buried by avalanche.

Verglas *(Fr)*   Thin layer of ice covering rock.

Vibram   Cleated rubber soles.

CLIMBING GRADES

BRITISH ROCK

In order of rising difficulty: **Moderate** *(Mod)*

Difficult *(Diff)*

Very Difficult *(V Diff)*

Severe *(S)*

Very Severe *(VS)*

Hard Very Severe *(HVS)*

Extremely Severe *(E1, E2, etc)*

ALPINE ROCK *(with approximate British equivalents)*

In order of rising difficulty: **I** Moderate

II Difficult/Very Difficult

III Severe+

IV Very Severe+

V Hard Very Severe+

VI *(and upwards)* Extremely Severe

ALPINE *(mixed routes)*

F *(facile)*   Straightforward, with no technical difficulties. Easy glaciers and snow slopes, rock scrambling.

PD *(peu difficile)*   Moderately demanding. Rock climbing to grade II and/or snow requiring considerable care.

AD *(assez difficile)*   Expect rock pitches of grade III or possibly IV. Steeper, more technical snow/ice.

D *(difficile)*   Hard

TD *(très difficile)*   Very hard

ED *(extrêmement difficile)*   Very hard and serious

LIST OF THE AUTHOR'S ASCENTS OF ALPINE FOURTHOUSANDERS

The numbers alongside the heights refer to the sequence in which the author made her first ascents of the peaks on *Collomb's List of 4000m Separate Mountains*.

1970 **Lagginhorn**, 4010m – № 1
Traverse from Fletschhorn, 3996m, via Fletschjoch and
North-North-East Ridge (AD-);
descent via West-South-West Ridge (PD)
with Les Swindin and Geoff Causey.

Matterhorn, 4477m – № 2
Hörnli Ridge (PD)
with Les Swindin. The party also included Geoff Causey and John Oaks,
Pat Nind and Andrew Reynolds.

1972 **Mont Blanc du Tacul**, 4248m – № 3
North-West Face (PD-)
with Les Swindin and John Parry.

1973 **Gross Grünhorn**, 4043m – № 4
South-West Ridge (PD)
with Les Swindin. The party also included Geoff Causey, Stuart Cooke,
Richard Heery and Andy Thompson.

Strahlhorn, 4190m – № 5
West-North-West Flank (PD)
with Les Swindin. The party also included Geoff Causey, Stuart Cooke,
Katherine Heery, Richard Heery and Andy Thompson.

Allalinhorn, 4027m – № 6
East-North-East Ridge – Hohlaubgrat (AD)
with Les Swindin. The party also included Geoff Causey, Stuart Cooke,
Richard Heery, Andrew Reynolds, Pat Reynolds and Andy Thompson.

Piz Bernina, 4049m – № 7
Ascent via Biancograt (AD);
descent via Morteratsch Glacier (PD-)
with Les Swindin. The party also included Geoff Causey and Andrew Reynolds,
Andrew Hodges and John Oaks.

Mont Blanc, 4807m – № 8
Traverse via Goûter Ridge and North-West Ridge to Col Maudit;
descent to Col du Midi (PD-)
with Les Swindin. The party also included Andrew Hodges and John Oaks.

Mont Maudit, 4465m – № 9
from Mont Blanc (PD)
with Les Swindin. The party also included Andrew Hodges and John Oaks.

1974   **Dent Blanche**, 4357m – № 10
South Ridge (AD)
with Les Swindin. The party also included Colin Wornham and Sue Wornham.

Barre des Ecrins, 4102m – № 11
North Face and West Ridge (PD)
with Les Swindin.

1975   **Aiguille de Bionnassay**, 4052m – № 12
North-West Face (AD/AD+); descent via East Ridge (AD-)
with Les Swindin and Colin Wornham.

Zinalrothorn, 4221m – № 13
North Ridge (AD)
with Les Swindin. On the descent, the party also included John Oaks,
Myles Plant and Colin Wornham.

1976   **Bishorn**, 4153m – № 14
East Ridge (AD)
with Les Swindin. The party also included Andrew Hodges and John Oaks.

Dom, 4545m – № 15
North-West Ridge – Festigrat (PD+)
with Les Swindin. The party also included Andrew Hodges and John Oaks.

Nadelhorn, 4327m – № 16
North-East Ridge (PD)
with Les Swindin.

1977   **Weissmies**, 4023m – № 17
North Ridge (AD without the Grande Dalle)
with Les Swindin. The party also included Andrew Hodges and John Oaks.

Lagginhorn *(2nd ascent)* South Ridge (AD)
with Les Swindin. The party also included Andrew Hodges and John Oaks.

1978   **Alphubel**, 4206m – № 18
South-East Ridge (PD)
with Les Swindin.

Liskamm, 4527m – № 19
East Ridge (AD)
with Les Swindin.

1979   **Castor**, 4226m – № 20
via Zwillingsglacier to Felikjoch, and South-East Ridge (F) on ski
with Les Swindin, Paul Luton and Jeremy Whitehead.

Alphubel *(2nd ascent)*
East Flank (PD)
– on ski with Les Swindin, Paul Luton and Jeremy Whitehead.

Finsteraarhorn, 4274m – № 21
South-West Flank and North-West Ridge (PD)
with Les Swindin. The party also included Allan Brindley, Geoff Causey,
Dave Hicks and John Oaks.

Gross Fiescherhorn, 4049m – № 22
Ascent via South-East Ridge; descent via North-West Ridge (AD)
with Les Swindin. The party also included Allan Brindley, Geoff Causey,
Dave Hicks and John Oaks.

Mönch, 4099m – № 23
South-East Ridge (PD)
with Les Swindin. The party also included Allan Brindley, Geoff Causey,
Dave Hicks and John Oaks.

Täschhorn, 4491m – № 24
Ascent via North-West Face – Kin Face (AD+);
descent via North-North-East Ridge (AD+/D-) to Domjoch
followed by traverse of Dom
with Les Swindin. The party also included Allan Brindley, Geoff Causey,
Dave Hicks and John Oaks.

Dom (*2nd ascent*)
Traverse from Domjoch via South Ridge (AD);
descent via North Flank (PD)
with Les Swindin and John Oaks. The party also included Allan Brindley,
Geoff Causey and Dave Hicks.

Alphubel (*3rd ascent*)
West Ridge – Rotgrat (AD+)
with Geoff Causey. The party also included Allan Brindley and Dave Hicks.

1980   **Aiguille Verte**, 4122m – № 25
West Ridge – Rotgrat (AD+)
Whymper Couloir (AD)
with Les Swindin and Pete Fleming.

Aiguille de Rochefort, 4001m – № 26
West Ridge – Rochefort Arête (AD)
with John Howe. The party also included Ian Stirrups and Sue Stirrups.

Grand Combin, 4314m – № 27
Ascent via West Ridge of Combin de Valsorey (AD);
descent via North-East Flank
with Les Swindin and John Howe. The party also included Ian Stirrups and
Sue Stirrups.

Bishorn (*2nd ascent*)
North-West Flank (F)
with Les Swindin.

Weisshorn, 4505m – № 28
Ascent via North Ridge (AD+);
descent via East Ridge (AD)
with Les Swindin.

1981   **Dürrenhorn** (Dirruhorn), 4035m – № 29
South-South-East Ridge from Bordier Hut (AD)
with Les Swindin.

Hohberghorn (Hohbärghorn), 4219m – № 30
North-North-West Ridge from Dirrujoch (AD)
with Les Swindin.

Rimpfischhorn, 4199m – № 31
North Ridge (AD)
with Les Swindin.

Pollux, 4092m – № 32
West Flank (PD)
with Les Swindin. The party also included Ian Stirrups and Sue Stirrups.

Breithorn, 4165m – № 33
Traverse from East to West (AD)
with Les Swindin. The party also included Ian Stirrups and Sue Stirrups.

Monte Rosa Group – traverse (AD):
Nordend, 4609m – № 34
Dufourspitze, 4634m – № 35
Zumsteinspitze, 4563m – № 36
Signalkuppe, 4556m – № 37
Parrotspitze, 4436m – № 38
Piramide Vincent, 4215m – № 39
with Les Swindin, Ian Stirrups and Sue Stirrups.

1982   **Aletschhorn**, 4195m – № 40
South-West Rib (PD+)
with Les Swindin and Pete Fleming.

Dent d'Hérens, 4171m – № 41
West-North-West Face (AD/AD+)
with Les Swindin. The party also included Pete Fleming and Andrew Hodges.

1984   **Gran Paradiso**, 4061m – № 42
West Flank from Vittorio e Emmanuele Hut (F)
– on ski with Les Swindin and Paul Luton.

Barre des Ecrins *(2nd ascent)*
South-North traverse (AD)
with Les Swindin and Pete Fleming.

Grandes Jorasses, 4208m – № 43
South-West Side via Point Whymper (AD-)
with Les Swindin

Hohberghorn (Hohbärghorn) *(2nd ascent)*
North-North-West Ridge via Dirrujoch from Dom Hut (AD)
with Les Swindin and Pete Fleming.

1985   **Aiguille de Rochefort** (2nd ascent)
West Ridge – Rochefort Arête (AD)
with Les Swindin and Pete Fleming.

Dôme de Rochefort, 4015m – № 44
South-West Ridge (PD+)
with Les Swindin and Pete Fleming.

Piz Bernina *(2nd ascent)*
Biancograt
with Les Swindin and Pete Fleming.

1986   **Bishorn** *(3rd ascent)*
East Ridge (AD)
with Les Swindin and Pete Fleming.

Gross Fiescherhorn *(2nd ascent)*
Traverse west to east (AD)
with Les Swindin and Pete Fleming.

Finsteraarhorn *(2nd ascent)*
South-West Flank and North-West Ridge (PD)
with Les Swindin and Pete Fleming.

Obergabelhorn, 4063m – № 45
East-North-East Ridge with descent via Arbengrat (AD)
with Les Swindin.

1988 **Allalinhorn** *(2nd ascent)*
South-West Ridge (PD)
with Les Swindin.

Weissmies *(2nd ascent)*
Traverse from Weissmies Hut to Almageller Hut (PD)
with Les Swindin and Pete Fleming. Members of the Alpine Club including
Jeremy Whitehead were also present.

1989 **Dent du Géant**, 4013m – № 46
South-West Face (AD)
with Les Swindin and Pete Fleming.

Gran Paradiso *(2nd ascent)*
West Flank from Vittorio e Emmanuele Hut (F)
with Les Swindin and Pete Fleming.

1st unsuccessful attempt to climb Aiguille Blanche de Peuterey, 4112m with
Les Swindin. The party also included Pete Fleming and Andrew Hodges,
plus John Mercer and Maz.

1990 **Allalinhorn** *(3rd ascent)*
West-North-West Ridge (F) – on ski
with Les Swindin, Allan Brindley and Brian Cox.

Strahlhorn *(2nd ascent)*
West-North-West Flank (PD) – on ski
with Les Swindin, Allan Brindley and Brian Cox.

Jungfrau, 4158m – № 47
South-East Ridge (PD) – on ski to below Rottalsattel
with Les Swindin.

Schreckhorn, 4078m – № 48
South-West Ridge (D-)
with Les Swindin.

Lauteraarhorn, 4042m – № 49
South Face Couloir and South-East Ridge (AD-)
with Les Swindin.

Lenzspitze, 4294m – № 50
South Ridge (PD+)
with Les Swindin.

Les Droites, 4000m – № 51
South Ridge (AD)
with Les Swindin and Pete Fleming.

1993 **Gran Paradiso** *(3rd ascent)*
West Flank from Rifugio Chabod (F)
with Les Swindin and Pete Fleming.

Aiguille de Bionnassay *(2nd ascent)*
Traverse from Gonella Hut via East Ridge (AD-) with descent via
South Ridge (PD+) with Les Swindin. The party also included
Pete Fleming, Alan Jonas, Bill Turner and Fiona Turner.

2nd unsuccessful attempt to climb Aiguille Blanche de Peuterey with
Les Swindin and Pete Fleming.

BIBLIOGRAPHY

BOOKS

Adam Smith, J. A., *Mountain Holidays* (London, The Travel Book Club with J. M. Dent & Sons Ltd, 1946)

Angell, Shirley, *Pinnacle Club, A History of Women Climbing* (The Pinnacle Club, 1988)

Asher, Rebecca, *Shattered – Modern Motherhood and the Illusion of Equality* (London, Harvill Secker, 2011)

Birkett, J. & Peascod, B., *Women Climbing* (London, A. & C. Black, 1989)

Coffey, Maria, *Where the Mountain Casts its Shadow* (London, Arrow Books, 2004)

Collomb, Robin, *Mountains of the Alps, Vol. 1: Western Alps* (West Col Productions, 1971)

Dumler and Burkhardt, *The High Mountains of the Alps, Vol. 1: 4000m Peaks* (London, Diadem Books, 1993)

Fleming, Peter, *One Man's Fourthousanders – Mountaineering in the Alps* (Peter Fleming, Limited Edition, 1995)

Irving, R. L. G., *The Mountain Way – An Anthology in Prose and Verse* (London, J. M. Dent & Sons Ltd, 1938)

Jordan, Jennifer, *Savage Summit* (New York, Harper, 2006)

MacFarlane, Robert, *Mountains of the Mind* (London, Granta Books, 2003)

Magnusson, Anna, *The Sky's the Limit* (Edinburgh, Black & White Publishing, 2007)

Mallalieu, Peter, *The Artists of the Alpine Club* (London, Alpine Club, 2011)

McLewin, Will, *In Monte Viso's Horizon* (Edinburgh, The Ernest Press, 1991)

Moran, Martin, *Alpes 4000* (Newton Abbot, David & Charles, 1994)

Pilley, Dorothy, *Climbing Days* (London, The Hogarth Press, 1989; first published by G. Bell & Sons Ltd, 1935; also published by Secker & Warburg. Reprinted by permission of Random House Group Limited.)

Shipton, E. E., *Nanda Devi* (London, Hodder & Stoughton, 1936)

Thompson, Dorothy, *Climbing with Joseph Georges* (London, Ladies' Alpine Club, 1962)

Thompson, Simon, *Unjustifiable Risk* (Milnthorpe, Lancashire, Cicerone, 2010)

Unsworth, Walt, *Peaks, Passes and Glaciers* (London, Allen Lane, Penguin Books Ltd, 1981)

Whymper, E., *Scrambles amongst the Alps* (London, Thomas Nelson & Sons, 1900)

Wilberforce Smith, Peter and Beryl, *A Little Walk on Skis* (Surlingham, Norfolk, Dickerson, 1987)

Williams, Cicely, *Women on the Rope* (London, George Allen and Unwin Ltd, 1973)

Williams, Cicely, *Zermatt Saga* (London, Allen and Unwin Ltd, 1964)

Winthrop Young, Eleanor and Geoffrey, *In Praise of Mountains – An Anthology for Friends* (London, Frederick Muller Ltd, 1948)

JOURNALS AND MAGAZINES

Ladies' Alpine Club Annual Report (Yearbook): 1916, 1917, 1928, 1935, 1953, 1961, 1967, 1975

Year-Books of The Ladies' Alpine Club INDEX 1910-1975, London, The Alpine Club Library, 2000

Alpine Journal: 1980, 1987 (Obituaries), 1988/89 (Obituaries), 2007

Alpine Club Newsletter 3/2009

Climber, May 2012, '*Jacky's Indian Summer*', Article by Libby Peter

La Montagne vol. XXIII, CAF Paris, 1927, Article by Mary Paillon

Lincoln Mountaineering Club: 50th AnniversaryJournal, 2009

GUIDEBOOK

Griffin, Lindsay, *Valais Alps West*, London, Alpine Club, 1998

INTERNET

Dictionary of National Biography, Oxford University Press, 2011

INDEX

ACKNOWLEDGEMENTS

In addition to the four people I mentioned at the end of the Preface who helped me with their recollections, advice and encouragement, and by reading and criticising early drafts of the manuscript, I would like to thank all the following who contributed their memories and opinions to this book: Geoff Causey, Katherine Heery, Paul Luton, John Oaks, Andrew Reynolds, Pat Reynolds, Ian Stirrups, Sue Stirrups and Jay Turner. I also thank Lindsay Griffin and the late Peter Hodgkiss for their helpful advice when I first considered writing this book fifteen years ago.

More recently, the following people have helped me in various ways to bring this project to fruition: Tadeusz Hudowski of the Alpine Club Library, Veronika Meyer of the Swiss Alpine Club and my sister, Janet Nelson, who assisted me with historical research; Françoise Call of the AC who advised me on some technicalities in the French language, Peter Rowland, for retrieving photographs from the AC Library, and Susan Hare who assisted him; Keith Gage who initially helped me with map design; Les Swindin and the late Pete Fleming for the colour photographs; Tony Bird for his assistance with scanning; Steve Dean, Terry Gifford, Chris Harle, Jay Turner and the late Rupert Hoare, who all advised me with regard to finding an appropriate publisher. I especially wish to thank Jay Turner, who read the entire manuscript and kindly wrote the Foreword.

I am also indebted to Viv Cripps of Millrace Books for her painstaking editing of the final draft to be sent to the publisher; to Jon Barton, Jane Beagley and the team at Vertebrate Publishing; and the following for allowing me to quote from previously published books and journals: Stephen Goodwin and Hywel Lloyd of the Alpine Club, Helen Elliott of the Fell & Rock Climbing Club Chronicle, Jeremy Whitehead, Les Swindin on behalf of the late Tony Drake of the Gloucestershire Mountaineering Club, John Oaks of the Lincoln Mountaineering Club, Janet Davies, Helen Jones and Hilary Lawrenson of the Pinnacle Club; Bloomsbury Publishing, Granta Books, Random House, Monica Dickerson of Surlingham, Norfolk, Joy Hodgkiss of The Ernest Press, and Jonathan Williams of Cicerone; Lady Denise Evans (née Morin), and Will McLewin.

I apologise to any other people who have also helped me and whose names I have inadvertently omitted from this list. Every effort has been made to contact the publishers or copyright holders of all the books and journals from which I have quoted, and I apologise to those I have been unable to trace. I shall endeavour to rectify such omissions in any future edition.

Barbara Swindin